Family Life and Family Support

Family Life and Family Support

A Feminist Analysis

Brid Featherstone

First published 2004 by
PALGRAVE MACMILLAN
Houndmills, Basingstoke, Hampshire RG21 6XS and
175 Fifth Avenue, New York, N.Y. 10010
Companies and representatives throughout the world

PALGRAVE MACMILLAN is the global academic imprint of the Palgrave Macmillan division of St. Martin's Press, LLC and of Palgrave Macmillan Ltd. Macmillan® is a registered trademark in the United States, United Kingdom and other countries. Palgrave is a registered trademark in the European Union and other countries.

ISBN 0–333–97378–X

This book is printed on paper suitable for recycling and made from fully managed and sustained forest sources.

A catalogue record for this book is available from the British Library.

Library of Congress Cataloging-in-Publication Data
Featherstone, Brid.
    Family life and family support : a feminist analysis / Brid Featherstone.
        p. cm.
    Includes bibliogaphical references and index.
    ISBN 0–333–97378–X (pbk.)
    1. Family social work – Great Britain. 2. Family policy – Great
    Britain. 3. Family – Great Britain. 4. Sex role – Great Britain.
    5. Feminist theory – Great Britain. I. Title.

HV700.G7F39 2004
362.82'53'0941 – dc22   2003066371

10   9   8   7   6   5   4   3   2   1
13 12 11 10 09 08 07 06 05 04

Printed and bound in Great Britain by
J. W. Arrowsmith Ltd., Bristol

This book is dedicated to
Linda Colclough
who founded MOSAIC

Contents

Acknowledgements   x

Introduction   1
What is family support? The battle for meaning   1
Family support: a diverse picture   6
Feminism for family support?   7
Structure of the book   13

PART I   SETTING THE SCENE

1   Family Life Today   19
A changing world?   19
The 'meaning' of family   23
Changing employment patterns: the implications for
    family life   25
Changing patterns of partnering: the 'outcomes' for
    children   30
What do children say?   36
Discussion   38
Concluding remarks: the implications for family support   39

2   Why Feminism?   41
The family: reform or abolition   42
Beyond reform or abandonment: deconstruction and multiplicity   45
The battles were over but who had won?   47
The 1990s – mapping complexity   49
Feminism for family support   56
Concluding remarks   61

3   Family Support in Perspective   63
Postwar welfare   64
Whose responsibility? Whose rights?   67
State paternalism and protection in the 1970s and 1980s
    and its critiques   70

The 1990s   74
Family support under the Act – a new balance?   77
Feminism – from marginalisation to incorporation to
    revitalisation?   81
Concluding remarks   85

4 Family Support Under New Labour: A New Era?   87
Locating and exploring New Labour and 'the family'   88
Building or overturning – a new era in 1997   89
Parents and parental responsibilities   93
The social investment state   96
Feminist critiques   100
Creating responsible parents   103
Bringing daddy back – but not for everyone?   106
Concluding remarks   108

5 Family Support: Diversity, Contradictions and Gaps   109
Prevention and support – new services for a new
    approach   111
Statutory settings and family support   117
Why feminism? How can it help?   120
Concluding remarks   126

PART II DELIVERING FAMILY SUPPORT

6 Working with 'Families'   129
Working with complexity and diversity   129
Family group conferences   134
Working with minority ethnic families   137
Working with 'couples': the possibilities   139
Concluding remarks   141

7 Working with Men in a Changing World   142
Locating 'fathers'   143
Men speak out as fathers   146
Working with men: the issues which emerge   148
Working with men in family support: the barriers and the
    possibilities for workers   150
Discussion   154
Concluding remarks   155

8 Working with Women   157
Locating women today   158
Family support: expanding mothers' identities or a new
    form of regulation?   159

Feminist social work – opportunities and constraints   166
Concluding remarks   189

9   **Children, Young People, Gender and Family Support**   **170**
Thinking about the 'here and now'   171
Working with boys and girls around their futures   176
The implications for family support   179
Concluding remarks   182

Conclusion   **183**
It's all in a name – the importance of language   183
Family practices and democratisation   184
The question of 'care'   185
Concluding remarks   188

References   189

Index   203

Acknowledgements

I would like to acknowledge the helpful comments provided by Barbara Fawcett, Nick Frost, Jim Goddard, Nigel Parton and Pat Wilkinson on various drafts of this book. I would like to thank Ruth Lister for her helpful input and Rhian Stone for the many discussions on policy. They bear no responsibility for its many limitations. I would also like to thank the men, women, boys and girls who shared their insights with me in the differing projects I have been involved with in the last few years. Thanks to Sue Hanson for her practical and personal support in producing the manuscript and to Catherine Gray at Palgrave Macmillan for her patience and encouragement. Finally to my 'family of friends' – I could not have done it without you all.

Brid Featherstone

Introduction: Family Life and Family Support – a Feminist Analysis

Terms such as family life, family support and feminism are vastly contested terms which encompass a range of topics and have received considerable attention as discrete subjects. In terms of their interrelationship, whilst feminist scholarship in relation to family life is extensive, there has been less attention paid within the feminist literature to family support or to feminism within the family support literature.

This book, therefore, has a very specific remit which is to highlight insights from feminist scholarship for those who practise in or who plan to practise in family support and/or those who seek to critically interrogate the field of family support. Given the vastness of the topics covered it can often act only as a signpost to complex debates. Moreover, given the diffuse nature of family support and family support activities (points which will be returned to below and throughout this book), its key aim is not to document such activities in exhaustive detail, but rather to introduce neglected insights from feminism into unsettling the thinking behind and the doing of such activities.

In this introduction I explore the contested term 'family support' and signpost key themes from feminism which are developed throughout the book.

What is family support? The battle for meaning

Whilst the term 'family support' can be used to refer to activities such as supporting those who care for relatives, both adults and children, with mental health difficulties, it is, however, more usually applied to policies and/or practices with dependent children and/or their families. In this book I concentrate on family support in relation to families and dependent children.[1]

As Penn and Gough (2002, p. 17) note, family support is one of those 'phrases that is used so often it has almost lost its meaning; or rather it encompasses so many meanings that it is difficult to disentangle them' (see also Pinkerton, 2000; Frost, 2003). There appears to be a range of diverse and often interlinked sets of meanings attached to the term in relation to aims, methods and processes. Penn and Gough (2002, p. 18), for example, note the array of authors who mobilise the term as an aspect of community care and empowerment (Stevenson and Parsloe, 1993); in the pursuit of better parenting (Pugh *et al.*, 1994); preventing child abuse (Gough, 1993); as a service response to cases of child abuse (Thoburn *et al.*, 2000); and as a service response to children in need more generally (Tunstill, 1997). Such writings coexist with a variety of broader analyses from a range of countries which seek to expand both the aims and what is done under the name of family support – *why* and *what* (see, for example, Gilligan, 2000; Canavan *et al.*, 2000). There is also an associated literature which seeks to look at the *how* – how activities are negotiated and delivered and crucially the role of service users in defining their needs and how they should be engaged with (see, for example, Pinkerton, 2000; Frost *et al.*, 2003).

Influential and widely used definitions of family support such as those provided by the Audit Commission – 'Any activity or facility provided either by statutory agencies or by community groups or individuals, aimed at providing advice and support to parents to help them bringing up their children' (1994, p. 39) – would underscore that its remit is infinitely elastic.

I have found it useful in thinking about the term to see it as an 'empty category' – that is, one to which a host of meanings can be attached and whose boundaries can be drawn and redrawn in ways which meet the needs of differing policy contexts. Attempts at definition are therefore mistaken if aimed at capturing some essential quality or activities. What is necessary is to unpack the spaces it occupies at both policy and practice levels in particular periods, and to identify how such spaces are contested and debated. My intent is to introduce into such battles for meaning neglected insights from feminist scholarship which open up alternative possibilities at both policy and practice levels.

Tunstill, an advocate of family support, has helpfully pointed out the importance of locating family support within explorations of the relationship between child, family and the state (Tunstill, 1997, 1999). There would appear to be some measure of consensus that

> One of the key aspects of the way children are perceived in the UK . . . is the way children are viewed as being primarily the responsibility of their individual family. This is central to the philosophy of the New Right, though it was also an important underlying principle of the post-1945 Beveridge model of welfare. (Daniel and Ivatts, 1998, p. 228)

The centrality of notions of individual family responsibility and associated concerns about family privacy have ensured a residual-ist approach to services of a variety of types and Chapter 3 will trace the implications in the post-1945 welfare state. This legiti-mated services being directed at those defined as problematic, although the boundaries of what is considered problematic have varied. It has also meant that notions of family responsibility have assumed and in practice reinforced women's responsibility and interventions have been focused upon women as mothers.

This view – that the child is primarily the responsibility of indi-vidual parents – has posed well-rehearsed dilemmas for 'the state'. For example, Frost and Stein (1989) note that one such dilemma is how can state institutions attempt to influence families while ensuring that they maintain their private character (see also Donzelot, 1980). Parton (1991), in a compatible observation, notes that a key dilemma has been how can the state establish the rights of individual children while promoting the family as the natural sphere for raising children and hence not intervening in all fami-lies thus reducing family autonomy. He identifies the development of philanthropy and subsequently social work and the emergence of 'the social' as central in managing this tension.

Until the 1980s 'prevention' rather than 'family support' was the term used to refer to the activities engaged in by services in both the statutory and voluntary sectors – this encompassed services designed in a narrow sense to prevent children coming into state care and broader services designed to assist families with their dif-ficulties, including the harms caused to children. The advent of family support was designed to signal the desirability of a broader focus – a signal which was strengthened by its use in the guidance associated with the Children Act 1989 (Department of Health,

1991). However, this does not mean that the term 'prevention' was superseded and indeed it and family support have become firmly entrenched as part of the policy and practice landscape established under New Labour (see Chapters 3, 4 and 5).

Since 1997, with the election of a New Labour[2] government in the UK, the policy context has altered, after years of New Right dominance. This has led to a complex picture generally in relation to 'family policy' although it would be unwise to paint a seamless picture of the direction of Conservative policies in relation to families and children or to overestimate the degree of difference between Conservatives and Labour. This is explored further in Chapters 3 and 4 of this book. It has also meant the recasting of family support, a point I return to below and develop in more detail in Chapters 4 and 5.

With the publication of a consultation document on family policy, *Supporting Families: A Consultation Document* (Home Office, 1998) and the emergence of an array of initiatives in terms of direct service provision to parents and children, as well as associated changes in terms of the benefit system largely directed at those bringing up children, it is possible to argue that a 'new' era has to some extent emerged.

There has been a limited move away from a central tenet of the welfare system which is that bringing up children is largely the responsibility of their individual families with a 'postmodernist' mix of universal and targeted developments at a range of levels (Lewis, 2001). Whilst the emphasis particularly in relation to service provision strongly inclines towards targeted provision for specific groups, according to observers such as Lister (2002a) an important development under New Labour has been the National Childcare Strategy. She argues that, despite all its difficulties, it does represent a breakthrough in British social policy in that it is the first time that a government has accepted that childcare is a public as well as a private responsibility. As Land (2002) has noted, a fundamental split in postwar welfare developments was that the care and education of children were separated, with the state assuming responsibility for universal welfare provision in relation to their education but not their care. Developments in relation to childcare in the UK thus contrasted with those in a country like Sweden where a social democratic understanding of the relationship between family and state resulted in a system where the 'provision, socialization and care of children are regarded as responsibilities to be shared between parents and the welfare state, supported by employers' (Björnberg, 2002, p. 36). This system has a number of aims, principally meeting the needs of children but also promoting gender equality.

Under New Labour, however, it is possible to argue that the primary aim seems to be to increase the stock of childcare as part of an overall aim to facilitate the entry of parents into paid work and needs to be located more widely within its development of what has become known as 'the social investment state' (Giddens, 1998; Jenson and Saint-Martin, 2001; Lister, 2002; and Chapter 4). The social investment state is about integrating people into the market, whereas the old welfare state contained possibilities even if limited for protecting people from the market. The key route for integration is through paid work for all, men and women included (Land, 1999).

In a social investment state investing in children is crucial. They hold the promise of the future, and state spending, which in general is seen as undesirable, is legitimate to support and educate them in order to increase their employability. Early childhood initiatives and childcare strategies are very important policy instruments as are targeted strategies to prevent early difficulties in relation to school truancy and criminality escalating into threats to social cohesion. It is also legitimate to help parents as a means to realise the investment in children and there has been a raft of initiatives directed at supporting parents. These coexist with the extension of initiatives more clearly directed at controlling particular categories of parents. Such initiatives, whilst posed in gender-neutral terms, do have gendered implications.

It is in this policy context that I would argue many of the current family support developments need to be seen – as part of a project to 'remake individual subjectivities and recast social identities' (Newman, 2001, p. 151). Crucially, this remaking is concerned with creating 'responsibilised citizens' (Rose, 1996, quoted in Newman 2001 p. 151). The role of the state as a major provider of welfare is limited in a social investment state and there is an overwhelming emphasis on the importance of people taking responsibility for their own welfare, primarily as indicated through the involvement in paid work on the part of both men and women.

A key context for developing and inculcating responsible citizens is within 'strong families', according to the Prime Minister, Tony Blair (1997). Whilst there are considerable indicators from Mr Blair, particularly that such strong families should consist of conjugal, heterosexual parents, in practice New Labour have trodden a slippery and often pragmatic path in relation to pronouncing and legislating on what constitutes a suitably strong family. In practice it is *parents* who are central to many strategies, particularly those packaged as family support, reflecting a pragmatic recognition that in a climate of considerable change in family composition, the notion of 'family' may be too unstable to base strategies upon. There is an apparent attempt to reorder here with the reinforcing of a construction of parenthood as tied to biology and carrying life-long responsibilities, and there is therefore a partial disentangling of marriage and parenthood. Whilst notions of 'parental responsibility' are not new and became entrenched in key legislative developments under the Conservatives, this process has continued and expanded under Labour.

The enforcing of parental responsibilities has become part of the remit of family support developments which have emerged in relation to youth justice, principally through the use of parenting orders under the Crime and Disorder Act 1998 (see Ghate and Ramalla, 2002; Chapter 4 of this book). The importance of encouraging parental involvement in paid work is a key aspect of programmes such as Sure Start (see Chapters 4 and 5) and family support activities are being mobilised to support this, as indeed they are to reduce behaviours such as smoking in pregnancy.

Family support: a diverse picture

As indicated, family support activities are currently dispersed across a range of practice sites in the pursuit of policy goals such as encouraging parents' employability and preventing children's criminality. These activities coexist with other understandings of family support which appear to work with a different set of meanings attached. In particular, they coexist with older understandings of prevention and family support, linked to but predating the Children Act 1989. Here, with differing emphases by differing constituencies, family support was located within a project which involved preventing children being removed from their families and/or being harmed. A considerable amount of attention has been paid to the issues in relation to this second construction of family support over the 1990s (see Chapters 3 and 5). In broad terms there are those who, whilst welcoming the focus on family support within the Children Act 1989, have expressed concerns about its insertion into a project which encouraged rationing by its linkage with the concept of 'children in need'. Furthermore, a considerable literature attests to the difficulties on the ground in terms of implementation (Audit Commission, 1994; Tunstill, 1997; Gardner, 2002a). The concept of 'children in need' was the subject of more fundamental criticism by those such as Moss *et al.* (2000) who argued that it supported the construction of services such as family support around a deficit model of children and childhood (see Chapter 9). Another set of criticisms has sought to uncouple family support both organisationally and conceptually from activities, which have also proved ambiguous and difficult to pin down, in relation to the protection of children from an array of harms including parental abuse (Kendall and Harker, 2002). Whether there should be boundaries and where and how they should be drawn between 'family support' and 'child protection' have been and continue to be the subject of considerable discussion by academics, policy-makers, managers and practitioners (see, for example, Laming, 2003).

Whilst there is a range of debates and battles over the meanings of family support in evidence today, in general many such debates tend to use gender-neutral language such as 'parent' and there appears to be little attention paid to thinking about what the 'family' in family support should or does encompass, despite the consistent anxieties around what *is* or *should be* a family which emerge in wider discussions (see, however, Frost, 2003). The failure to deconstruct who or what exactly is being referred to when making claims in relation to 'family support' is linked with an often associated failure to make explicit whether there are particular family practices to be supported and/or controlled/proscribed. The role of the state in family support, moreover, complicates questions of support and control and the balance which can or should be struck between them.

This book identifies the role a feminist analysis can play in the rethinking of family support which is required in a contemporary landscape where notions of 'family' are complex and gendered divisions and inequalities persist, particularly in relation to caretaking and violence. Such rethinking involves interrogating the values and assumptions underpinning the policy spaces in which family support activities operate currently.

Feminism for family support?

Feminism reemerged at the end of the late 1960s after a long period where there had appeared to be little overt activity by women in relation to their situation as women. Initially known as the women's liberation movement, and later as second-wave feminism, it proved very different in tenor and content from much of the feminism which had preceded it earlier in the century (see Jagger and Wright, 1999) in that it embarked on a very wide-ranging and diverse critique of women's lives, men's power and institutions such as 'the family'.

By 1999, thirty years after its reemergence, a number of pre-millennium books appeared in the UK which engaged in a reevaluation of how far things had changed. Whilst they differed in their assessment of how helpful or valuable feminism had been, they argued that some of the key issues it had placed on the agenda, such as the inequality of women in the workplace, men's violence, and strategies and policies which supported the combining of paid work and caring responsibilities, continued to be matters of considerable concern and had not been resolved (Benn, 1998; Franks, 1999; Segal, 1999; Walter, 1999).

Analyses were also to appear, however, questioning feminism's relevance to the new millennium, arguing that it had become a straitjacket which continued a language of women's victimisation preventing an honest engagement with the reality of the advances women had made and the disadvantages now being experienced by boys and men (see, for example, Coward, 1999).

In advancing the need for a feminist perspective, it is important to bear in mind Coward's injunctions for the need to be critical and reflective and for the importance of attending to the complexities of our current times. Early feminism, whilst contested and diverse in its approaches, did speak to a period where a particular model of family held sway at the level of prescription and to a lesser extent practice – the male breadwinner model which offered men considerable power in terms of access to economic resources and restricted women to the familial and the maternal as well as rendering the caring work they did invisible (see, for example, Barrett and McIntosh, 1982; Segal, 1995). We are in different times in a host of ways and Chapters 1 and 2 document the evidence in relation to the changes in family forms and family life. For example, changes in the labour market for both women and men have emerged, complicating simple assumptions of male advantage and female disadvantage as well as increasing inequalities between women and between men:

A world was created in which many of the old work patterns disappeared for good. What has emerged is not exactly the world dreamt of by feminists – a world of easy sharing and mutual fulfilment – but then again neither is it the world feminists originally set out to attack. It is no longer a world where men dominate the economic activity of the country or monopolize power, nor does 'the family' automatically imply a male breadwinner and a dependent wife repressed emotionally and sexually and struggling to retain a separate identity. (Coward, 1999, p. 57)

Whilst Coward considerably understates how much men continue to dominate economically and in terms of power (see, for example, Franks, 1999; Segal, 1999; and Chapters 1 and 2), she is right to signal that there have been changes in relation to economic activity generally and 'the family', changes which have transformed the gender landscape for all men and women.

Whilst versions of feminism which insist that nothing has fundamentally changed and that men as a monolithic category still have power over women are not helpful in developing the understandings and practices needed, there are approaches which can help explore what is happening to men, women, boys and girls in a world where fixed markers in relation to masculinity and femininity are challenged, and there have been complex changes in the labour market and living arrangements. Contrary to Coward's arguments, these approaches can help explore what is happening to unemployed and unskilled men and the destructive consequences of inequalities between men which 'do indeed have a gender dimension as boys and men anxiously compare themselves and compete with each other' (Segal, 1999, p. 163; Ruxton, 2002).

How can feminist ideas form part of a relevant and helpful project for family support? There are four key issues I would highlight. First, feminist perspectives oblige attention to the role of language. This has particular relevance for the use of the terms 'family' and 'parent'. Feminist research, alongside other research (Marsh and Crow, 1998), indicates the importance of questioning and/or expanding notions of 'family' with a recognition that the subjective meaning of family is changing as a result of a host of contemporary developments (see Chapter 1). Many people's family

maps . . . are a long way away from the idealized picture of mother, father and two siblings, and even where the standard stock of kin appear . . . others may now find a place, disrupting the taken-for-grantedness of primacy of blood and marital relationships. (Silva and Smart, 1999, p. 9)

Not only do feminist insights map such diversity – they offer important pointers into the impulses, particularly on the part of women, which have fuelled such diversity and the complex and contradictory consequences for all concerned.

Attention to language also obliges caution about the use of ungendered terms such as 'parent' and 'parental responsibility'. The challenges involved in exploring why gender matters are considerable and complex (see Chapter 2). To put it briefly here the term 'parent' can obscure the multiple and differing investments men and women continue to make in mothering and fathering, and the complexities that may be arising as a result of a range of changes in how mothering and fathering may be being carried out. The term 'parent' can obscure both the fixity and fluidity which are apparent. Whilst it can herald welcome moves towards gender equity, it can also act as a rhetorical device to obscure and confuse. To give an example, gendered divisions in childcare continue to be entrenched, with women of all classes and occupations doing the bulk of such work, although there is evidence also of some fluidity (O' Brien and Shemilt, 2003). The term 'parent' speaks to the fluidity to some extent but not the persistence of many entrenched features. For example, research into who is obliged to engage with parenting programmes under the Crime and Disorder Act 1998 would indicate that it is poor women who, in the main, are taking on the reality of exercising parental responsibility (see Chapter 4).

Second, feminist perspectives oblige close attention being paid to what have become known as 'family practices'. The displacement of fixed notions of what it is be a man or woman and the attendant emergence of an emphasis on working things out in the absence of straightforward rules means a range of possibilities are open if not always equally available for the 'doing' of family life. A key issue here is that scripts premised upon male authority and the subordination of women and children are questioned to varying extents and the fall-out for all concerned has been considerable (see Chapter 2).

The rather ungainly concept of 'democratisation' has emerged to capture some of what is happening even if there is considerable disagreement about what it means and how far it has developed (see Chapters 1 and 2). In broad terms, it appears to refer to increased opportunities for settlements based upon the unquestioned authority of men within the home to be challenged by women and children. For some writers this is to be welcomed and should underpin welfare interventions with families. For example, Ferguson (2001a, p. 8) argues that such interventions should encourage the building of 'democratic families': 'where children are heard as well as seen and feel safe, women as well as men are treated with respect, and men as well as women are enabled to have expressive emotional lives and relationships'.

A fundamental aspect of 'democratic families' is that violent and abusive behaviours have no place and their proscription is central to the activities of those seeking to build such families. By signposting the reality and consequences of male violences to women and children, feminists started a process which continues to be necessary. *Which* men and *why* are questions which require ongoing exploration at a range of interlocking levels in relation to gendering, economic, social and cultural processes. To signpost the responsibility of men for much of the violences practitioners encounter in family life is to begin rather than end that process. Whilst it is inadequate in terms of capturing the range of violences which practitioners encounter, it does, however, continue to be necessary in alerting us to the continued reality of men's violence. Moreover, an associated feminist project which explores the complexities of mothering and rescues it from assumptions of naturalness or instinct has considerable potential for understanding the difficulties which may arise in relationships between mothers and children. Such insights are urgently required in a context where contemporary policy and practice discourses appear dominated by ungendered explanations which posit child abuse as attributable to 'families being under stress' (see Chapter 5 for further discussion of how child abuse is being constructed in policy developments currently).

Furthermore, current discourses in family support can, as indicated, reproduce a distinction between 'family support' and 'child protection'. Feminist insights in relation to violence of all forms open up important possibilities for the rethinking and indeed transcending of this distinction as they direct attention to questions about gendered and generational power relations and wider cultural and material practices around violence and abuse. They therefore refuse an assumption that abusive practices can be easily categorised within particular families, or an associated assumption that control and support are or should be dichotomous activities, or that control is always a problematic activity. In relation to the first point, for example, the ubiquity of domestic violence would contest any notion that abusive activities can be narrowly located within a small number of families (Humphreys, 2001). Second, the control of one person who is violent or abusive will usually imply the support of others. Finally, a key aspect of many feminist interventions into welfare practices has been the advocacy of social control measures in order to offer possibilities in relation to voice, self-actualisation and safety for women and children (see, for example, Gordon, 1986, 1989; Featherstone, 1999). These points are returned to in Chapters 3 and 5.

The importance of active engagement by those on the receiving end of controlling and supportive strategies with how needs are defined and the opening up of dialogue in relation to definitions and strategies has been underscored by feminists and located within wider developments in relation to welfare policies and practices generally (Williams, 1999). This could contribute to contemporary discussions within the family support literature (see Frost, 2003).

Finally, in starting the process of rendering visible the work involved in 'caring', feminist insights play a key role in a project which is concerned with profoundly important questions about caring and how it should be recognised and supported. The work on 'the political ethics of care' which has emerged from a diverse range of sources, primarily feminists, poses an important challenge to the basic values underpinning the social investment state and the associated welfare policies being developed under New Labour (Williams, 1999, 2001). It is rooted in concerns which form the very bread and butter of current family support practices. What is caring? Who does it? How can it best be 'recognised' in the sense of valued properly? Moreover, what kinds of policies are required to support the kinds of caring practices we want to foster? It offers a direct challenge to the current valorisation of paid work as *the* badge of responsible citizenship which is being promoted by New Labour and it also opens up the possibility of broadening out debates on how a wider set of balances can be struck in relation to the doing and supporting of caring activities.

The implications for family support can thus be summarised as follows:

- There is a need to pay attention to language and to interrogate terms such as 'family' in order to engage with the complex and multiple meanings which it can carry today.
- The term 'parent' needs to be constantly deconstructed in order to engage with the fixity and fluidity of contemporary practices in relation to caretaking.

- Family support activities should be explicitly located within a project which is concerned with building 'democratic families', thus paying attention to the concerns of men, women and children and recognising the importance of both support and control activities. This involves engaging in ongoing dialogue around how such support and control activities should be carried out.
- Finally, the policy context within which such practices are promoted is vital in terms of providing an infrastructure which can support the building of 'democratic families'.

Structure of the book

Part I of the book concentrates on locating *what* is done within a broader engagement with *why* and on the policy landscape and goals family support is aimed at. Part II engages directly with practices, the *what* and the *how*, in a variety of settings. The focus on categories such as men, women, boys and girls throughout Part II is not usual in books on family support and illuminates a key thesis of my approach which is the continuing importance of engaging with gender at the level of both language and material practices.

As Frost *et al.* (2003) have noted, given the diversity of family support, it is almost inevitable that any one book will contain problematic omissions. This book is no exception and in Part II this becomes particularly acute. Part II makes no claims to be an exhaustive account of family support activities. Rather the purpose is to highlight specific issues from a variety of settings in relation to men, women, boys and girls which are less often engaged with in the general literature. The chapters in Part II draw from small-scale pieces of research and voluntary work which I have been involved with over the last few years. These projects have included an evaluation of a family support project in a school setting and two projects working with fathers. The experience of being involved in a project working with mothers of children who have been sexually abused is also drawn on in Chapter 8. Finally I am involved in a range of capacities with three Sure Start projects. Whilst, for reasons of confidentiality, none is referred to explicitly, that experience is drawn on to make some general remarks.

Chapter 1 explores empirical research into a range of developments in family life, outlining how such developments are expanding understandings of 'family'. It explores how children are both positioned and positioning themselves in relation to the consequences of changes in adult men and women's relationships.

Chapter 2 expands on the arguments offered in this introduction, locating the origins of contemporary feminist insights and outlining the contours of contemporary discussions in relation to family life and welfare policies and practices. Chapter 3 explores how the postwar welfare state constructed boundaries around family responsibilities and support. It offers a historical backdrop to contemporary debates in relation to family support via an examination of the development of children's services. It has a broad sweep taking us post-1945 to 1997 where it is argued in Chapter 4 that a 'new' chapter in relation to the welfare state appears to have been opened. This has been accompanied by a range of policy and service development initiatives in relation to children and families which appear to have recast family support and opened up new sites of practice. Chapter 5 explores some of the tensions and dilemmas which are emerging at the levels of policy and organisation and identifies the progressive possibilities feminist approaches hold in relation to dealing with such tensions and dilemmas.

Part II focuses on what is happening in practice in a range of settings in the statutory and voluntary sectors and is designed to identify the possibilities and constraints attached to developing the kinds of practice approaches this book promotes as desirable. Chapter 6 outlines the possibilities and constraints of practising with an expanded notion of family or what Frost (2003) calls inclusive notions of family. Chapters 7, 8 and 9 concentrate variously on working with men, women, and boys and girls, exploring what issues are emerging in practice in a variety of settings and the opportunities available alongside the constraints in relation to a project around building 'democratic families'. An important observation about Part II is that it is not designed to lay down prescriptions for practice but to draw out observations from a range of settings which can open up possibilities as well as highlighting the difficulties for practice and practitioners.

The Conclusion draws together the themes dealt with throughout the book and outlines some ways forward particularly in relation to how an 'ethics of care' could begin to revision family support at the level of policy and practice.

Notes

1. This book, because of the author's location, concentrates in the main on developments in England particularly in the post-1997

context. However, developments in Wales have run a compatible trajectory. Whilst there are differences either in legislation or organisational arrangements for the delivery of family support in Scotland and Northern Ireland, there are also considerable similarities across all four countries. Moreover, there is considerable synergy between all four countries and the Republic of Ireland in relation to thinking about and arguing for particular conceptions of family support.

2. Using the term 'New Labour' signifies the nature of the political project. It does not imply it is 'new' chronologically.

PART I

Setting the Scene

Family Life Today

This chapter confines itself to a discussion of the issues in relation to families with dependent children (see Cheal, 2002, for a broader discussion). It identifies features of the contemporary landscape germane to understanding family life as it is being lived by men, women and children. These include diversity in family form, changes in employment patterns and the implications for the unpaid division of labour. It identifies how children are both being positioned and positioning themselves in relation to these changes. Finally, it signposts some of the implications for family support practitioners which are developed further throughout the book, particularly in Part II.

A changing world?

'[T]here have been some changes within the patterns and trends in the organisation and practice of family life since the end of the 1960s, and some of these patterns and trends contrast quite sharply with those of the 1950s in particular' (Peplar, 2002, p. 150). In questioning whether changes in patterns and trends represent a change in the quality of family life, Peplar cuts to the heart of contemporary anxieties. Developments such as the rise in divorce and two-parent involvement in the paid labour force are lamented precisely because it is assumed they lead to a deterioration in the quality of family life, particularly for children (Etzioni, 1993). The rise in cohabitation, divorce and lone motherhood are also lamented because they are seen to represent a decline in adherence to a particular *ideal* of family life which involved marriage as a lifelong commitment.

Historical analyses point to the importance of taking a longer-term view of contemporary developments. Gillis (1996) argues that the fragmentation and instability so commonly felt today has been apparent in Western societies since the Middle Ages and traces how nostalgia about a previous period of apparent stability has recurred throughout preceding periods. Humans have been imagining and reimagining families throughout recorded history as their actual families have always been too fragile to satisfy the existential need for a sense of continuity and belonging. There have, therefore, been the families we live *with* and the families we live *by*. What is important about today, according to Gillis, is that in the past people could find the families they lived *by* in a range of locations such as religion or communal institutions. Currently, many in the West have collapsed the families they live *with* into the families they live *by*, thus burdening actual family members with considerable expectations. The family thus takes on a greater cultural and emotional significance and moreover mediates wider tensions and contradictions.

Today nostalgia about the past is apparent in the tendency to freeze the 1950s as a period of stability and desirability (Stacey, 1991). This period in many Western countries was a time where a particular model of family life – male employed head of household, homemaker wife and dependent children in a nuclear arrangement – was both the dominant form of arrangement and the ideal to be supported. The anxieties mobilised by changes to this particular model can make it hard to hold on to historical evidence of its specificity (Stacey, 1991; Somerville, 2000).

Onto its decline are mapped anxieties about the decline in the quality of family life, or more catastrophic concerns about the demise of family altogether. The usage of the term 'family' to cover a diverse array of arrangements (see Silva and Smart, 1999; and discussion below) would indicate that there may be a persistent investment in a language of family which complicates such assumptions. However, there would appear to be complex changes in *who* that family might encompass, as the evidence below would indicate. Linked with this is the emergence of a greater degree of uncertainty and instability in men and women's relationships than in the more recent past. Children can, therefore, come to bear the weight of adult expectations about belonging and rootedness (Beck and Beck-Gernsheim, 1995; Jenks, 1996).

Generally, current trends cannot be read straightforwardly:

We might say that there is both continuity and diversity in family life . . . This means that although there is a numerical dominance in the form of two parent families, this organization no longer defines so exclusively what it is like to live in a family, or what a family is. We live in a context where the normative European model of the conjugal couple living in a nuclear household is losing force. (Silva and Smart, 1999, p. 4)

Preliminary returns from the census conducted in April 2001 would support Silva and Smart's observations (http://www.statistics. gov.uk/census2001). The family picture of England and Wales reflects a shift away from the model that dominated for most of the twentieth century. But of all households with dependent children, 59 per cent are married-couple households, 11 per cent cohabiting couples and 22 per cent lone-parent families.

Lone parents account for 10 per cent of households and nine out of ten lone parents are women. The percentage of married couples is declining and there has been an increase in the percentages of single (never married) people and divorced people. The number of households made up of cohabiting couples accounts for less than one in ten of all households and all adults. This compares with just over one in 20 households in 1991. Nearly 40 per cent of cohabiting-couple households contain dependent children.

Lewis (2001) argues that 'the facts' of family change in relation to marriage and cohabitation, for example, are real and hard to exaggerate and she also argues that trends towards cohabitation are more pronounced among the poor: 'in the lower third or so of the income distribution the rate was almost half as high again, and among couples with children drawing benefits it was more than two and a half times as high' (p. 4).

Marriage and parenthood have become separated and this is particularly pronounced amongst those who are poor (see Joshi et al., 2000). This is reflected in the growth in cohabitation but to some extent also in the growth in numbers of lone parents (Mann and Roseneil, 1999). Another key feature of today is that parenthood has become to some extent disassociated from biology (Bainham et al., 1999). This is due partly to technological developments but also to the growth in divorce. For example, children may now spend all or parts of their childhood being parented by adults with no biological connection to them.

Somerville (2000) has, however, cautioned against a simple acceptance that we are in a 'new era'. She argues that the average duration of marriage in the UK has actually changed very little in a hundred years.

the numbers of multiple marriages, children living with step parents, step siblings and relatives other than their parents or in public care, were just as great in the distant past and at the height of Victorian values as they were at the end of the twentieth century. However, the cause in these instances was death not divorce. (Somerville, 2000, p. 7)

We see a discontinuity therefore in trends in relation to the duration of marriage only if we measure current trends against the postwar period. However, the ending of marriage through divorce is a discontinuity and its widespread availability and use since the 1970s is an important development historically.

Whilst there appear to have always been a wide range of family forms, 'new' family forms have emerged partly as a result of technological developments and the articulation of recognition claims by formerly invisible groups such as gays and lesbians. The mobilisation of the term 'families of choice' by gays and lesbians reflects new claims on their part, but can also reflect an increase in the significance of adult friendship networks, which are incorporated into and sometimes supplant families of origin (Weeks et al., 1996; Peplar, 2002).

Lewis argues that 'while at the demographic levels families and family building are becoming ever more diverse there is convergence in terms of the negotiated nature of commitment and responsibility' (Lewis, 2001, p. 28). To support her claim she refers to research she has carried out with married and cohabiting couples. There were more similarities than differences between those younger couples who cohabited and those who married in terms of how they divided their responsibilities and discussed who did what. All appeared actively engaged in everyday negotiations around the doing of family life, in contrast to their parents who alluded to their experiences of living in a time when notions of responsibility and commitment were fixed and tied to a unitary understanding of marriage. It is important to recognise, therefore, that even within what may be seen as 'traditional' arrangements, new normative guidelines are emerging and that distinctions between differing family forms in terms of practices may not be clear-cut (Silva and Smart, 1999).

Exploring diversity through a concentration on enumerating family forms and particularly relying on statistical evidence to do so are called into question further when one considers the intersection of diversity in terms of form with issues such as ethnicity/race. For example, more than one-third of African-Caribbean women are registered heads of households, which is higher than any other group. Around 50 per cent of all African-Caribbean births are to single women and 25 per cent of all African-Caribbean women are single mothers (Somerville, 2000). However, as Reynolds (2002) cautions, although traditional definitions in Britain and the USA present the female-headed household as a fixed and unitary black family structure, this structure is one of the many stages of family life that black women continue to move through during their lifetime. She argues that an overconcentration on form (for example, marriage versus non-marriage) as opposed to processes which are concerned with daily lived experiences of support and commitment obscures the complexity of what is actually happening. Clarke and O'Brien (2002) have also cautioned against reading off simple assumptions from the statistics in relation to South Asian families. Whilst there would appear to be considerable evidence to indicate that such families exhibit a particular family structure and particular norms – male breadwinner, rates of women working outside the home are low, divorce is uncommon and births outside marriage are actively discouraged – there is also evidence of considerable negotiation emerging which belies simple assumptions of a stereotyped patriarchal settlement.

There is a complex association between family form and material disadvantage (Joshi et al., 2000). Lone-mother families, for example, are much more likely to suffer material disadvantage and materially disadvantaged women are more likely to become lone mothers (Somerville, 2000). Divorce impacts adversely upon the material welfare of women and children and stepfamilies may suffer material disadvantage although forming a stepfamily may alleviate the poverty of some lone mothers (Golombok, 2000; Batchelor, 2003). Rates of early marriage and marriage breakdown are highest among the poorest. However, poverty rates among minority ethnic families such as Bangladeshis which have low rates of marriage breakdown are among the highest of all (see Platt, 2003, for an analysis of 'the severe and persistent' poverty among minority ethnic groups generally).

The 'meaning' of family

Silva and Smart (1999) argue that what a family *is* appears intrinsically related to what a family *does*. A major change in the concept of family is that 'it has come to signify the subjective meaning of intimate connections rather than formal, objective blood or marriage ties. This subjective appreciation binds together people who live in separate households for part of the time, or all of the time, as well as people who have legal links, or people who simply choose to belong together as a family' (p. 7). In this context of fluid and changing definitions of families a basic core remains which refers to the sharing of resources, caring, responsibilities and obligations. Family refers to what is done rather than what is.

Contemporary research frequently asks participants to map who they consider family:

> In some instances the maps which are produced are considerably removed from the idealized pictures of mother, father and two siblings, and even where the standard stock of kin appear within the circles, others may now find a place, disrupting the taken-for-grantedness of primacy of blood and marital relationships. (Silva and Smart, 1999, p. 9)

A new vocabulary is not emerging, however, to deal with these new relationships and the notion of family is being used to cover everything. Silva and Smart see this as open to two competing understandings. On the one hand, using the concept of family to cover such a variety may obscure the changes which are occurring and create an impression that little is really happening. On the other, the continued usage of the term may also reflect a resistance to giving up the qualities associated with the idea of family such as caring, intimacy, responsibility and loving, particularly in a culture which still devalues other kinds of relationships.

Whilst Silva and Smart are correct to associate the persistence of a language of family with positive qualities attached to the idea of family, it important to remember that the term can encode difficult and painful meanings also, particularly when it is associated with a prescriptive project which implies that there is a particular model to be adhered to.

In Silva and Smart's view there are advantages to stretching the concept of family in that it disrupts the boundaries which are presumed to exist between proper families and less desirable families and can ultimately carry wider connotations by dissolving the idea that only one kind of family can produce desirable citizens. Accepting diverse forms of intimacy and caring as legitimate forms of family life will decentre the nuclear family through a process of gradual cultural change. It can also reinforce claims for change at the level of law and social policy in order that diversity is more fully recognised and supported.

Silva and Smart argue for the development of diverse, inclusive understandings of family and signpost the importance of attending to individual perceptions rather than imposing top-down definitions. Whilst important, their linking of such perceptions with what is *done* rather than what *is*, may, however, underestimate the importance of ties based upon blood, for example. As we shall see below, children do attach different meanings to birth parents and step-parents and there are complex issues around identity and belonging posed for those who for whatever reason cannot live with any birth relatives (see Chapter 3). Furthermore, it is also important to be alert to the possibility that the notion of family in itself may need to be mobilised with caution for those who feel excluded from or damaged by particular families.

There is an important opening up of the possibilities attached to what it means to be or 'do' family today which can, as Silva and Smart indicate, be obscured by the use of the language of family in an uninterrogated way. This has obvious implications for those concerned with family support, requiring ongoing attention to be paid by practitioners to the definitions of those they work with.

Changing employment patterns: the implications for family life

The male breadwinner model which cohered around a division of labour in which men took part in the paid workforce whilst their wives took responsibility for unpaid domestic and caring tasks has proved a powerful symbol as well as being a key assumption underpinning the establishment of the welfare state (see Chapter 3). It was never a model that was accessed by all sections of the population, partly because male working-class wages could not support it (see Land, 1999). It has also been a model which has been available differentially to groups of men (see Franks, 1999; Ruxton, 2002).

By the end of 1996, women outnumbered men in paid employment for the first time in peacetime. However, Franks (1999, p. 40) cautions that raw figures of women's workforce participation can be misleading as there is a widening gap between those highly educated, usually full-time women who have entered well-paid secure employment and the majority, over 90 per cent, who occupy lowly, insecure and badly paid jobs.

The growth in women's employment until the mid-1980s was predominantly in part-time work, although since then full-time female employment has also been increasing. Women, in particular mothers, are still predominantly represented in the part-time labour force although African-Caribbean mothers have consistently been represented full-time in the paid labour force. There have been considerable debates about whether part-time work represents 'choice' on women's part or is simply to do with what is available and the constraints of childcare provision. Moreover, there have been debates about whether it reflects a rejection by many women of a 'career' identity in favour of an identity which prioritises their caring responsibilities (Hakim, 1996; Lewis, 2001; Glover, 2002).

Women appear to have entered the workforce at a time when work is changing:

> Women . . . have been encouraged to embrace work, just at a time when the workplace is going through its own frenzied transformation and work has coincidentally become more unwelcoming to everyone. The results of the changes are deregulation, rising workplace inequality, longer hours, and greater pressures for the smaller numbers of full-timers, combined with insecurity and uncertainty of life for the growing periphery of temporary workers and part-timers, where women are over represented from lecturers to cleaners. (Franks, 1999, p. 2)

Ruxton (2002) notes the impact upon different groups of men of economic restructuring and unemployment particularly in the 1980s and 1990s. He argues that while some men have clearly increased their power, others have experienced 'downsizing' and 'retrenchment' and become unemployed. The outcomes in terms of poverty, stress and loss of social support have been serious for such men (see also Coward, 1999). Ruxton notes that whilst women remain disadvantaged overall in the labour market (the gender gap in pay in relation to full-time workers is still at 18 per cent according to Rake, quoted in the *Guardian*, 22 November 2002), there have been considerable changes for certain groups of men. There are particular issues for those who have become detached from employment. Since the 1980s one of the most significant changes has been the large rise in the number of men of working age, especially older men, who have become 'economically inactive', that is, not employed or recorded as unemployed. While official figures fail to acknowledge unpaid work, the transformation of the position of men within the figures is striking. At the end of the 1990s the group of inactive men outnumbered the recorded unemployed by more than two to one. Whilst this does reflect government encouragement in the 1980s for claimants to move off the employment register and onto disability and sickness benefits, and tighter approaches to staff selection by employers, it may also be that some men have retreated from increasingly difficult circumstances into incapacity. There are particular issues in relation to men in areas where traditional industrial jobs have disappeared, areas such as South Wales, the North East of England, Merseyside, Clydeside and South Yorkshire where 30 per cent of the entire population of 25–64-year-old men are economically inactive and long-term unemployed.

The economic position of young men generally appears to have deteriorated over time and job prospects for young men from ethnic minorities appear particularly bleak (Platt, 2003). Ruxton notes research which indicates that although few young men made distinctions between jobs for women and jobs for men, in practice they ruled out jobs on the basis of the skills and pay involved:

> Many of these jobs would typically be done by women, suggesting that young men's choices draw upon long-standing perceptions that have consistently devalued the real level of skill of 'women's work' (both reproductive work and work for pay). Within the context of the changing labour market, where interpersonal and communication skills and high standards of customer service (skills more traditionally associated with women) are frequently at a premium, it seems likely that marginalised young men's expectations in terms of status and pay will increasingly not be met. (Ruxton, 2002, p. 37)

Whilst it is important to explore differences for men and women in relation to employment, it is also important to note that employment appears to have become more difficult for both men and women. Increases in the amount of work accompanied by a rise in antisocial hours and fear of losing jobs, especially in areas where traditional manufacturing industry has declined, are apparent (Ruxton, 2002). In a study of 1,165 mothers it emerged that in only 12 per cent of families where both parents worked did both parents work 'typical' hours (defined as 8.30 a.m. to 5.30 p.m. with no Saturday or Sunday work). In 88 per cent of families either the mother (9 per cent), father (36 per cent) or both parents (43 per cent) were working atypically (Dean, 2002). Moreover, it would appear that 'atypical' hours tended to be imposed upon low-income families, who unlike professional parents were much less likely to feel that the working arrangements suited them.

The rise in antisocial hours would appear to be a particular issue for children. Asked what they think about their parents' work patterns, *when* parents work does matter (Ghazi, 2003). Weekend working is very unpopular, as is late evening work. Nine out of ten children when asked specifically about their fathers felt they did not have enough time with them, which appeared linked to the long hours they spent at work.

Changes in employment patterns pose a range of implications for service providers. *Who* is available to be worked with and *when* are obvious practical issues but there are also deeper concerns about how changing employment patterns are impacting upon the identities of mothers and fathers. The complexities are posed here when the evidence in relation to who does what in the home is considered.

What happens in the home?

Are men doing more in the home as women do more in the workplace? Franks's (1999) review of the research evidence suggested not. She argued that in households where both partners work full-time, women spend over three times as many hours as men on domestic chores and over twice as many on childcare and these are the households where work is more equally shared. The division of labour between women working part-time and their partners barely differs from those households where the woman is not involved in paid work. Men who have no paid employment actually spend less time on childcare than they did in the 1960s and their time spent on domestic work has barely altered.

More recent research on working fathers, however, would indicate that working fathers are doing a third of all childcare but are struggling with a 'long hours' culture which prevents many of them from seeking what they feel is a more appropriate balance. Nearly two-fifths usually worked more than 48 hours a week and one in eight usually worked 60 hours or more (O'Brien and Shemilt, 2003). This research argues that in two and a half decades the amount of time fathers spend with their children has shot up – from less than 15 minutes a day in the mid-1970s to two hours by the late 1990s and that is during the week; it is more at the weekends. However, for one father this research is 'seriously flawed'. He argues that whilst men might say they wish to care more for their children and bewail obstacles such as the long-hours culture, in practice men say one thing and do another (Seaton, 2003).

It is hard to predict what might happen if there was a better balance at the level of policy and employment practices. However, some of the research does point to a change in behaviour in the here and now. Lewis's (2001) research with a small research cohort showed that both married and cohabiting couples were engaged in considerable amounts of negotiation and discussion around the unpaid division of labour and this was not evident in the accounts of their parents who had much more fixed understandings of what the roles of husband, wife, mother and father entailed. Her research led her to perceive a 'democratic possibility' rather than democratic reality. However, as Lewis's accounts attest, there are considerable tensions attached to such tendencies. She found that couples needed to engage in considerable amounts of negotiation which she contrasted with the more tranquil climates established by their parents. Franks (1999) notes the results of the National Child Development Study which showed that while the happiest women were those whose partners contributed most in the home, the unhappiest men were those doing the most.

Indeed, it is argued that the instability of contemporary adult relationships may be linked to the difficulties associated with putting democratising approaches into practice (Jamieson, 1998). Certainly, accounts from working mothers in the 1990s which are explored further in the next chapter would indicate that it has in the main been women who have had to bear the brunt of changes in employment patterns through shouldering a double burden (Freely, 1996; Benn, 1998).

With regard to men who cannot access the economic provider role or have lost it, it is clear that many find the possibility of transition to another role in the home difficult and may suffer a considerable lack of confidence in terms of taking it on as well as significant difficulties in rethinking an identity in the context of loss (Ferguson, 1998). Ruxton documents views from service providers, Fathers Plus, attempting to engage men in a changed economic climate in the North East of England where specific areas have been strongly impacted upon by economic changes.

With the cultural expectations of fathers as providers and mothers as carers still entrenched despite the changing employment culture many men are unprepared for the new role of fathers as parents and primary carers. They come to the role reluctantly and lacking in confidence, being thrown in to the job for negative reasons. Their loss of self-esteem through ongoing unemployment, and sensitivity at their seeming inability to fulfil responsibilities as provider makes for unstable foundations from which to nurture their offspring. (Ruxton, 2002, p. 81)

Changing patterns of partnering: the 'outcomes' for children

There has been considerable discussion about the implications for children's welfare, particularly in relation to changing patterns of partnering. What has excited most professional attention in the UK, particularly in relation to those developing family support and/or prevention policies and practices, has been long-standing concerns about the outcomes for children who are living apart from any blood relatives and/or family however defined (for example, in residential or foster care) (Fox Harding, 1991; Daniel and Ivatts, 1998). Concern about such outcomes has prompted considerable action on the part of New Labour since 1997 (Fawcett *et al.*, forthcoming), but in general such concerns do not receive the widespread attention that developments such as divorce and the growth in lone motherhood do.

It is argued that changes in adult relationships in recent decades have impacted upon the meanings adults attach to childhood and children (Beck and Beck-Gernsheim, 1995; Jenks, 1996). In a context where adult relationships come and go children can become relied upon for stability and 'childhood' can become a precious space to be protected. However, the very instability of adult relationships can itself mobilise considerable anxieties about the stability that can be offered children.

Certainly there seems to be considerable interest in the outcomes for children of contemporary changes in family forms. The concern with outcomes can encompass a wide range of psychological and social indicators such as self-esteem, educational attainments, involvement in criminality, ability to sustain relationships and so on and has been exhibited by a diverse range of constituencies so that research evidence to support or refute particular positions has been mobilised accordingly.

The interest in outcomes can itself be seen as evidence of an agenda which constructs children and their future development as central, thus precluding adequate attention being paid to issues as to why men and women are divorcing, and women are choosing to have children on their own or parenting in partnership with other women. However, it is important to interrogate outcomes for children not only for children's sake but also because of the pointers they offer us towards understanding adults' lives.

Lamb's (1999) edited collection from the USA brings together the research on outcomes in a range of what is termed 'non-traditional' families and care arrangements: maternal and dual-earner families; non-parental childcare; primary care-giving fathers; non-custodial families; divorce and stepfamilies; adoptive families; families headed by lesbian and gay parents. The collection also explores children's development in black, Latino and multiracial families. It contains valuable research reviews of the US literature, at the same time as reflecting how widely boundaries can be drawn in relation to what is considered 'non-traditional'. As Lamb acknowledges in the introduction, this is a risky project, however, as it assumes rather than interrogates the category 'traditional'. Moreover, it leaves what would appear to be a historically constructed notion of what constitutes traditional uninterrogated in terms of what outcomes it produces and their desirability.

Golombok (2000) reviews both UK and US evidence on outcomes for children's 'healthy psychological development' in a range of family types emerging from technological and social developments. She considers the research evidence in relation to a number of contested questions. Is it necessary to have two parents; a father present; parents who have a genetic link with their child; parents who are heterosexual?

Golombok argues that the research would indicate that those most at risk of adverse outcomes are those in single-parent families and stepfamilies – 'families in which children have commonly been exposed to hostility between their parents, their parents' separation or divorce often resulting in a loss of social and financial support and the transition to a stepfamily necessitating the negotiation of new family relationships' (Golombok, 2000, p. 101).

Some key themes emerge, therefore, which centre around conflict between parents, socio-economic difficulties and the issues involved in negotiating transitions and new attachments. In relation to divorce, for example, there has been an ongoing debate about the relative importance of key variables such as parental conflict pre- and post-divorce and the changes in socio-economic circumstances which often accompany divorce. Most research would indicate that conflict between parents at all stages impacts adversely upon children and therefore if divorce, for example, stops or alleviates such conflicts then children are less likely to be adversely affected by the divorce itself. 'Most family members experience substantial psychological and emotional disturbance around the time of divorce, although this is sometimes mixed with more positive feelings, especially where there is relief regarding resolution of the problems leading to divorce' (Lamb *et al.*, 1999, p. 126).

There is variability in the length of time it can take to achieve a new equilibrium. Most children experience: a decline in their economic circumstances; abandonment or the fear of abandonment by one or both of their parents; the diminished capacity of both parents to attend meaningfully and constructively to their children's needs because they are preoccupied with their own distress including their economic circumstances; and diminished contact with many familiar or potential sources of support as well as familiar living settings. 'As a consequence the experience of divorce is a psycho-social stressor as well as a significant life transition for most children. Some children from divorced homes show long-term behaviour problems, depression, poor school performance, acting out, low self-esteem and (in adolescence and young adulthood) difficulties with intimate heterosexual relationships' (Lamb *et al.*, p. 127). However, whilst stressing that divorce is a painful experience that increases children's psychosocial vulnerability, they caution against exaggerating the long-term impacts. The majority of children do go on in the long term to 'develop within the normal range' – that is, without identifiable psychosocial scars or other adverse consequences.

The formation of a stepfamily, post-divorce, can be highly complex and take many forms (Batchelor, 2003; Chapter 6). There can be a formal process involving remarriage or cohabitation. One adult may join a mother and her children; two adults both with children may form a household. It is a transition for all concerned and response to a transition to some extent depends on what has preceded it (Hetherington and Stanley-Hagan, 1999; Batchelor, 2003). The move to a stepfamily can increase financial resources if it is from a single-parent family and another adult can provide additional emotional and child-rearing support. However, there can be considerable financial difficulties attendant upon the imperatives of supporting more than one household. There can be difficulties with the new step-parent being viewed as an intruder and there may be particular difficulties where the child/children have had a close relationship with the resident parent or indeed an involved non-resident parent. New more complex networks emerge and there are variations in how the challenges are met. There is evidence that expecting the stepfamily to fit the model of a traditional biological family can lead to new problems and exacerbate existing ones:

> Stepfamilies that weather the initial challenges of family formation tend to be those that recognise that building a sense of family takes time, family boundaries must be flexible to accommodate existing ties to non custodial parents and extended family and step-parents cannot replace biological parents and may need to develop a separate non-traditional parenting role. (Hetherington and Stanley-Hagan, 1999, p. 139)

Despite the above it is estimated that the numbers of children who experience severe lasting problems are relatively small. Most children adapt and develop well, although clearly all experience considerable challenges.

What about children in 'single parent' families? The terminology is often contested here, linking into concerns to deconstruct what can be portrayed as a unitary category.

This category can include: those resulting from parents' separation or divorce; death; and those which contain a mother from the start, a category called solo mothers by Golombok (2000).

Most single-parent families are headed by a mother rather than a father with the small number of single-father families usually resulting from the death of a mother or after separation or divorce. When the latter happens it is usually because the mother is unable to care for the children because of mental or physical illness although Jackson's (1994) accounts from mothers who leave their children could indicate that though small in number, there can be a diverse range of reasons. There have been few studies into single-father families and in what follows I am mainly looking at research which has explored single-mother families. The research on such families highlights gender issues in relation to poverty and conflict which are often masked in the gender-neutral language employed in the studies outlined above.

Again the outcomes for children need to be integrated into an understanding of what preceded the transition to a family headed by a mother. Golombok (2000) identifies the range of variables which are involved here. For those children where divorce has preceded the transition, 'conflict' between parents pre- and post-divorce seems crucial. Furthermore, a mother's reduced ability to function effectively when she is feeling vulnerable can combine with children being more distressed and demanding:

> For newly single mothers the demands of looking after difficult children while in a poor emotional state themselves can be more than they can take, and their ability to function as effective parents may diminish at this time . . . But the improvement in children's adjustment following divorce is paralleled in the emotional well-being of their mothers. (Golombok, 2000, p. 8)

Golombok notes the result of a study by Hetherington and Stanley-Hagan (1995) which found, for example, that by two years following divorce three-quarters of divorced women reported they were happier currently than they had been in the final year of their marriage and most felt that it was easier to raise their children alone than with a husband who was either disengaged or undermining or where there was conflict including violence.

Financial hardship commonly accompanies the transition to a single-parent family which is linked to gendered inequalities in the labour market. Ferri's (1976) research with children in single-parent families compared with children in two parent-families at their eleventh birthday found that the children were more likely to have emotional and behavioural difficulties and to be doing less well at school. She concluded that the difficulties could be explained almost entirely by low income. More recent research makes compatible points (Golombok, 2000).

Lack of support has been implicated in the difficulties experienced by single mothers and their children, although that can encompass a range of dimensions. It is also quite complex, as some research on the presence of men in family life would indicate that men's presence can add to the pressures women experience in bringing up children (Oakley and Rigby, 1998). But mothers would indicate that the lack of anyone to take over or with whom to talk parenting issues through can be difficult (Golombok, 2000).

Some research is being done with mothers who have been single from the start. This can include women who did not plan to have children or had assumed that the father would be involved, but it is also becoming more common for women to actively choose to have children on their own – a category which can include lesbians (see Kershaw, 2001, for a discussion of lesbian-mother families and the research evidence in relation to outcomes for children).

Many of the children whose mothers have been single from the start are likely not to have experienced a parental separation or to have been exposed to hostility/violence between their mother and father. Second, they and their mothers will not have experienced the difficulties outlined above in relation to the transition to single motherhood although they may of course experience both financial difficulties and a lack of social support. The small number of studies open up interesting questions which need to continue to be researched. One study by Golombok *et al.* (1997) focused on the quality of family relationships and the emotional well-being of children raised from infancy by financially secure single mothers and found that the children experienced greater warmth and involvement with their mothers and were more securely attached to her than a comparison group from two-parent homes. However, the children felt less competent in physical and intellectual activities.

This research underlines the complexity of the variables which may need to be taken into account but there are additional issues in relation to children's demands about their father. Whilst not all will want to find their father, most are curious. There are particular issues emerging in relation to those conceived through the use of the sperm of an anonymous donor and Blyth (2001) argues that the 'search for their origins' is not only becoming an issue as many reach adulthood but deserves recognition.

Golombok (2000) argues, in conclusion, that there is more learning to be done in terms of doing research on mothers who have been single from the start and who are financially secure with supportive family and friends to ascertain whether growing up in a one-parent family in itself is bad for children.

What the above research indicates is the importance of considering complex sets of variables and their interactions when evaluating outcomes for children. The persistent identification of issues such as poverty and conflict/hostility between adults also opens up important questions in relation to gendered inequalities within the labour market and directs attention to the urgency of exploring what this conflict/hostility encompasses in terms of its sources and meanings for men and women.

However, what has emerged in contemporary discourses is the phenomenon called 'harm-ism': the tendency to see only harm, even where the evidence is more complex than this (Smart *et al.*, 2001, p. 37). There would appear to be a need for research which is multifaceted and not as outcome-focused (see Rogers and Pryor, 1998, in relation to divorce research). Outcome-focused research can preclude adequate attention being paid to how all involved perceive their experiences.

What do children say?

There has been a considerable growth in interest in researching children's own views on family change and transition across disciplines and through multidisciplinary work.

For example, from within developmental psychology, Dunn and Deater-Deckard (2001) have researched children's views about the changes in their families that occurred during and following parental separation, divorce and repartnering. They looked at children's views about the support they received from family members, friends and more formal support services and contrasted children and adult's views of such relationships. The children were in four family types: non-stepfamilies; single-mother families; step-father families; and stepmother/complex families in which both parents brought children from previous relationships.

This research offers important pointers towards what children feel they need and where they found support when their families were in transition. In many cases communication with parents, particularly fathers, was limited and grandparents and friends became important sources of confiding. The children distinguished between birth parents and step-parents, with less close relationships with step-parents and confusion over what kind of role a step-parent should play. Moving between two households had advantages, although those who were more involved in discussions about this were more positive. Children who described their relationship with their parents as high in conflict, criticism and negativity or who were frequently involved in conflict between their parents were likely to have higher levels of adjustment problems. Moreover, where there were poor parent relationships, the ability or opportunity to confide in peers may be especially unlikely. Positive mother–child relationships may be particularly important for the development of close friendships and children in lone-parent families reported less extensive contact with friends although the quality of their friendships did not differ from those in other families.

Smart *et al.* (2001) researched children's views post-divorce/separation from a sociological perspective. They found evidence of children rethinking what 'family' meant, which could lead to a certain degree of 'optionality' in the child–parent relationship. They noted that ties between children and parents have always been regarded as exempt from the voluntarism which it has been recognised can characterise kin relationships generally. For example, Finch (1989) has argued that the degree of liking and affection between adult kin rather than the positional relationship between them is central to determining what kinds of interactions occur between them. Although children's relationships with parents have seemed immune from such judgements, Smart *et al.* noted how often children in their study spoke of liking or not liking particular parents: 'They may have felt that their parents hold a unique position in their lives which could not be taken over in any absolute sense by other adults, but they no longer feel bound to them in the same way. We found that respect and liking significantly influenced the commitment as well as the closeness they felt towards them' (2001, p. 84).

However, Brannen *et al.* (2000) also from within sociology paint a wider and more complex picture in research looking at four different types of family setting: two-parent families; lone-mother families; stepfamilies; and foster care They addressed the following issues: children's reflections upon family life both in terms of its meanings and its importance to them and the ways in which they considered family life 'ought' to be enacted in the context of moral or normative guidelines.

Their findings support and question Smart *et al.*'s findings: 'children's representations of family life suggest that love and care, especially that provided consistently and on an everyday basis, are far more important to children than family structure. Most children held inclusive notions of family which encompassed different types of family forms, including lone parenthood and step families' (Brannen *et al.*, 2000, p. 204). However, no matter what form they lived in they still considered both birth parents to be very important to them. Foster children who lacked the continuity of at least one parent made the case most starkly, including parents they rarely or never saw in their inner circles of significant others in spite of the most unpromising circumstances or relationships. By contrast, step-parents had to earn their significance and work at the relationships, which would appear to support Dunn and Deater-Deckard's (2001) findings.

Gender differences between children in relation to outcomes and perceptions have been interrogated to some extent (see Golombok, 2000). A particular issue has been that family forms where a father is absent have been seen as having particularly deleterious consequences for boys. The research evidence would indicate a more nuanced picture which emphasises the quality of the relationships established between fathers and mothers and between fathers, mothers and children generally (Lamb, 1997). Where there do appear to be considerable concerns are in relation to the supports available to and the ability of boys to access supports when negotiating a range of difficulties in their lives (see Chapter 9).

Discussion

There would appear to be a considerable need to take outcomes for children seriously and to explore what children require. Alongside this must be located a concern to understand what is happening to relationships between adult men and women. Why does there appear to be so much 'conflict' and hostility between adults, what does this conflict and hostility encompass and how much of the latter is actually men's violence to women?

Of particular importance for practitioners is the recognition that there are complex links between poverty and diversity in family forms. There is, therefore, a considerable need to explore what is happening in poor men and women's relationships. In the USA it has been argued that a dramatic decline in the prospects of young black men is linked to a decline in their perceived eligibility by women. According to Franks, in the UK 'men who cannot support a family do not form one; nor are women eager to marry them' (Franks, 1999, p. 144). Whilst Mann and Roseneil (1999) are correct to argue that it is important to recognise the level of agency that may be being exercised by poor lone mothers in the same way as other financially secure lone mothers are doing, this exercising of agency does need locating in the context of restricted choices in relation to what men have to offer.

Giddens (1992), however, would argue that the increased diversification of patterns in relating between adult men and women, and in particular the shift away from lifelong fixed commitments, both reflects positive changes in women's aspirations and embodies and carries the potential for a 'democratising' of the intimate which is to be welcomed. Whilst his thesis has been criticised (Jamieson, 1998), it has also been welcomed by those who seek to rescue the motivations of those who divorce, for example, from what they see as dominant constructions of immorality or selfishness and who seek to explore the gendered causes and consequences of divorce (Smart and Neale, 1999).

Explorations which seek to explore the contradictory impulses and consequences of contemporary developments and to emphasise the importance of developing holistic understandings of what is going on for men, women and children are increasingly to be found in research influenced by feminist perspectives which are the subject of the next chapter.

Concluding remarks: the implications for family support

This chapter has charted key features of contemporary family life. It identifies how the continued usage of the term 'family' can obscure the diversity apparent and signposts the importance of recognising that the term 'family' does not have a singular meaning. It obliges ongoing attention to the self-definitions of individuals on the part of practitioners.

The chapter identifies the destabilisation of a particular model of family life – male provider and economically dependent wife. It highlights the way in which the emergence of 'a flexible economy' requires the emergence of 'flexible men and women' particularly among the poorest, who are working antisocial hours.

The implications for service providers are only just becoming apparent in terms of who is available to be worked with as well as how changes in traditional work patterns appear to be leaving groups of men without a clear compass. Such men are more likely to be disadvantaged and to be those encountered by family support practitioners (see Chapters 7 and 8 for practice implications).

There has been considerable concern expressed about the outcomes for children, particularly of the growth in divorce, lone motherhood and stepfamilies, and the chapter has explored the research evidence in relation to such outcomes. It argues that there is an important need to locate such research within understandings of how all concerned are making sense of their lives. Attention to adults' choices and well-being are important not only for the sake of the adults concerned but also for their children.

CHAPTER 2

Why Feminism?

As I explored in Chapter 1 the term 'family' can encompass considerable diversity in family forms. Moreover, men's and women's roles within family life are subject to debate and a degree of change. To argue, however, that feminism can both help understand what is happening and offer pointers towards policies and practices which are attuned to the diversity and complexity which are apparent is controversial. Feminism does not have a good reputation, for example, in the areas of either family law or policy according to Smart and Neale (1999), as it has been considered to be only concerned with the needs and interests of women, assumes children's needs and interests are synonymous with those of their mothers, and pays scant regard to, if not actively trampling over, those of men.

I will argue here that for those interested in developing policies and practices in relation to family support, certain versions of feminism have a great deal to offer. First, they help illuminate *why* there have been changes in adult men and women's relationships which have led to differing family forms and differing practices in family life becoming more prevalent. Second, feminist analyses can offer important and neglected insights into the consequences for all concerned – men, women and children – crucially through demonstrating why gender continues to matter. Finally, they offer important pointers for those concerned to locate family support practices within a policy framework which can actively support the building of more democratic families.

First, it is important to trace and locate contemporary approaches, not only to understand where they come from, but also to signpost the complexity and diversity of feminist thought. Such complexity and diversity are often not recognised in the simplistic characterisations which are used to argue that feminism is either irrelevant or dangerous or both (Segal, 1999).

Such characterisations often rest upon constructing feminism as a singular phenomenon with fixed meanings. However, there have been multiple feminisms available with highly conflicting views on a range of issues. Indeed, it used to be common to assign feminism and feminists to categories such as radical feminist, socialist feminist and so on which had its own dangers in terms of simplifying and unnecessarily counterposing complex positions, but did have the merit of undermining simplistic characterisations of 'feminism' and of drawing attention to important differences between feminists, particularly in relation to how far it was a project solely for women (see, for example, Eisenstein, 1984; Tong, 1989). Such categorisations are currently not widely used although there are considerable differences between those who call themselves feminists (Segal, 1999; Bryson, 2002).

Currently, there is also a wide range of constituencies including researchers, policy-makers and campaigners who do not use the term 'feminist' at all but are using concepts such as gender and/or ideas from feminism in their approach to a wide variety of issues which impact upon family life. This is partly because such ideas have become part of general currency and are particularly apparent in debates about welfare.

This chapter concentrates initially on exploring the differences between feminists in relation to understanding 'the family' and then moves on to exploring a range of contemporary developments which seem informed by feminist ideas. Because of space constraints, it limits itself to the ideas and strategies which have emerged since the late 1960s, from what have become known as second-wave feminists. It is important to remember, however, that there is a considerable history of feminist activity in relation to family life dating back to the nineteenth century (see for example, Gordon, 1986, 1989; Jagger and Wright, 1999; Somerville, 2000).

The family: reform or abolition?

The emergence of visible activity by women, in relation to their situation as women in the 1960s in many parts of the West but particularly in the USA and the UK, has had far-reaching consequences. A key early demand was that women should be freed from their confinement to the domestic and enabled to work outside the home. This, argues Bryson, was central to liberal feminism. Betty Friedan's book, *The Feminine Mystique* (1963), spoke to the discontent of many American housewives and was to prove pivotal in the establishment of the National Organisation for Women, an organisation which continues today aimed at bringing women 'into full participation in the mainstream of American society now, exercising all the privileges and responsibilities thereof in truly equal partnership with men' (Bryson, 2002, p. 11). This approach built on both general liberal and previous feminist aspirations in relation to equality.

Whilst Friedan undoubtedly spoke to the desires of many women with her critique there were many who rejected it on the grounds of its narrowness and/or the liberal assumptions underlying it. What Friedan was criticising was a very specific model of family life based on the male breadwinner and his economically dependent wife who took responsibility for the domestic and caring activities generally. This was a model which began to change particularly with the rise in lone parents in the 1970s (Barrett and McIntosh, 1982), but it was also not one which was available to all women. Working-class and black women were not confined to the home and indeed in the USA particularly often were to be found working for white middle-class women (hooks, 1984).

Others rejected and indeed continue to reject liberal, including liberal feminist, aspirations towards equality because of the assumptions about human nature underpinning them. Bryson summarises such criticisms (2002, pp. 12–13). There are different versions of liberalism but at its heart is the notion of the independent autonomous human being. There is a crucial flaw in this notion in that it treats people as autonomous and self-sufficient and abstracts them from their physical bodies and social relationships. The neglect of both physical bodies and social relationships has considerable implications for women. Not only does this ignore the work they do to maintain physical bodies and social relationships but the promotion of notions of equality with men can offer little support towards developing strategies for how such work should be carried out.

Furthermore, an uncritical acceptance of male norms is reflected in the assumption that women's aim should be to become like men and to seek success within existing structures and according to existing rules, rather than seeking to change such rules. Finally, liberalism's traditional distinction between public and private and its insistence that the latter cannot be a matter of political concern draws an artificial distinction between the two and works to obscure or deny the existence of power relationships within the family and the ways in which inequalities within the private restrict women's ability to operate in the public.

Other forms of feminism were to emerge which addressed such power inequalities directly. Radical feminists such as Millett (1970) developed the concept of patriarchy to describe a social system based upon male domination and female subordination. Men's power was maintained by a process of socialisation which began in the family and rested upon economic exploitation, state power and sexual violence. This was not a completely new way of looking at matters and had precedents in early versions of feminism but it was to prove both more popular than hitherto with women calling themselves feminists. The concept of patriarchy has been endlessly debated and disputed (see, for example, Walby, 1990). Other key insights have been both influential and contested. Radical feminists insisted that personal relationships are not matters of individual choice but reflect and maintain men's power and that men's con-tinuing failure to accept their fair share of domestic responsibilities is linked to their refusal to give up a position of privilege. This restricts women's employment prospects, maintains women's financial dependency and is reinforced by the use of violence by men (see Bryson, 2002, for a summary).

These insights did indeed open the way for ongoing and con-tinuing analyses of what happened in relation to unpaid care and the domestic division of labour and provided the key impetus for exploring men's violent and abusive behaviour but there was also a very clear backlash against attempts to map such analyses onto a rejection of men, marriage, heterosexuality or indeed family life (see Somerville, 2000). Moreover, concrete proposals such as those of radical feminists such as Firestone (1970), which advocated col-lective arrangements for the raising of children and were based on the voluntary agreement of a number of adults to cooperate in caretaking, were not influential.

At the risk of oversimplifying, it is possible to see liberal femi-nists as clearly targeting a particular model of the family – the male breadwinner model with an economically dependent housewife – and advocating approaches to get women out of the home and into the paid labour force, whereas radical feminist proposals seemed to counsel a more wholescale abandonment certainly of marriage and for some of heterosexuality.

Beyond reform or abandonment: deconstruction and multiplicity

For Marxist feminists such as Barrett and McIntosh (1982) it became crucial for feminists to acknowledge that 'the family is a constructed "unity" rather than a term whose real referent or meaning can be agreed. It is now widely recognized that the tendency to think in terms of an "essential family" creates serious theoretical problems and confusions' (p. 95). Moreover, they argued that the confusion by early feminists of 'the family' with a particular model was misguided given how much that model had begun to change particularly with the growth in lone mothers as early as the 1970s. They argued that a more fitting object of critique for feminists was an ideology which assumed that the language of family was a positive or exclusive signifier for human needs in relation to security and emotional fulfilment. They also argued for the collectivisation of many of the tasks associated with women in the home. Marxist and socialist feminists became associated with analyses which sought to understand the economic importance of women's domestic and caring labour and the interconnected, if conflicting, ways in which capitalism and men benefit from it. Where they clearly cohered with radical feminists was in their insistence that it was *vital* to both understand and challenge what happened in the home and who did what. Socialist feminists also opened up important issues which continue to be relevant, particularly in terms of exploring the role of the state and especially the welfare state in reproducing gendered inequalities (see Segal, 1987; and Chapter 3).

As will be discussed below, feminists studying families currently eschew attempts to speak of 'the family' or to construct it as an institution (Smart and Neale, 1999). However, the call by Barrett and McIntosh for a rejection of a familial ideology was to founder quite quickly in the face of a backlash from a diverse range of sources, including feminists, against any attempts to portray feminists as 'anti family'. Their call for the collectivisation of tasks such as caring were also to be challenged.

What emerged quite quickly and continues in the twenty-first century was a complex and tension-ridden set of imperatives towards developing more plural understandings of women's desires in relation to children, men and family life. Black women not only exposed the specificity of the particular model being criticised by feminists such as Friedan but also pointed out the ways in which historically black people's kinship patterns had been destroyed, and indeed the healing space family relationships could offer to those suffering racist oppression (hooks, 1984; Somerville, 2000; Bryson, 2002). Compatible issues emerged over time from disabled women who pointed out that feminist critiques privileged the voices of care-givers. This did not engage with the understandings of those who received care as well as their concrete experiences of being denied the right to engage in family life (Williams, 1992, 1999).

A complex literature on mothering emerged from the mid-1970s onward which had a range of implications. Whilst seen by some observers as problematic and a move from radical critique to a regressive celebration of mothering and motherhood (Segal, 1987, 1995), it did open up spaces for women who did not wish to abandon motherhood but rather to change the conditions under which women mothered. This exposed considerable divisions. For highly influential radical feminists such as Rich (1976), the logic of what was advocated was that women should create a female culture in order to truly reclaim mothering, whereas for others from a more psychoanalytic perspective, such as Chodorow (1978) and Dinnerstein (1976), it was imperative that women give up their monopoly on mothering. Although Chodorow's and Dinnerstein's analyses differed in important respects they both argued that exclusive caretaking by women damaged both girls and boys, producing boys who overinvest in autonomy and girls who overinvest in caring. As Snitow (1992) notes, these writings exposed a key division within feminism which continues today: is the goal to share childcare with men or to mother without men? Chodorow's and Dinnerstein's analyses clearly point towards a project to reform family life, whereas Rich's would point towards a more thorough transformation with radical implications for men's involvement.

The writings on motherhood also exposed important tensions between feminists in relation to thinking about mothering. Chodorow with Contratto (1982) argued that those such as Rich had fallen prey to the fantasy of the 'perfect mother'. Such a fantasy allowed the displacement of all the difficulties mothers experienced onto the social conditions in which they mothered. This did not engage adequately with the complexities of the feelings evoked within the mother–child relationship and implied that mothers would naturally be good mothers if patriarchal constraints were removed.

Such tensions continue between feminists and have been particularly posed for workers who seek to understand mothers' abusive behaviour towards their children (see Featherstone, 1997; and Chapter 8 in this book).

Whilst Rich's analysis undoubtedly was pertinent to many lesbians, here too a plurality of voices has emerged. Although many lesbian families argue that the heterosexual nuclear family is inherently oppressive, a lesbian perspective can also see marriage and the family as privileged forms of social organisation from which same-sex couples are unfairly excluded (Bryson, 2002). Moreover, there is evidence of lesbian mothers actively encouraging male involvement in their children's lives (Kershaw, 2001). One cannot therefore map rejection of heterosexuality onto rejection of men onto rejection of marriage or family.

In conclusion some early feminists raised considerable concern about a particular model of family which reinforced many women's economic independence. Others highlighted patterns of power in relation to caring and violence which were more widely focused than one model of family life. From very early on, however, there were considerable battles in relation to the meaning of family or motherhood.

In the next section I explore how the 1980s changed the landscape in which feminist ideas and strategies operated. This section concentrates explicitly on what was happening in the UK.

The battles were over but who had won?

By 1978 feminism in the UK no longer had a national focus, although feminist activity continued in a range of forums, and by 1979 a Conservative government with a woman prime minister had been elected (Lovenduski and Randall, 1993). The numbers of lone mothers and divorce rates continued to rise, leading to the ongoing proliferation of family forms removed from the nuclear. Male unemployment rose and more women including mothers entered the labour force. Having children continued to be a private responsibility throughout the 1980s and the management of work and home issues continued to be resolved at an individual level. Collective strategies in relation to childcare were still pursued by feminists amongst others such as the DayCare Trust (formed in 1980) but fell on stony ground (Lovenduski and Randall, 1993).

Inequalities between women increased with some high-profile women doing very well (Coward, 1993; Benn, 1998). There was evidence of a 'bourgeois feminist triumphalism' which seemed to celebrate women as individual achievers who could have it all, career and motherhood, and the ultimate embodiment was Margaret Thatcher. However, many were struggling as were men in a changing job market (see Chapter 1).

In 1987 a book by the socialist feminist Lynne Segal was highly critical of directions in feminism throughout the 1980s. She argued that radical feminist analyses had triumphed within feminism and were also increasingly the public face of feminism. Polarised thinking was dominant, constructing all men as wielding power over women through violence and women as essentially peace-loving and virtuous. There had been a retreat into pessimism about men and the possibilities of building political alliances with men, a retreat which was matched by the difficulties of advancing progressive approaches generally. She also linked the promotion of categorical thinking with the difficulties feminists had experienced in dealing with differences between women. She argued that the focus on men as monolithic oppressors was designed to obscure or evade dealing with how women oppressed each other as a result of racial, class and other inequalities.

At the same time as the more monolithic focus decried by Segal, however, there was a flowering of feminist activity in the academy and a growth in women's studies, and a focus on differences between women received considerable impetus with the emergence of controversial theoretical currents such as postmodernism. Here early feminist projects to understand 'the family' or women's lives foundered at the feet of critiques which emphasised the importance of moving away from singular and universalist theories which purported to speak to and for all women and to identify any one arena as 'the' site of women's oppression (see Nicholson, 1990).

At a media level, feminism became associated with a range of confusing and contradictory negatives in the 1980s: it was constructed as victim-focused and puritanical as well as anti-men. So it offended those who wanted to emphasise women's strength and power and it also offended those who wanted to build lives with men (Coward, 1993).

In summary the 1980s were confusing times for women and men and were central to the emergence of changes in employment patterns as well as changes in how family life was being lived out.

Feminists were often bitterly divided and there was no clear national focus for feminist activities. A difficult political climate seemed to offer unprecedented opportunities but at great costs for individuals, particularly those who wished to be mothers and to work.

The 1990s – mapping complexity

From the mid-1990s onwards we can identify the emergence of what has been called both a 'new feminism' or 'third wave' feminism. This strand of writing has been characterised by pragmatism with many of the accounts written by journalists in highly accessible formats (see, for example, Freely, 1996; Walter, 1999; Benn, 1998; Franks, 1999). These accounts have brought into the public domain issues such as inequality at home and work, issues which were either ignored or rendered irrelevant in the 1980s. Partly because many of the accounts are from journalists they appear to have received considerable and often considered media attention.

Freely (1996) and Benn (1998) both exemplified Somerville's observations that 'Taking as their philosophy, pragmatism rather than purity, these writers concentrate on motherhood as both a source of satisfaction and joy and an obstacle to equality at work. This approach enables them to avoid the clash of political absolutes over the nature of the family as an institution' (Somerville, 2000, pp. 212–13). Whilst Freely rather unfairly castigated early feminists for forgetting motherhood, she also reflected and reinforced feminist concerns about the difficulties of marrying public involvement in the world of work with attending to the care of children. Benn explored mothers' accounts from a range of backgrounds and argued that working women were living in two worlds with different priorities – the world of work and the world of home – and argued for a new political language and infrastructure which would seek to reconcile these priorities. Researching in the period before and just as a New Labour administration was elected she appeared to signal a new confidence on the part of feminists about engaging in a changed political climate.

What emerged from this strand was the importance of family life, particularly motherhood, to women and also the difficulties of combining work and motherhood and the impact motherhood had upon equality. According to Somerville they offered an analysis which pointed out that women had accommodated the economic and social transformations of the second half of the twentieth century but there had been little change in the division of labour within the home and in effect men had not changed enough. Until men changed, and that meant change at both the public and private level, women would continue to meet obstacles to their full participation in public life and children and caring generally would be second-best activities. However, it is important to note that whilst critical of men, they clearly saw what they were advocating as a project which included men. These accounts fed into a wider project around rethinking care and caring responsibilities generally which was to find academic recognition in the funding of a large research project at the University of Leeds, Care, Values and the Future of Welfare (CAVA) and the work on rethinking citizenship by Lister (1997).

Varying strategies have been promoted by these diverse if interconnected strands, reflecting ongoing debates on how caring work, which has in practice been women's work, is to be financially recognised without reinforcing women's responsibility for it. As Bryson (2002) notes, some feminists have over the years controversially called for 'wages for housework'. This has never been widely accepted by feminists, however, as it has been feared that it would be interpreted as 'wages for housewives' and because any achievable wage rates would be unattractive to men, it would entrench women more firmly within the home. Benn (1998) called for a carer's income which both men and women could apply for, although in practice Bryson notes that this has the same dangers as the call for wages for housework. Lister (1997) discussed the idea of a basic 'citizen's income' which should be paid to all adults as a gender-neutral way of providing a degree of economic independence for all. However, Lister expresses concerns about the lack of specificity it has in that it fails to distinguish between those who are contributing to society by their caring work and those who are not and moreover it could actually weaken women's links with the labour market. Her preferred model which is explored further in Chapter 4 is that of the 'universal caregiver' model which is an avowedly normative and prescriptive approach to developing an infrastructure which supports both men and women's involvement in care and paid work.

A range of discussions has emerged in relation to what has been called variously the work–life balance and family-friendly policies (see Chapter 4). Williams (2001), for example, has argued for a rethinking and refocusing of working practices around an 'ethic of care' or 'the political ethics of care'. By recognising that we are all interdependent and will give and receive care at varying points of the life cycle, she has sought to broaden the discussion away from mother/child responsibilities and to displace involvement in paid work as the central organising principle of human activity. Strategies here could include a wide variety of changes particularly in relation to working practices. Somerville (2000) notes the emergence of a range of other demands from a variety of sources which call for differing strategies in relation to employers, the state and men so there is no unanimity among feminists. What is apparent is a reenergised engagement with old concerns about the balancing of work and care.

Moreover, feminist concerns in this area increasingly dovetail with those of a range of other constituencies around a belief that the financial and social costs of current working patterns are unacceptably high. As Bryson (2002) notes, these are no longer seen as 'feminist luxuries but central political demands' (p. 147) (see also Chapter 4).

Another important set of developments from the academy in the 1990s was the emergence of research into diverse family forms. Stacey's (1991) detailed ethnographic study from the USA of 'the unpredictable, often incongruous and contested character of contemporary family practices in the postindustrial United States' (p. 5) was an important landmark. She explored two extended kinship networks of primarily white working-class people and named the relationships she found as 'postmodern', arguing that like postmodern culture the family arrangements were diverse, fluid and unresolved:

> The postmodern family is not a new model of family life, not the next stage in an orderly progression of family history but the stage where the belief in a logical progression of stages breaks down. Rupturing evolutionary models of family history and incorporating both experimental and nostalgic elements, 'the' post-modern family lurches forward and backward into an uncertain future. (Stacey, 1991, p. 18)

Whilst it is important to recognise the specificities of the USA (Stacey, 1986, 1991, 1999), her work is of relevance to what happened in the UK in relation to academic developments. Crucially, her emphasis on 'practices' and her eliciting of accounts from multiple perspectives in relation to the doing of everyday life, as well as her mapping of how relationships which are not defined by blood or marital ties are negotiated, have clear resonance with work that emerged in the UK (see, for example, Silva and Smart, 1999; Smart and Neale, 1999; Smart *et al.*, 2001).

The term 'family practices' has emerged which seems to sum up the shifts which have occurred in feminist theoretical and empirical work (Morgan 1996; Smart and Neale, 1999). This term is used to challenge the idea that 'the family' is a thing or an institution and thus moves away from early feminist critiques of it as the key site of women's subordination. This reflects the influence of a range of critiques such as those outlined above as well as the influence of theoretical currents such as postmodernism. It also reflects the evidence of a dispersal of practices across a range of households and involving a range of blood, kin and non-kin relationships:

> The term 'practices' emphasises fluidity. More than this the term 'practices' allows us to conceptualize how family 'practices' overlap with other social practices (for example, gendering practices, economic practices and so on). Moreover, while 'practices' are historically and culturally located, they allow us to imagine the social actor who engages in these practices and who may choose to modify them. (Smart and Neale, 1999, p. 21)

The feminist approach to family practices as developed by Smart and Neale (1999; Smart *et al.*, 2001) concentrates on looking at men's, women's and children's accounts of what 'doing family' means in post-divorce/separation contexts. It is therefore very clearly not about providing a voice for women, which is what earlier versions quite appropriately, given women's invisibility, did. It looks at what 'family' means to those sharing care and living across households with a range of participants who are not linked by blood or marital ties. It interrogates how mothers rethink their identities in contexts where they are not the sole caretakers and how fathers redefine what fathering means in situations of non-residence. What is happening to gendered settlements in relation to caring? How do new settlements emerge? What are the implications of treating men and women as equal before the law when in practice many have negotiated unequal settlements around caretaking and paid work? How do children negotiate the more fluid terrain of post-divorce family life? It also opens up issues around how women and men who are no longer tied together as marital partners renegotiate their relationships as parents.

Studies have emerged which address lone mothers' under-standings about how they should fulfil their responsibilities towards their children (Duncan and Edwards, 1999). Lewis (2001) has explored both cohabiting and married couples' understandings of commitment and responsibility. All of these appear influenced by earlier work by Finch (1989) which explored family obligations between adults in a period of social change.

Whilst clearly addressing different arenas a key theme which emerges from all these studies is the importance of engaging with 'bottom up' understandings of family life and examining partici-pants' own beliefs about how they should or should not discharge their responsibilities towards each other. Gendered understandings of what is the right thing to do emerge as both significant and complex, particularly in Smart and Neale's and Duncan and Edwards's studies. Both studies point out the difficulties with top-down impositions of a language around parenthood, as it does not always engage with how identities are constructed in relation to fatherhood and motherhood, or it fails to address how men and women may interpret notions of parenthood.

Many of these studies are feeding into the broader project identified above, CAVA, which attempts to develop what Williams (1999, p. 675) has called a 'moral grammar' from below. A range of research projects exploring questions such as who looks after children when parents work, who lives where after divorce, or who do single people go to for support is ongoing. These look at what values and moral frameworks are being used to resolve the dilemmas and what difference class, gender, ethnicity, disability, age and/or sexuality make to these dilemmas. Clearly a broad project in which gendered analyses intersect with a range of other social divisions, this feeds into a rethinking and revisioning of welfare practices and policies.

Smart and Neale's research continues a feminist focus on power which raises interesting issues. They explicitly distance themselves from what they see as earlier feminist assumptions about how power operates, indicating that they do not assume that it auto-matically operates in a particular way, that is, in a top-down way in terms of men exercising power over women. They observed from their research that there appeared to be two modes of exercising power and two types of experiences of powerlessness. 'Debilitative power' was deployed in some circumstances and seemed to impact primarily upon women in that it was experienced as an effacement of the self in contexts where women needed to become more 'them-selves'. Issues of space and independence, for example, were a common theme for many of the mothers but in post-divorce par-enting women often experienced the men as not respecting such space and independence.

They also identified the deployment of 'situational power' which derives from the reality that women are mostly the primary caretakers of children while men are usually responsible for finan-cial support. It is, however, they argue, only the latter – situational power – which was regarded as a legitimate source of complaint. Women's need to find their own space was not defined as legiti-mate whereas men's concerns in relation to either sharing care or debating financial responsibilities was.

They recognise other manifestations of gendered power which continue to need addressing such as the use of physical violence. Both men and women acknowledged the potential for violence by themselves in times of difficulty which did not characterise the nature of the relationship prior to breakdown. This was identified as mainly a 'one off' phenomenon. There was a second type of vio-lence which was 'destructive of the self' which was rarely a 'one off'. It was the sort of violence which had a long history and which had generated physical damage as well as psychological damage and was predominantly carried out by men. They argued that sus-tained and/or destructive violence occurred in at least 15 of the 60 cases they looked at, which meant that one in four women were experiencing violence which could be said to be damaging to their self-esteem and sense of self.

They do not explore this violence in terms of its meanings for the men or try and identify any links between this and the men's backgrounds. In this they reflect a common difficulty in feminist thinking about men's violence which will be explored below.

What did, however, emerge in the mid-1990s and continues today was an interest in and contested focus by feminists on the role of fathers. This emerged in a climate where from the early 1990s onwards there had been a clear political campaign against lone mothers as well as the emergence of discussions, influenced by debates in the USA, of the implications of the growth in lone motherhood for the welfare of adult men and boys (see Williams, 1998, for a discussion of two key discourses around father absence and father presence which preoccupied a range of constituencies in the 1990s). As noted above there had been tensions exemplified by the oppositional views of Rich and Chodorow in relation to the role of the father and of men in family life from the mid-1970s onwards. Summarising some of the disagreements, Coward (1999) suggested that many feminists were unable to see any role for men other than as supports for women or as dangers to women and children. She, however, argued that men were entitled to develop their own paternal journeys which feminists should support and they had an important and distinctive role to play in children's lives.

The debates, however, often seemed unable to move beyond polarised positions which rested on categorical thinking about men as fathers. As Williams (1998) noted, there was a need to move beyond such categorical thinking and to engage with the complexities of men's wishes and behaviour. For example, she noted Connell's (1995) research which found that individual men could have contradictory feelings and wish to both cooperate with the mothers of their children and undermine them. There was a tendency, however, to think of them as either problems or victims.

An influential development was the emergence of a book by Burgess (1997) which wished to 'reclaim fatherhood' from a variety of negative and barrier-laden constructions, including feminist constructions of men but also earlier feminist constructions of care as oppressive. This has fed into contemporary developments which pose men as 'resources' in family life and has fuelled a number of service developments, which are explored further in Chapters 4 and 7. It has also fed into the broader project which seemed to be emerging, as outlined above, in relation to developing a more pragmatic approach to the balancing of work and care, particularly obvious in the work of Freely, Benn and Walter.

Overall, it is apparent that in the 1990s a complex body of work emerged from a variety of sources which is concerned with exploring bottom-up understandings of family life as it is currently being lived. There is evidence of attempts to explore multiple perspectives in terms of men, women and children and there is evidence of work which foregrounds gender as well as integrating it within broader understandings. An important development alongside more explicitly academic developments has been the emergence of pragmatic and populist attempts to bring concerns particularly in relation to the balancing of caring and employment onto the policy and cultural agenda.

In the next section I offer a broad overview of what I consider are the key strengths of continuing to use feminist insights when trying to understand family life, in particular for those involved in the doing of family support.

Feminism for family support

I argued in the Introduction that the emergence of feminism is important in understanding *why* some contemporary developments emerged. It opened up possibilities for rethinking what family meant and for doing family differently. In this it was part of wider economic, technological and cultural developments. For example, women's involvement in paid work, which has offered opportunities for avoiding relationships with men, leaving relationships with men or doing relationships differently, can be seen as linked to economic imperatives. Indeed some would argue (Mitchell, 1986) that feminism merely acted as a midwife to the needs of the capitalist economy in encouraging women's involvement in the paid labour force. However, few women, despite all the difficulties involved, would wish to return to a situation where they did not have the opportunity to be economically independent of individual men. The ability to take up such opportunities is often sorely circumscribed and there have been restrictions placed upon those for whom reliance on the state benefit system has provided such opportunities (see Chapter 3 for developments in relation to child support). But it does remain an important aspect of contemporary developments that marriage is not the only way women can acquire a meal ticket today and feminism has supported this development. It has also actively supported changes in taxation and benefits systems in order to reinforce women's economic independence from individual men.

Feminism has also supported changes in expectations of intimate relationships which have both altered the meanings attached to marriage particularly and made possible the doing of everyday life differently. Giddens (1992) argues that women, aided by feminism, have pioneered a profound transformation in the social world and in particular are promoting a restructuring of intimacy. Whilst there are those who argue that the changes in intimacy are neither as recent nor as transformatory as he proclaims (Jamieson, 1998), his contention that developments have had profound implications for contemporary heterosexual relationships and particularly for marriage is seen as important by others seeking to understand and research divorce, for example (Smart and Neale, 1999).

Giddens argues that women no longer accede to male dominance and that both sexes are being forced to come to terms with the implications. In this landscape 'Personal life has become an open project, creating new demands and anxieties. Our interpersonal existence is being thoroughly transfigured, involving us in what I shall call everyday social experiments' (Giddens, 1992, p. 8). In the process a restructuring of intimacy is occurring. There was an almost inevitable connection between love and marriage for many women in the earlier periods of modern development. However, we are now in the territory of the pure relationship. A pure relationship refers to a situation in which a relationship is entered into for its own sake, for what can be derived by each person from a sustained association with each other, and which is continued only in so far as it is thought by each party to deliver enough satisfaction for each individual to stay within it. Love used to be tied to sexuality through marriage but now the two are connected more and more through the pure relationship. Marriage has veered increasingly towards the form of a pure relationship and this pure relationship is part of a restructuring of intimacy. There is a clash here between the pure relationship and traditional forms of romantic love:

> Romantic love depends upon projective identification, the projective identification of *amour passion* as the means whereby prospective partners become attracted and then bound to one another. Projection here creates a feeling of wholeness with the other, no doubt strengthened by established differences between masculinity and femininity, each defined in terms of an antithesis. (Giddens, 1992, p. 61)

Giddens argues that in the era of the pure relationship what emerges is confluent love which presumes equality in emotional give and take. Love here only develops to the degree to which each person is prepared to reveal concerns and needs to each other and be vulnerable to the other. Confluent love is therefore active and negotiated and is at odds with the forever-one-and-only quality of romantic love. Romantic love was bound up with fantasies about the loved one and these fantasies were gendered. Fantasies of invulnerability in men sustained by both partners rested upon women doing the emotional work and carrying men's emotional vulnerability. Giddens argues that the separating and divorcing society of today is an effect of the emergence of confluent love rather than its cause.

Giddens has argued that in the field of intimacy there is a move towards greater equality which is leading to changing relationship patterns, a thesis which is much debated. He recognises that violence and coercion make it impossible to construct equal relationships. Not only is it vital to locate this not just in the context of constructing such relationships, it also continues to be an important reason for relationship breakdown. The Exeter Family Study, for example, found that one in four women separated because of domestic violence (Cockett and Tripp, 1994; see also Humphreys, 2001).

The rethinking of self and personal life more generally which Giddens points to – a trend, pioneered by women, to live lives which are not just characterised by unthinking adherence to tradition – can be seen as concerned with a project around self-actualisation rather than solely due to the need to flee abusive relationships. This trend links with a wider process of individualisation in Western society. 'We now live in a post-traditional order where processes of individualization have resulted in the self becoming a reflexive project. Identities are now to a large degree constructed by individuals themselves rather than inherited' (Ferguson, 2001b, p. 50). A key aspect is that this is a process open to women (Beck and Beck-Gernsheim, 1995). In contemporary contexts the question 'who shall I be?' is inextricably linked up with 'how shall I live?' Everyday life therefore becomes open to discussion and negotiation rather than fixed. Intimate relationships are clearly central here and provide the terrain for demands often by women in relation to men's behaviour and communication. As Beck and Beck-Gernsheim (1995, p. 62) note, 'studies on the reasons for divorce show that women expect a good, emotionally fulfilling life together much more than men do.

Smart and Neale (1999), who have carried out a considerable amount of empirical research into divorce and post-divorce parenting, argue that the most compelling aspect of Giddens's argument is that the dominant form of intimacy, namely heterosexual marriage, cannot remain unchanged in contemporary circumstances. However, they argue that he fails to explore how the pure relationship is mediated by differences such as ethnicity, religion, access to material resources and so on. They are not implying here that only the secular white wealthy communities and those in full-time employment can access the pure relationship, as they reason that it might be the poor, urban unemployed white sectors who are less enmeshed in property concerns and for whom marriage might entail financial impoverishment who incline towards this model. This is an interesting point to consider in the context of the findings highlighted in the last chapter, which note a strong correlation between family form and poverty.

Certainly, it requires more empirical investigation. Research in the last chapter would suggest a tempering of Giddens's optimism. For example, although he does indicate that men in general may be struggling with constructing new narratives of self in contemporary conditions he does not anchor such observations.

Those who have used gendered understandings to explore poor men's lives would indicate the considerable challenges posed by changes in both economic and gender relations for such men (Stacey, 1998; Ferguson, 1998, 2001a; Ruxton, 2002). Stacey notes, for example, that there are clear indicators that men seem much less well-equipped to deal with the hazards and opportunities posed by a changing gender and economic landscape. Exploring physical violence by men to women (admittedly only one form of violence and complexly linked to psychological sexual and economic violence) would reinforce such concerns. Whilst this is a phenomenon which extends across classes, ethnicities and social backgrounds, Ruxton (2002), for example, argues that the onset of unemployment needs further investigation in terms of its potential to trigger such violence.

Feminists have been anxious to stress the links between the range of violences women experience both in intra-familial and extra-familial settings. They have been concerned to gender the language and explanations offered and they have also been instrumental in opening up spaces for children's voices to be heard particularly in relation to the sexual abuse they experience. However, there are important differences between feminists in relation to understanding and countering what has become known as the continuum of sexual violence (Kelly, 1988). In particular there are those who have stressed the importance of deconstructing men and deconstructing sexual violence, seeing neither as a unitary phenomenon (Segal, 1990). These debates are explored more fully in Chapter 3 in terms of how they have informed developments in relation to family support and child protection practices.

However it is important to signpost here the insights of those such as Ferguson (2001a; 2001b), who has directly applied the work of Giddens and feminist writings on violence to practices in family support. He argues that supports of both an emotional and practical nature are crucial for women and children to negotiate more democratic settlements with men and each other. He argues that understanding and working with the consequences of past and present violence and abuse can free up women and children from old toxic attachments and patterns and combined with practical help can open up important possibilities for them to develop better self-understandings and relationships with each other. He also argues that work with men is essential in order to engage with their vulnerabilities and their violent behaviour.

More generally, there is considerable evidence that whilst there are similarities in how men and women respond to contemporary developments such as divorce and separation, for example, there are also differences which would point to the continued importance of using feminist insights to map the consequences of contemporary developments in family life for all concerned.

Day Sclater's (1999) work, for example, indicates that both adult men and women continue to make profound psychological investments in marriage and family life which are not adequately addressed by notions, such as Giddens's, of the pure relationship which implies a rather cool, calculating attitude to moving on if things are not good enough. She argues from a psychoanalytic perspective that divorce involves engaging with profound feelings of loss and indeed can be likened to a bereavement. Furthermore, she critiques the current emphasis on adults behaving cooperatively as this fails to acknowledge adequately the psychological coping strategies which people need to mobilise to cope with the emotions that are involved in loving and losing. Conflict is routinely attributed in contemporary discussions to the influence of adversarial court processes. She argues that this is too simple in that it obscures the profound emotions which are mobilised in contexts of loss. The current context fails to acknowledge the vulnerability of adults whilst emphasising that of children. In the process children become lost as individuals and are constructed as the objects of adults' concerns.

However, in research into how parents negotiated post-divorce contact arrangements, Day Sclater and Yates (1999) noted the importance of using gendered approaches to understand what was going on. Gendered interpretations were made routinely by divorcing men and women which both raised questions about the psychological investments that women and men make in disputes about divorce and fly in the face of the gender neutrality of family law and its central concept of parental responsibility. Given Giddens's comments about the difficulties that men may have in constructing new narratives of self in contemporary circumstances, it is perhaps not surprising to find in Day Sclater and Yates's research that what united the fathers' narratives was a strong sense of vulnerability and loss which was overlaid with appeals to notions of justice and rights in order to salvage something for themselves:

> The fathers in the study made different interpretations of the welfare discourse; for some ironically it presented them with an opportunity to pursue a rights-based discourse, for some it was inseparable from financial issues and all felt a profound sense of injustice *vis-à-vis* women in general. (Day Sclater and Yates, 1999, p. 280)

Mothers also invoked the welfare discourse but this was frequently challenged by what the researchers called the 'independence' discourse with which it was frequently in conflict:

> The welfare discourse emphasises the priority to be given to children's interests and the apparent need for parents who are in harmonious contact with each other. The independence discourse on the other hand emphasises the needs of a woman for a final and complete separation from the former partner, and the pursuit of personal autonomy after divorce as a valued and motivating goal. (Ibid., p. 273)

Day Sclater and Yates focus attention on the considerable emotional costs involved in divorce for the adults concerned. In the current climate the costs for children are what is emphasised and adults are often solely located as the source of children's distress and subject to rational injunctions about behaving cooperatively. They also explore how gender differences manifest themselves in dealing with such distress. This research pinpoints the implications for services of the distress which may be experienced and acted out in different ways by men and women, physical and emotional distress which leads a significant proportion to seek out the services of a range of health and welfare professionals.

Concluding remarks

A number of issues emerge from this chapter which are explored further, particularly in Chapters 6, 7 and 8 in relation to the practice implications. One issue is that changes in family forms, in particular through the more widespread usage of divorce, signal changes in both women's aspirations and the possibilities available to them. This is how feminism helps us to understand *why*.

However, what is also important to note is that the complex and contradictory consequences of such changes and the gendered implications of such consequences need to be mapped. In particular, men appear to be having difficulties both within relationships and when separation/divorce occurs. These difficulties may be particularly accentuated for those men who are disadvantaged (see Chapter 8 for a discussion of the implications for practitioners).

Feminism can help explain and has also contributed to contemporary cultural discourses which speak of men and women's disappointment with each other, if not their hostility. But it can also offer pointers, even if they are tension-ridden, towards different settlements. In particular, it argues that attention to the well-being of children should be part of a broader project which looks at how caring activities are supported generally. Whilst there are no easy answers here it argues that old settlements which would involve the suppression of women's desires and needs are not acceptable. New settlements will involve posing opportunities and challenges for men to become more involved in care. This needs to be located in a broader project which looks at the role of welfare policies more generally and poses a considerable challenge to current policies which seem to emphasise both involvement in paid work and responsible parenting in the absence of an adequate infrastructure of support (see Chapter 4).

CHAPTER 3

Family Support
in Perspective

This chapter takes a step back from the contemporary concerns of Chapters 1 and 2 in order to locate what has become known as the ambiguous and elastic concept of 'family support' within an understanding of the 'battle for hearts and minds about the role of the family', and in particular the role of the state in relation to family and child in these battles (Tunstill, 1997, p. 40). It locates its explorations within a specific time frame, the post-1945 expansion of welfare by the state. This is because this postwar welfare settlement has been crucial in terms of understanding key developments and is currently the subject of significant and explicit rethinking and reordering. This rethinking and reordering forms the subject of the next chapter.

I explore how the postwar welfare settlement established the boundaries of what was known as prevention until the 1980s and 1990s, when the term 'family support' became much more widely used, a usage strongly boosted by the guidance attached to the Children Act 1989 (Department of Health, 1991). Prevention and family support are, however, used alongside each other and to a certain degree interchangeably in contemporary policy and practice developments and this is particularly apparent in the initiatives which have emerged under New Labour (see Chapters 4 and 5).

Feminist analyses have been influential in rethinking and reshaping the discipline of social policy itself and a key object of study is the welfare state (Lewis *et al.*, 2000). Feminist contributions to critiquing or rethinking the specific policies and practices which have emerged under the umbrella of prevention and family support have been more tentative and have been conducted in the context of debates about the role of the state in protecting children and women from abusive men. Such contributions are obviously crucial to the concerns of the book and are explored in terms of their strengths and limitations. It will be argued that feminist insights as they have developed in the 1980s and 1990s have become increasingly pertinent to developing practices within family support which resist the counterposition of protection and support and rethink prevention.

Postwar welfare

According to Clarke *et al.* (2000), highly particular assumptions about family, work and nation were central to the postwar construction and development of what became known widely as the welfare state (see also Williams, 1989). Whilst they point out that it is more accurate to see what was constructed as a new mixed economy of welfare, in that welfare was provided through a range of institutions, the term 'welfare state' which was used was highly significant and the popularity of the term did capture a shift.

A key point is that whilst there was an expansion of state provision postwar, this was framed by the presumption that 'most welfare needs would be satisfied by the family and the market' (Clarke *et al.*, 2000, p. 37). Only in education and health care was it the state's role to be the primary agency of provision (although here private provision continued). This led, for example, to a distinction being made between the care of children and the education of children, with education free to children on a universal basis. However, childcare provided by the state was fee-based, a distinction which has proved harder and harder to justify and which is currently the subject of considerable debate (see Land, 2002; and Chapter 4).

In addition to its direct role in the provision of health care and education, the state was required to support the market and the family, filling gaps where the market and the family failed and with no intention of replacing them as the main support to individuals:

> In their different ways the programmes of public housing, income maintenance, services to neglected children and so on, assumed that needs would be met primarily through male (waged) work and the services

that a wage could buy, and through the services provided within the family by wives/mothers. (Clarke *et al.*, 2000, p. 37)

Thus was assumed a particular mixed economy of support based upon an economic and social architecture in which the family wage was the cornerstone and in which a gendered division of labour was embedded. In practice much welfare work was expected to be undertaken within the family either by spending some of the 'family wage' or by women looking after the young, the ill and the dependent. State welfare was designed therefore to supplement and support this hidden welfare work. Embedded in the postwar welfare regime were three core assumptions: waged work would be the primary source of income; the political task of maintaining full employment would be achieved; and full employment meant full male employment. However, it was recognised as crucial that provision for and insurance against unemployment and illness were built in.

The model of the family underpinning the tax and benefit systems was therefore that of the male breadwinner supporting a dependent wife and children. Although normatively accepted, it was a model to which many working-class families did not conform. Moreover, as time went on, with the return to pre-Second World War deregulated flexible labour markets and the growth in lone parents, this assumption was to become more and more problematic and the benefits system changed accordingly (see Land, 1999).

The postwar settlement rested in a very practical sense on the unpaid work of mothers and women. It is also argued that it rested on a belief in 'mother love' which was to support a psychological as well as material rebuilding project after the horrors of war (Walkerdine and Lucey, 1989). Thus, the work of those such as Bowlby (1953) spoke to the desires of the times as well as offering a compass for the building of a better world based upon offering security and attachment at a psychological level alongside that at a material level.

Feminists have devoted considerable attention to making visible the unpaid work women, especially mothers, did, securing social entitlements for these women and demonstrating the gendered implications of the mixed economy of welfare provision which emerged (Williams, 1989; Lewis, 2000). They have also been part of a project which explored the assumptions about nation underpinning the development of the welfare state. Until the Second World War national identity and British cultural supremacy linked the development of welfare policy to imperialism. With the collapse of empire:

> The welfare state became central to the reconstruction of post-war Britain. Britain's civilizing mission as an imperial power was to be brought home. The welfare state embodied this spirit of reform and improvement. It was to be built with the bricks of the family and the mortar of national unity, by the labour of low-paid women and newly arrived black workers. Ironically, it was often these groups of workers to whom the benefits of the new welfare state were restricted. Black male workers may have built council houses, but discriminating allocation criteria meant that they weren't eligible to live in . . . Working-class white and black women may have cleaned hospitals but they were not necessarily entitled to sickness benefit in their own right. (Clarke *et al.*, 2000, p. 35)

The creation of the welfare state played an important role in compensating for both imperial decline and loss of status to the USA in the new postwar era which emerged. The eugenic themes of the Beveridge Report with its imperialist emphasis on the role of mothers in ensuring the adequate continuance of the white race and the adequate continuance of British ideals in the world reflected some of this.

Although the postwar settlement was based upon particular assumptions as outlined above, this does not mean that there were coherent policies developed in relation to supporting a model of 'the family'. Indeed for much of the postwar period it was argued that the UK had either implicit or no family policies (Kamerman and Kahn, 1978; Land and Parker, 1979). As Fox Harding (1996a) notes, different state policies emerged over time which were in conflict with one another, with a particular family form or family role being rewarded in one part of the system but penalised in another. This was to become very apparent in the 1970s and 1980s as economic and demographic changes became starkly posed. For much of the Conservative rule from 1979 to 1997, for example, despite considerable rhetoric to the contrary, successive administrations did little to reinforce a particular family form and moreover facilitated economic developments which rendered solo male wage-earning families either unachievable or undesirable.

Very complex tensions have been apparent at particular periods about the role/responsibility of the state in relation to the care and welfare of children within families.

Whose responsibility? Whose rights?

According to Daniel and Ivatts, although there have been differing emphases:

> it is, nevertheless, important to stress that throughout its history, and whatever its current emphasis, child care policy in the UK has always operated within a broader political context which is inimical to state intervention in the family. This as posed as the 'liberal dilemma'. . . On the one hand, children are seen as the responsibility of families who, in turn, are entitled to autonomy and privacy in their child-rearing role. On the other hand, it is accepted that the state has a duty to protect children from abuse and neglect within the family. (1998, pp. 197–8)

The resultant liberal compromise has been to devise a legal and policy framework which does not convert all families into clients of the state (Dingwall *et al.*, 1983; Hendrick, 1994; Daniel and Ivatts, 1998).

Hendrick (1994) argues that the specific welfare of children was not much more than an afterthought in the grand schemes which brought in the welfare state in the UK, except with respect to problems likely to arise after the end of evacuation. The plight of evacuated children who could not go home began a discussion about those other children who were unable to live at home and led to two issues being discussed: the nature of postwar childcare services and who should be responsible for them. The death of Dennis O'Neill at the hands of his foster parents in 1945 gave added impetus to such discussions. The subsequent report criticised the lack of coordination between different authorities and social workers and located the problem of childcare within the whole system of administration. The Curtis Committee in 1946 lay claim to being 'the first enquiry in this country directed specifically to the care of children deprived of a normal home life' (quoted in Hendrick, 1994, p. 214). Its key recommendations were to locate central responsibility for all deprived children in one government department, with responsibility to be exercised locally by new children's committees and the appointment of local authority

Children's Officers who would be well-qualified academically and have chief officer status and their own department. Boarding out, or what is now called fostering, was the preferred form of care for deprived children and this system should be extended through vigorous efforts by local authorities. These recommendations were accepted by the government in 1947. The main principles of the Children Act 1948 echoed strongly the recommendations of the committee: a new emphasis on boarding out in preference to residential homes; restoration of children in care to their natural parents; greater emphasis on adoption where appropriate; and partial responsibility by the children's departments for young offenders.

The Act was not specific about the amount of time to be given to preventive matters but a Home Office Circular in 1948 stressed their significance. As Hendrick (1994) notes, psychological research and economic factors relating to the cost of residential care and foster breakdowns gave strong impetus to a policy preference for 'maintenance of the family' and prevention of children leaving families. There was at this time little regard for arguments that children might be endangered by the desire to keep families together.

In 1948 local authorities were given responsibility for the development and provision of personal social services but these were considered a low priority in the development of welfare services and were not accorded the financial resources given to health and education, for example. They were seen as residual services rather than universal – picking up the pieces where the family could not. Moreover, Finlayson (1994) acknowledges that although greater responsibility for welfare had shifted to the state, there was still a significant role for the voluntary sector to play. They continued to provide a high range of personal social services – for the blind, elderly people and unmarried mothers in particular. Grier (2001) explores the role of two children's charities post-1948 and notes the considerable degree of enthusiasm on the part of the Labour government for voluntarism.

By the mid-1950s prevention in the sense of prevention of the child leaving the family was the dominant aim of these residual services. Statutory recognition of the importance of prevention was to come in the Children and Young Person's Act 1963, Section 1. This Act was primarily concerned with delinquency but Section 1 gave local authorities the specific powers they had been seeking in order to practise preventive work. This included being able to make provision in kind or in exceptional circumstances to give money and other material aid in order to prevent children coming into local authority care.

According to Frost and Stein (1989), by the end of the 1960s the childcare service had developed considerably with a powerful group of mainly women workers who provided both substitute care and preventive work. The extent to which this work was psychoanalytic has been contested but there was certainly a strong belief that emotional difficulties lay at the root of many of the problems children experienced and this was extended to understanding delinquency. The focus was on families, mainly mothers rather than on children.

However, a variety of developments were to change this picture. From the mid-1960s the consensus that childcare services were to do with rescuing those who were unable to fit in with the mainstream and partake of the general affluence around had begun to evaporate generally. The rediscovery of poverty was to be crucial in puncturing the consensus (Frost and Stein, 1989). It became harder to argue that it was only the few who could not cope and therefore needed help.

The Seebohm Committee was appointed in 1965 and promoted a family-oriented service which was, however, community-based. 'The move towards a "family service" did not develop naturally out of experience; it was predicated on a developing Fabian theory of social democratic welfare *vis-à-vis* working class families' (Hendrick, 1994, p. 236) and encompassed dealing with the 'depraved' and the 'deprived' as a result of concerns about juvenile crime. This was promoted as a move away from the residualist approach which saw the role of services as to intervene with those who, for whatever reason, could not fit in with or be part of the general affluence. The objective of the new social services departments was to reach out 'far beyond the discovery and rescue of social casualties, enabling the greatest possible number of individuals to act reciprocally giving and receiving services for the well-being of the whole community' (Seebohm, 1968, para. 2).

These recommendations were incorporated into the Local Authority Social Services Act 1970. As Bamford (1990) notes, this was a quarter of a century after the developments in health and education. However, this expansion was threatened almost immediately by the economic crisis of the mid-1970s which put paid to the expansion of local government generally. Furthermore, according to Parton (1985), the fall-out from the death of Maria Colwell in 1973 who had been returned home from foster care was to prove catastrophic in terms of confidence in and within the newly established departments. The departments, particularly in terms of childcare services, were to be narrowly focused on 'casualties with the vast majority of children and families having no contact with the departments – they receive no services and fall outside its surveillance' (Daniel and Ivatts, 1998, p. 198).

Whilst cautioning against generalisations and oversimplifying the past, Fox Harding (1991) has argued that with the benefit of hindsight 'it is now fairly easy to identify the 1960s in England and Wales as the "prevention" decade when policy and social work practice favoured supporting the natural family and minimising time in care, and the 1970s as the time of "child protection" spurred on by concerns about child abuse' (p. 217). The term 'prevention' was the forerunner of the term 'family support' which was not to emerge until the 1980s. Prevention offered possibilities for a minimal approach to children and families in the sense that it could be defined quite narrowly as literally preventing children from being removed, but it also could be used to offer considerable support including some financial help. The emergence of a concern with the 'protection' of children in the wake of the death of Maria Colwell was, however, to pose considerable tensions for a mixed economy of welfare which had relied upon the family as a crucial component.

State paternalism and protection in the 1970s and 1980s and its critiques

Fox Harding (1991) identifies four value positions or perspectives in childcare policy: laissez-faire and patriarchy; state paternalism and child protection; the modern defence of the birth family and parents' rights; and children's rights and child liberation. As she recognises, all such categorisations carry considerable dangers in that they can render quite complex positions unhelpfully coherent and imply a level of fixity to people's positions which is inaccurate. However, they did capture a sense of the diverse range of perspectives around in the 1970s and 1980s. These perspectives can be summarised as follows. Laissez-faire and patriarchy is essentially a perspective which argues that power of adult males over women and children in the family should not be disturbed and the role of the state should be a minimal one. State paternalism and child protection legitimate extensive state intervention to protect and care for children. Good quality substitute care is favoured when the care of the biological parents is found to be inadequate. The modern defence of the birth family and parents' rights legitimates state intervention but of a supportive kind. It is a position which wants the expansion of welfare provision and highlights concerns that it is often poorer and socially deprived parents who are seen as victims of heavy-handed state action rather than offered support and help. Finally, children's rights and liberation advocate the child as a subject, as an independent person with rights, which, taken to extremes, are similar to the rights of the adult.

Published in 1991, this outline captures the debates in the 1970s and 1980s well. Fox Harding identifies the 1970s as a period which saw the emergence at a policy and practice level of the second perspective: that of state paternalism and child protection. This perspective was of course of much longer standing, as she documents, but it did reemerge in the 1970s in a particular form. There was a greater emphasis when compared with preceding decades on protecting children from their families and on the use of substitute care. 'More was seen of the controlling state than in the previous decade; the family oriented support work of the 1950s and 1960s was giving way to a greater readiness to focus on the child as a separate individual and to act coercively, if need be, on her behalf' (Fox Harding, 1991, p. 91).

Parton (1985) has argued that the preoccupation which emerged in the 1970s and extended into the 1980s with child abuse in the UK, and the readiness to use legal powers to remove children from families, stemmed from deeper moral anxiety about the decline of the family as a socialising agent and this was linked with wider fears about the social order. It is interesting therefore that the response appeared to be to remove children from what were seen as problematic families as the Children Act 1975 exemplified. This was undertaken rather than attempting to change or reorder families. The Finer Report on One-Parent Families (Department of Health and Social Securing, 1974), for example, does indicate that there was considerable concern about the rise in numbers and the implications for state expenditure. However, one-parent benefit was introduced and a number of other state benefits and provisions were adjusted to take into account the special circumstances of the lone parent (see Lewis, 2002, for an extended discussion of the Finer Report).

The emphasis on protection excited considerable critique. At the risk of oversimplifying, by the middle of the 1980s it was possible to ascertain a consensus emerging from such critics which went something like this. The preventive ethos has been superseded by a focus on child abuse and child protection – this took children away from their parents, penalising the poor doubly.

Research by Bebbington and Miles (1989) pinpointed the issues very starkly, contrasting the chances of two children being admitted to state care – Child A and B. They found that Child B in a lone-parent household in receipt of Income Support, with four or more children, of mixed ethnic origin, in privately rented accommodation with one or more persons per room, had up to a one in ten chance of coming into state care. By contrast, Child A, a white child in an owner-occupied house with two resident parents and not dependent on social security benefits had a one in 7,000 chance.

The critics of a system which they saw as essentially about judging and disciplining the poor developed a consensus which maps to some extent onto Fox Harding's third perspective: the modern defence of the birth family and parents' rights. This encapsulates the idea that birth or biological families are important both for parents and children and should be maintained wherever possible, and where families have to be separated, links should be kept up. The role of the state is seen as ideally neither paternalist nor laissez-faire but as supportive of families, providing the various services that they need to remain together. Class, poverty and deprivation are seen as important. Fox Harding identifies the most consistent advocate of this approach as Bob Holman (1988). He not only espoused much of the above but also gave an important role to voluntary bodies in preventive childcare work and explicitly promoted a mixed economy of welfare, welcoming initiatives which actively involved members of families and communities in the provision of support to each other.

Holman (1988) documented how through the 1980s the key national childcare charities had developed an enthusiastic commitment to prevention. They were represented by the National Council of Voluntary Child Care Organisations which by 1985 had approved the following statement:

> It is important to help children by enabling families to stay together. A positive response to the need for preventive work has become increasingly apparent among member organisations. We believe that the principles and practices which we here summarise will contribute to the prevention of disadvantage, neglect or abuse of children and young

people and to the achievement of their individual progress. (Quoted in Holman, 1988, p. 111)

In contrast to laissez-faire approaches and the state paternalists where psychological bonds formed between children and their primary caretakers are more important than any notion of a blood tie, for this perspective, links with original biological parents appear crucial. Yet, as Fox Harding (1991) points out, the third perspective can also draw on the work of psychological theorists such as Bowlby. Holman, for example, invokes Bowlby's work. However, she argues that they go beyond psychology to support the importance of biological ties per se. One way of looking at this is that this perspective is acutely aware that in a society where society defines family in biological terms, then to have lost some of one's nearest biological relatives is to be socially defined as having something missing. Therefore Holman can be seen as supporting biological ties because they are socially defined as normal.

Unlike the state paternalists this perspective sees parents' needs and interests as important in themselves and does not treat parents only as a means to the end of child welfare. The emotional importance to a parent of a biological bond is seen as important and there is considerable concern for those parents who are poor, single and deprived.

This perspective focuses on the nuclear family as a unit rather than seeing the child as separate. Policy and practice should support the welfare of this unit and this is the most effective way of enhancing child welfare. While the emphasis is mainly on the nuclear family, wider kinship links may also be seen as valuable.

Moreover, it has a particular view of society and social problems. Society is characterised by social divisions and inequalities. 'Part of the reason why the state is able to remove children from their parents, override those parents' rights, and to keep children away permanently, is to do with the powerlessness of poor people' (Fox Harding, 1991, p. 120). This perspective is very attuned to the importance of class divisions. It can see the state as able to act in an enabling way through more redistribution and an extension of the welfare state. State intervention should be supportive rather than coercive and there is a preference for help to be offered on a voluntary basis. This perspective is the one which maps most closely onto that of the most influential proponents of family support in the twenty-first century. The problems in its thinking are therefore very relevant. It had a clear tendency to connote control as automatically oppressive and fails to address whether differing family members might have differing needs and interests which would warrant control strategies for some in relation to others' abusiveness. It was not until the events in Cleveland (Department of Health and Social Security, 1998) that the issues here were to become very sharply posed.

According to Corby (2002), events in Cleveland, where over 100 children were removed from their homes because of suspected sexual abuse, and the subsequent inquiry were to prove a watershed in thinking about, and responding to, child abuse in Britain. He argued that state paternalism was seriously questioned and this coincided with an emphasis on family autonomy and a questioning of professional authority by those on the political right. But there was also a strong critique of state paternalism, as outlined above, from social democrats and the left.

However, the issue which the Cleveland Inquiry was concerned with – sexual abuse – had considerable potential to disrupt assumptions such as that either 'the family' is a unit which should not be interfered with (family autonomy approach) or it is a unit which should be supported with an array of welfare rather than controlling measures (pro birth family/parents' rights). Whilst there is evidence of a more specific recognition that children's interests needed to be at least ascertained separately as in the Children Act 1989, Cleveland did not, however, lead to a widespread recognition that the 'family' needed to be deconstructed or an associated discussion about what causes sexual abuse. That this did not happen is due to a range of factors but of crucial importance was the limited remit of the inquiry which did not explore why sexual abuse happens and the marginalisation of feminist approaches at the time which were due to factors intrinsic and extrinsic to feminism. This is explored in more detail below.

The 1990s

The decade opened with a brand new piece of legislation. The Children Act 1989 was the most wide-ranging piece of legislation introduced since 1948 and remains the underpinning legislation today. Parton (1991) provides a detailed account of the genesis of the Act. It had an unusually explicit and rational history in that it was preceded by a review of childcare law and was informed by a set of empirical studies (Tunstill, 1999). Events in Cleveland seemed influential in that there was a clear attempt to try and narrow down the grounds for legal intervention through the concept of 'significant harm' (Section 47, Part 1) and to offer parents a range of legal safeguards in relation to legal interventions.

It was also considered to place the child centre stage in a host of ways. The child's welfare was paramount and there was an obligation to ascertain the wishes and feelings of the child. It introduced advocates for children called guardians *ad litem*, which underlined the idea of children as individuals in their own right and established complaints procedures for those looked after alongside giving children limited rights to choose where they lived and with whom they had contact. Over the years children's rights advocates have both questioned its efficacy and continue to push the boundaries of children's participation (J. Roche, 2002).

The notion of 'parental responsibility' received some attention in terms of whether it signalled a new set of balances between parents and the state in the upbringing of children. Fox Harding (1996b) argued that since 1979 the Conservatives had developed an interest in the issue of family responsibility, the scope of state responsibility and particularly the amount of state expenditure involved:

A rhetoric of family behaviour has been developed in which certain themes, such as individual responsibility and the undesirability of dependence on the state, have become central to the aim of restoring or revitalizing family responsibility. A major preoccupation has been the area of *parental* responsibility. (Fox Harding, 1996b, p. 130, emphasis in original)

Parental responsibility became a theme uniting the Child Support Act 1991, the Criminal Justice Act 1991 and the Children Act 1989. Whilst the different types of parental responsibility within the three Acts are not always consistent, the concept was used 'as a powerful instrument of social policy in shaping the family' (Edwards and Halpern, 1992, quoted in Fox Harding, 1996b, p. 136). It was promoted in place of state responsibility, although it was also a mechanism of greater state control. It meshed with a wider strategy which promotes more private dependency and fewer state-dependent families as well as broader family responsibility.

Fox Harding (1996b) explores the emergence of the Child Support Act 1991 as an instance of concern with state expenditure and undesirable family forms. This Act aimed to shift responsibility away from the state through making absent parents, invariably fathers, pay child maintenance. It can be seen to reverse historical trends within the twentieth century away from private patriarchy, where women were dependent upon individual men, to public patriarchy where women became less dependent upon the support of individual men, although they remain subordinated. But the 'new' forms of private patriarchy instituted by the Child Support Act do not force women to stay in or form households with individual men. It reinstates the financial dependence of lone mothers but women do not do have to do anything for these men in return for their financial support. Moreover, individual men are also controlled by this legislation.

In general, childcare observers did not highlight the gendered implications of parental responsibility in relation to the Children Act and interrogated it more in terms of whether it increased or decreased state powers to control or support parents. Eekelaar (1991) argued that the Act encoded two notions. Parents must behave dutifully towards their children and responsibility for childcare belongs to parents rather than the state. The second idea came to be the dominant one according to Eekelaar and this has led to a weakening of the state's supervisory role in relation to parent–child relationships. Parental responsibility is defined as individual responsibility, cannot be surrendered voluntarily to the state and remains undiminished even when care is shared with the state. For others such as Daniel and Ivatts (1998), the notion that responsibility for childcare belongs with parents weakens the possibility of the state supporting parents and fits with a long-standing trend in British social policy. Parton (1991) located it more obviously within the policy context of the time whilst recognising its historical links:

> While the family was constructed as an essentially private institution and the primary institution for rearing children, parents were seen as having responsibilities towards their children rather than holding, in effect, parental property rights as in the past. The role of parents was cast in far more active terms, terms consistent with the Government emphasis on individuals and families taking responsibility for both their own behaviour and the quality of life of their dependents. While the state was seen to have an important role to play, this was to ensure that parents fulfilled such responsibilities. The role of the state was confirmed as residual and supportive rather than primary. However, it

should work in partnership with parents on behalf of children in need. (p. 155)

The definition of 'children in need' is contained in Section 17(10). It has three categories: a reasonable standard of health or development; significant impairment of health or development; and disablement. Section 17 of Part 3 of the Act gives local authorities a general duty to safeguard and promote the welfare of children in need and to promote the upbringing of such children by their families by providing an appropriate range and level of services. Schedule 2 of the Act contains further provisions which are designed to help children in need to continue to live with their families and prevent the breakdown of family relationships.

During the 1990s childcare debates were to be largely dominated by whether the Act had facilitated a 'new' balance in the way the state worked with parents around support and protection issues. There was also a concern to elicit how well the Act promoted the abilities of children to make known their wishes and feelings.

Family support under the Act – a new balance?

Whilst the term 'family support' was not used in the Act, it was in the associated guidance (Department of Health, 1991). It was made clear here that the term marked an important shift in emphasis. The emphasis was on providing positive support to a child and their family which could include using local authority accommodation when children were looked after by the local authority in partnership with parents who maintained parental responsibility.

These developments in relation to family support were considered cautiously by those who wished to expand the remit of the state's supportive mandate for families. Tunstill (1997) argues that prevention provided the conceptual framework for children with their families from the 1950s to 1970s and was ousted by family support in the 1980s. She argues that family support in the 1980s had the potential to point towards an optimum childcare policy in a way prevention did not. She notes that prevention had often been interpreted narrowly as the prevention of children going into care without the offering of support, although there were those who argued for a wider perspective which avoided an exclusively problem-focused approach and looks well beyond the nuclear family unit. She argues, however, that the positive potential contained in the notion of family support became hijacked within the Children Act 1989 by being tied to the rationing concept of 'children in need' which led to filtering, with priority being given to professional judgements and resources.

Certainly the implementation of Part 3 of the Act was to become the subject of considerable interrogation in the 1990s. The slow and patchy pace of developments was to become quickly apparent (Aldgate and Tunstill, 1996). Two key developments in the 1990s, the Audit Commission Report, *Seen But Not Heard: Co-ordinating Community Child Health and Social Services for Children in Need* (1994) and the publication of *Child Protection: Messages from Research* (Department of Health, 1995), were central to opening up widespread discussions about the implementation of the Children Act and in particular the balance of work being carried out under Section 47 and Section 17.

The Audit Commission report suggested that social services' children and families departments change their priorities from a reactive service engaged in crisis intervention to one which offers support to children in need. It argued that social services' support is too narrowly focused and that prevention should be better than cure. An investment in more proactive services should improve the possibility of reducing the need for crisis intervention (Audit Commission, 1994).

The following year *Child Protection: Messages from Research* (Department of Health, 1995) was published which also opened up considerable debate about priorities and the appropriate balance between family support and child protection. Based on a range of research studies commissioned and funded in the late 1980s, an overview document, summarising the main themes, was published to considerable media fanfare. There was a key message from the diverse studies, according to the overview, which was that with the exception of a few severe assaults and some sexual maltreatment, long-term difficulties seldom follow from a single abusive incident or event:

> It was the overall context in which children lived which was crucial. Apart from the severe cases, the most damaging outcomes accrued in situations of emotional neglect where the primary concern was parenting style – what became known as 'low warmth, high criticism' contexts. These were however the contexts where practice seemed either least successful or were ignored. While there was little evidence that

children were being missed and suffering harm unnecessarily at the hands of their parents, as implied by most child abuse inquiries, and was thus 'successful' according to a narrow definition of child protection, this was at a cost. Many children and parents felt alienated and angry, and there was an over-emphasis on forensic concerns, with far too much time spent on investigations, and a failure to develop longer-term coordinated treatment, counselling and preventative strategies. (Parton, 1997, pp. 6–7)

It therefore called for a refocusing away from specific incidents of abuse and their investigation to earlier and broader assessments of family needs. Over time the publication of *Messages from Research* has occasioned considerable debate amongst a range of constituencies about the following: the adequacy of the research base; the problems of the dissemination process and its desirability; and the feasibility of the 'messages' being disseminated (Gardner, 2002a, offers a good exploration here).

A key concern is that in the main *Messages from Research* concentrated on what professionals did or did not do in their work with families, which gives a very partial picture particularly given the then lack of research into wider populations. For example, there is considerable evidence that those who are sexually abused do not approach professionals at all (Wattam and Woodward, 1996). One of the research programmes associated with *Messages from Research* (Kelly *et al.*, 1991) highlighted this and the linked implication that mothers and friends are the primary resources for those needing protection and support, but this was not highlighted in the dissemination process and did not inform discussion about what 'family support' might mean in such contexts (Colclough *et al.*, 1999).

Many of the research studies in the programme noted that there was a disproportionate representation of lone-mother families and reconstituted families on social workers' caseloads. However, there was little discussion encouraged about or reference to wider demographic trends in relation to family forms, which was all the more surprising given the promotion of 'family support'. What discussion there was condemned the 'myopia' (Department of Health, 1995, p. 65) exhibited by practitioners in their neglect of wider family networks. This remained caught up in traditional discourses about extended family kinship patterns, within the overview document certainly. Although it has over time fed into some limited discussions about whether new constructions of 'family' which were not exclusively based upon blood, marital or kinship patterns might be emerging (see Marsh and Crow, 1998; and discussion in Chapter 6).

High levels of violence and conflict between adult men and women were also apparent. The levels of violence noted were not located in the overview document in the context of any discussion of how they compared with levels within the wider community. Nor did they link in with discussions about why men and women might be in conflict with each other and whether there might be wider patterns to interrogate beyond the level of the individual couple, although the findings here do appear to have contributed to the placing of 'domestic violence' on the child welfare agenda in the policy context established post-1997.

The overview document, and in particular the introductory statements by the then Secretary of State, led to a tendency to establish a set of unhelpful binaries: family support/good versus child protection/bad. Whilst this was not what was intended by many of the researchers and was not the intention behind the Children Act, the splitting that the Children Act introduced between Section 17 and Section 47 has facilitated a binary approach developing. This, it will be argued, continues today although it has become more and contested (Department of Health, 2001). In particular, the inquiry into the death of Victoria Climbié and the subsequent report by Lord Laming (2003) have opened up considerable discussion about this (see Chapter 5).

Overall, the 'refocusing' project reduced refocusing to a voluntaristic project which relied upon changing social workers' attitudes and activities (Parton, 1996, 1997). Furthermore, despite numerous injunctions to the contrary, there were simplistic signals being sent out which counterposed protection and support/prevention despite the evidence that throughout the 1990s, the demand for *both* child protection and family support was unprecedented, and the first national inspection of provision for children in need which took place between 1993 and 1995 drew a picture of departments under siege (Department of Health, 1996). Departments were applying higher thresholds to stay within their budgets and facing alarming increases in the costs of specialised accommodation for children with complex needs, for example, those who sexually abuse others (Gardner, 2002a).

There were those who raised concerns about the desirability of 'refocusing' and the promotion of 'family support' as an appropriate response to the harms experienced by children and those who sought to protect them (see Colclough *et al.*, 1999). Such concerns were directly informed by attempts to bring feminist understandings to bear on debates in relation to protection and support. In the next section I locate such understandings and the complexities, strengths and limitations of the feminist understandings which had emerged over the 1970s, 1980s and 1990s.

Feminism – from marginalisation to incorporation to revitalisation?

In the 1970s and 1980s there began to emerge a tentative and still developing addition to the four perspectives outlined by Fox Harding. This was a position informed by feminism which had a number of contradictory and diverse elements. Whilst initially quite limited because of its concerns to provide a voice for women, it has over the decades emerged as an important contributor to developing a more integrated approach to the need for care and control, protection and support and to rethinking prevention. Currently, it obliges attention to the deconstruction of the assumption that there is something called 'the family' which should be either supported or controlled and argues that it is practices by people who are gendered which needed to be interrogated and either fostered or proscribed.

Its potential contribution to a child welfare project was not immediately obvious however. As Chapter 2 noted, the 1970s particularly were a period of considerable feminist activity in terms of both developing an array of analyses and being politically visible. It is then that the more radical critiques of the nuclear family emerged as a site of unpaid labour and of violence and abuse. Much of this focused on the implications for women rather than children and seemed to have little impact upon or relevance for debates in childcare. This was partly due to the difficulties many feminists themselves had initially in thinking about the role of the state particularly in relation to social control. Gordon (1986), writing from the USA in the mid-1980s, noted the paradox that feminists historically had 'been important advocates of modern social control. Yet contemporary feminist theoreticians and scholars have tended almost exclusively to condemn social control' (p. 62).

A small 'women and, social work' movement emerged in the UK which held a number of conferences in the late 1970s and early 1980s and local groups of women social workers were formed

(Brook and Davis, 1985). However, generally, there was a preference for developing strategies which did not involve the state or state employees. Women-run services located outside the statutory sector in the form of refuges and helplines, like Women's Aid and Rape Crisis, were set up. Services such as refuges provided for children also. State controls were sought in relation to punishing violent and abusive men but there was a considerable degree of suspicion about invoking the state to support women and, given its historical association with disciplining women, there was little attention devoted initially as to whether such disciplining was ever necessary in the interests of children.

In the 1980s the rediscovery of child sexual abuse, largely attributable to the efforts of survivors and feminist supporters, brought feminist and child welfare concerns together. However, this was not to be a straightforward project by any means.

In many ways the events in Cleveland already alluded to, which were to lead to the setting up of the Cleveland Inquiry in 1988, arguably set back considerably the possibilities of opening up a considered debate on the causes of sexual abuse and the strategies which should be employed to deal with it. The taking of over 100 children away from their family homes focused attention generally on the powers of the state and the rights of children to have their wishes ascertained and these fed into the concerns of family autonomy advocates, the defenders of the birth family and parents' rights and those who promoted the rights of children.

Why sexual abuse happens did not form a part of the inquiry's remit and was sidelined as an issue often in public discourses about overzealous professionals breaking up families. There was, therefore, no officially sanctioned space for opening up discussion about feminist insights or indeed any other insights into the causation of sexual abuse. Even if there had been such a space the difficulties were considerable. The naming by feminists of men as perpetrators in the main is uncomfortable, as are the consequent strategies which oblige exploring masculine socialisation practices, particularly in relation to sexuality (Frosh, 1994). It obliges a quite fundamental rethink about how men engage with women and children and with their own emotions and desires. It involves exploring both the commonalities and the differences between men and the ways in which men engage variously and often very anxiously with societal discourses which stress the importance of masculine mastery and control.

However, this does not mean that certain feminist insights in relation to sexual abuse did not start to become incorporated into practice in the 1990s post-Cleveland. This was, however, often in highly problematic ways. They more often coincided with prevailing policy and legal trends with a focus on removing the perpetrator rather than the child thus reducing the need for expensive local authority resources such as childcare. This also fitted with long-standing and ongoing concerns about the fate of children removed, particularly as evidence emerged in the 1990s of abuse in residential homes and poor outcomes for children placed in state care (see Fawcett *et al.*, forthcoming). Furthermore, the feminist emphasis on the reality of many mothers' protectiveness rather than their collusion became translated in practice into placing the burden of responsibility for support on the mother, again reducing the need for expensive resources. Feminists exposed the difficulties of this for individual mothers and it was an important finding of Farmer and Owen's (1995) research which was one of the research projects attached to *Messages from Research*. However, as Chapter 8 notes, in practice such support burdens continue and still have not been adequately addressed.

This is linked to the ongoing difficulties there have been with introducing a language around gender into debates. Thus there has never been any widespread commitment to exploring the implications of the gender neutrality of the notion of parental responsibility contained in the Children Act or in exploring whether in mistaking what might be a goal for a given, it would result in women/mothers actually bearing the burden of responsibility (Williams, 1998). Whilst it has never been clear how or whether gender neutrality might be acknowledged as an issue at a legislative level, there has been an ongoing need to monitor what is happening in practice and to point out the gaps between the legal and official language and the actual material realities. Furthermore, the emphasis which the Act placed upon uncoupling parenthood and marriage has meant that divorce did not end parental responsibility and tied adults together as parents. For feminists this has meant an ongoing concern with the consequences for women and children, especially where domestic violence has been an issue. The biggest gains seem to have been made in terms of identifying and gaining recognition for the links between violence to women and violence to children and in recognising the damage to children which can be caused by violence to women, although it is usually posed in gender-neutral language in official guidance (see Chapter 5). But the importance of addressing violence as an issue when contact arrangements post-divorce are being developed is also increasingly on the agenda (see Frost and Featherstone, 2003).

Moreover, it is important to acknowledge that there were intrinsic factors which led to feminism being less influential than it might have been. As Parton (1990) noted post-Cleveland, there was a worrying tendency by feminists at that time to extend the analysis which had been developed in relation to child sexual abuse to all forms of child abuse: 'many feminists assume the oppression of women and children to be the same – in form, cause and manifestation. There is a failure to disaggregate women and children as groups' (p. 17).

As Gordon (1986, 1989) noted, the physical and emotional abuse of children involving women often as victimisers did not fit neatly into feminist narratives which stressed women's victimisation. However, she argued that feminist insights were relevant to understanding such abuse. In particular, gender as an analytic category provided important pointers in trying to think through what features of women's and men's positions and their relationships with each other predisposed them to be involved in what types of harms to children and how children's relative powerlessness and gendered differences compounded this (see Featherstone, 1997).

This feminist perspective obliges attention therefore to questions such as: What does mothering signify to individual women? How possible is it for women to openly challenge discourses which stress the inevitability of instinctual maternal love? How do men negotiate feelings of power and powerlessness in intimate relationships? How available is a language of emotional vulnerability to them? These questions continue to be marginalised in government guidance especially, although Chapters 7 and 8, in particular, offer important evidence of their pertinence to practitioners.

A key contribution within which this book locates itself is that feminist insights currently offer strong support for a project which resists the counterposing of protection and support and rethinks and broadens out what is meant by prevention. This is developed further in the following chapters in relation to the debates and developments which have ensued under New Labour. The work of those such as Hooper (1992) in relation to the needs of mothers of children who are sexually abused and Ferguson's (2001a) work more generally argue for the interweaving of protective and supportive activities. They refuse assumptions that control strategies should be connoted as undesirable and indeed in Ferguson's work there is an explicit commitment to working in dialogue with all concerned around why and how a range of practices require fostering as well as an articulation of what needs proscribing.

As Chapter 5 indicates, feminist insights can also contribute to a project which opens up broader issues in relation to prevention. For example, it will be argued that the prevention of violent and abusive activities must incorporate a gendered dimension which engages with issues such as masculine socialisation.

Concluding remarks

Immediate postwar developments were concerned with developing a welfare settlement based on a particular model of family life and family functioning – wage-earning males with dependent wife and children. There were specific developments promoted for those who could not meet this norm or were displaced postwar.

For much of the postwar decades there was strong adherence to the assumption that children were best placed within their families and the shape of that family was neither questioned nor challenged. Prevention strategies largely assumed the prevention of children being removed from their families. The 1970s began a period of concerns about child protection with more evidence of state involvement in the removal of children from poor families, developments which excited a considerable counter-reaction particularly from those influenced by class critiques. The 1970s and 1980s were also to see the emergence of a range of family forms and of feminist critiques of the family and the emergence of sexual abuse onto the public domain.

The early 1990s too saw the most far-reaching piece of legislation in relation to children postwar – the Children Act. It reconstructed parents in gender-neutral terms as holding lifelong responsibilities towards children. It introduced the notion of 'family support' as a statutory responsibility to be developed for 'children in need' – a notion which appeared designed to supplant earlier notions of prevention. The mid-1990s saw the publication of key pieces of research which opened up debates about the balance between child protection and family support. Feminist insights can be seen to be complexly and uncertainly placed. Some were marginalised whereas others were incorporated but often in problematic ways. It is argued that they had and have considerable potential to contribute to the transcending of the protection/ support split which has increasingly been recognised as problematic and to a rethinking of prevention, a project of considerable pertinence in the policy climate ushered in by New Labour.

The election of a New Labour government in 1997 introduced an array of differing understandings and initiatives in relation to family support and uncoupled it from its linkage with child protection. It also opened up a renewed engagement with the notion of prevention. The next chapter sketches out the contours of the policy context and Chapter 5 expands more fully on the possibilities and constraints for a feminist engagement with the differing understandings of protection, support and prevention which have emerged.

CHAPTER 4

Family Support under New Labour: A New Era?

Supporting Families: A Consultation Document (Home Office, 1998) was published in 1998 by the Labour government elected in 1997 and is considered to mark the emergence of an explicit family policy for the first time in the UK (Land, 1999). An explicit family policy has been defined as: specific programmes and policies designed to achieve specified explicit goals regarding the family; (or) programmes and policies which deliberately do things to and for the family, but for which there are no agreed-upon overall goals regarding the family (Kamerman and Kahn, 1978, p. 3).

Certainly, there would appear to be an array of programmes and policies which deliberately do things to and for parents and children and there appear to be some clearly articulated goals regarding parents and parenting which are inextricably linked with an overall project in relation to ensuring children's welfare. This would appear increasingly not to be a project about promoting a particular family form but rather about ensuring that children, particularly poor children, are better supported in a host of ways and about developing a new balance between the state and parents in terms of supports and controls to ensure this.

Numerous writers continue to explore what New Labour is about and why. The very title 'New Labour' has been subject to considerable interrogation in itself, emerging as it did in the 1990s as part of a project which sought to distance the party from 'old' programmes, policies and images and as central to the construction of something different (see Fairclough, 2000). A range of analyses have emerged here in relation to understanding the overall project (Driver and Martell, 1997; Giddens, 1998, 2000; Jordan with Jordan, 2000; Newman, 2001). Whilst I do engage with these analyses, the chapter has a specific purpose which is to understand why developments in family policy have taken the trajectory they have and to sketch out the landscape within which many contemporary family support projects are being developed. In relation to the latter, the next chapter elaborates on this more fully.

A key argument is that it is important to identify how a dominant construction of children as *investments* and parents as carrying *responsibilities* links with a wider project, particularly in relation to the reforming of the welfare state and the emergence of the social investment state. This argument seems crucial in capturing key tendencies in what is going on, although it does not capture fully the complexity of what has happened and could lead to an assumption of coherence in the New Labour project in relation to family policy and family support.

Locating and exploring New Labour and 'the family'

First, it is important to acknowledge New Labour's legacy from the Conservatives. It inherited a modest and reluctant infrastructure particularly in relation to support for families, alongside a legislative infrastructure based upon the notion of 'parental responsibility'. Despite the rhetoric and the presence of a diverse constituency of pro-family values pressure groups, the Thatcher years did not present a picture of a Conservatism centrally concerned with the family and traditional values and the picture under the Major government was even more mixed (Fox Harding, 1999; Somerville, 2000). As Fox Harding (1999) notes, the mixed picture reflects not only a conflict between the ideology of the right and the family values approach but also a deeper conflict within right-wing ideology itself – between economic liberalists and traditional authoritarian conservatives. Whereas much of the ideology of the right emphasised a restricted role for the state generally, family values campaigners wanted more prescription and legislation. Equally, economic liberalists' emphasis on individual autonomy and the unfettered right of the market to dictate all forms of relationships clashes with that of the traditional authoritarians who espouse a strong state, commitment to nationhood, law and order and the policing of behaviour. This divide militates against a clear consensus on family issues and policies although in practice there was an accommodation of the conflicting ideologies. 'Libertarian Conservatism' adopted by the New Right in Britain and the USA supports laissez-faire economics and a strong state to maintain traditional and family values. This accommodation is uneasy, however, in the face of many issues, some of which became the subject of much concern in the 1990s. Should mothers of young children be in paid work? Should employers take any account of workers' family commitments?

In practice, whilst the Conservatives presided over an historically unprecedented increase in women, including mothers, entering the paid labour force, no Conservative administration supported the development of day care as a state responsibility. Moreover, family leave policies were among the worst in Europe (Coward, 1993; Benn, 1998).

There was evidence in a range of areas such as childcare legislation, juvenile offending and the Child Support Act 1991 of a preparedness to expand parents' responsibilities for children but not to offer parents support in the form of financial help, day care, parental leave or indeed services such as counselling and so on.

Building or overturning – a new era in 1997

When New Labour came to power in 1997 they inherited a landscape which had changed profoundly politically, economically and socially since 1979 when they were last in power. They had responded to the changes and to the successive electoral defeats they had suffered by a major reassessment of policies. This meant not only engaging with Thatcherism as a legacy but also reassessing 'Old' Labour thinking (Driver and Martell, 1997; Powell, 1999; Jordan with Jordan, 2000; Newman, 2001). The adoption of the title 'New Labour' was a conscious signposting of its distance from previous Labour thinking.

Alongside major changes to party democracy, the relationship with the unions and attitudes towards nationalisation, there had been a significant rethinking of attitudes to crime and the family and the links between crime and the family. Developing a distinctive position on the family was also part of a project which underlined the distance between 'Old' and 'New' Labour and made an electoral pitch for ground which had historically belonged to the Tories. Certainly, by the mid-1990s it seemed as if Labour had adopted the 'family values' rhetoric more often associated with the Conservatives.

Newman (2001, p. 170) sees New Labour and the associated project 'the Third Way' as representing an unstable political settlement. She identifies three arenas of instability: the attempt to combine neo-liberalism with a renewal of civil society; the attempt to forge a new social settlement which articulates elements of the radical politics of the late twentieth century's new social movements together with the moral orthodoxies of Christian socialism, communitarianism, ethical socialism and old Labour paternalism; and conflicts over power arising from the partial constitutional changes that have been introduced, and from the uneasy interaction between forms of centralisation and decentralisation.

The first two areas of instability and their intersection are particularly important in terms of decoding the twists and turns New Labour has taken in relation to family policy.

Neo-liberalism and the renewal of civil society

The fracturing of the postwar social settlement under the neo-liberal regime of the Conservatives was perceived as problematic by New Labour and they therefore developed a project which was concerned with building the right kind of social base to ensure that destructive forms of fragmentation do not occur (Barlow and Duncan, 2000). Crucial is the 'constitution of new subjects – self-reliant and responsible, moral and familial, community oriented and at the same time seeking new opportunities for themselves as individuals' (Newman, 2001, p. 143).

This is a daunting project for all concerned. For example, as a range of writers have noted, the emphasis on involvement in paid work as a central means of self-reliance poses considerable tensions, particularly in the context of an overall concern with renewing civil society. The tensions in today's globalised economy with its associated features of casualisation, insecurity and low wages for many with the apparent concern to encourage responsible parenting by both genders and involvement in community activities have been explored by a range of writers (see, for example, Barlow and Duncan, 2000; Lister, 2001).

Communitarianism

The complex body of thought called communitarianism has at times provided the justification for much of the themes within the Labour project in terms of its emphasis upon morality, responsibility, family and community. It has been invoked to provide the ideological glue for Labour as it appeared to offer a third way between neo-liberalism and the allegedly outdated social democracy which underpinned the postwar welfare settlement.

Driver and Martell (1997) have outlined the key themes within communitarian thinking as well as exploring the differing versions New Labour has variously associated itself with.

In opposition to New Right thinking, people in communitarian thought are not seen as asocial but are realised only through social relations. Second, they only develop fully in the context of communities. If communities are fragmented, people's development is hindered. Therefore, strong communities should be fostered and supported. Third, it is not possible to find universal foundations for human behaviour as these are relative to the communities in which they arise. New Labour allies itself explicitly with the first two claims, setting itself against Thatcherite notions that there is no such a thing as society and the New Right privileging of the market as the basis for human behaviour. In so doing it promotes the importance of strong communities, the bedrock of which is strong families. It appears to have more difficulty with the third claim as this could be seen to lead to relativism in terms of values, whereas it wishes to establish strong shared values in relation to acceptable behaviour.

There are many versions of communitarianism. According to Frazer (1999), communitarianism can generate a critique of corporate capitalism as easily as a critique of broken-down families. However, Labour's version veers much more towards a critique of broken-down families than corporate capitalism. It has embarked upon ambitious and wide-ranging attempts to recruit, cajole and control a range of players at a range of levels in a project which links economic efficiency with social and moral cohesion. This has implications for how 'family' is being reconstructed and the rights and responsibilities of parents and children.

In the course of what is seen as wrong or inadequate about individualism, many communitarians mention families as a place of special and particular relationships:

> that is, family relations stand as a counter-example and alternative to the voluntary, rights-based, market exchanges and contracts that are privileged in liberal theory. The family is an exemplar of unchosen relations and obligations . . . and is invoked as an inspiration or model for community – in the family there is a good greater than abstract justice,

there are relations that are not based on self-interest. (Frazer, 1999, p. 157)

Frazer notes the views of MacMurray, for example, who has been a strong influence on Tony Blair's personal beliefs. MacMurray argues that family is the original human community and the basis as well as the origin of all subsequent communities. He further argues that the more a society approximates to the family pattern, the more it realises itself as a community. As Frazer notes, other communitarians resist this, seeing the family as an imperfect model for political community and family relations as insufficient for civic virtue. Frazer argues that the two senses of family as community and family as the basis for community are straddled in the concept of the communitarian family which has been advanced by both American and UK communitarians concerned with political matters:

> The communitarian family is characterised as one where both partners are actively and deeply involved in their children's upbringing, and where all members are collectively active and participatory in the community. Parents' moral responsibility to bring their children up is a responsibility to the community. The communitarians argue explicitly that the two parent (different sex) family is best, and a variety of social scientific sources are cited in support of a range of reasons why this is allegedly so. (Frazer, 1999, pp. 157–8)

New Labour's communitarianism?

Whilst *Supporting Families* made it clear that the welfare of children was best secured by two resident parents who were married, in practice Labour have adopted a pragmatic and often inconsistent approach in their policies in relation to family form. This can be argued to reflect the second area of instability highlighted by Newman – New Labour attempts to appeal to a diverse range of constituencies. So any attempt to promote one family form such as marriage is tricky as it could offend sections of the population and open up New Labour to charges of hypocrisy which were levelled at the 'Back to Basics' campaign launched under John Major.

Whilst *Supporting Families* did articulate an agenda in relation to both strengthening marriage and expressing a preference for marriage as the best form in which to bring up children, this has not been followed through consistently by any means (Skinner, 2003). However, it is important to note that an agenda in relation to strengthening marriage does continue. An Advisory Group on Marriage and Relationship Support was established by the Lord Chancellor with a remit to develop a coordinated and proactive strategy for marriage and relationship support and to assess the impact of relationship breakdown. Funding continues to be made available to voluntary sector organisations providing marriage and relationship support and indeed there was an increase in this funding for 2002/3 (National Family and Parenting Institute, 2002).

However, Part II of the 1996 Family Law Act which aimed to save marriages was repealed for being ineffective. The Married Couples Tax Allowance has been abolished and no policies on marriage were outlined in the 2001 Labour Party Manifesto. Parental responsibility is to be extended to unmarried fathers. Debates over adoption legislation have signalled a willingness to include cohabiting couples and same-sex couples as suitable adopters. Same-sex couples are to be included in proposed legislation to recognise their status and rights, although not heterosexual cohabitees (B. Roche, 2002).

Parents and parental responsibilities

What *Supporting Families* highlighted and subsequent developments have strongly reinforced was a concern with the outcomes for children, particularly of poverty, and an allied concern with supporting and controlling *parents* to discharge their responsibilities towards children.

A key responsibility is economic. The emphasis on paid work with one of the focuses being lone mothers explicitly expresses this responsibility in gender-neutral terms. In so doing it reinforces involvement in paid work as a key responsibility of parenthood for both mothers and fathers:

> The ambivalence towards mothers with young children taking up paid employment, in particular full-time employment, which underpinned many social policies in the post 1945 welfare state has almost disappeared. The tax and social security systems have been reformed to assist mothers to behave more like fathers, i.e. as workers. (Land, 1999, p. 142)

However, whilst there is a central emphasis on paid work, an array of reforms have been instituted which are aimed at providing a continuing stream of income for families with children irrespective of whether the *adults are in work,* and which can be relied upon by families who move into work: to pay support for children to the main carer, in line with Child Benefit; to remove the stigma attached to claiming the traditional forms of support for the poorest families; by creating one system of income-related support for all families with children. (For a discussion of the range of initiatives at the time of writing and debates about their efficacy see National Family and Parenting Institute, 2002; see also Skinner, 2003.)

In order to encourage movement into paid work, apart from changes in terms of the benefit system a range of other policies have been introduced. The commitment to a National Childcare Strategy emerged and has developed from 1998 onwards (see Skinner, 2003). The aim of developing a National Childcare Strategy 'represents the first time the government has accepted that child care is a public as well as a private responsibility' (Lister, 2002a, p. 10). This is an important break from the dominant approach sketched out in the previous chapter where childcare services in the UK reflected a liberal philosophy of the separation of public and private spheres and intervention in the latter was mainly for those deemed problematic in some way. Furthermore, there has been an increasingly questioned separation of the care and education of children which had occurred in the postwar welfare settlement.

However, the welcome extended to the commitment has become more and more tempered over time. A range of concerns have been raised: the reliance on the private for-profit sector to supply a growing number of childcare places except in more deprived areas is one concern (Land, 2002). Others cohere around the cost of childcare, the inadequacy of the financial supports being made available and the gaps in provision (Pacey, 2002).

There has been an increase in maternity leave and the introduction for the first time of two weeks' paternity leave. Three months' unpaid parental leave has been introduced and parents have a right to request flexible working arrangements.

Again there have been a range of critiques, not surprisingly often from feminists, which will be returned to below. Suffice it to note Lister's (2002b) argument that the proposals seemed situated within an overriding concern with what the business community would find acceptable and that the reform objectives listed in the Green Paper *Work and Parents: Competitiveness and Choice* (Department of Trade and Industry, 2001) did not even mention gender equity.

A range of initiatives have been developed such as the National Family and Parenting Institute which does not offer direct services but is involved in research, dissemination and policy analysis. Direct service provisions include a phone line for parents (Braun, 2001) and the funding of time-limited specific projects under a funding stream (the Family Support Grant) based at the Home Office. This government department, which was also responsible for the publication of *Supporting Families*, has both a family policy unit and a funding remit. Through this funding stream both new and established services have received funding in relation to work on themes which are set annually. These have included work with fathers, minority ethnic parents and disabled parents. Furthermore, in relation to work with fathers, a new national organisation called Fathers Direct has been established post-1997. Its remit is not the direct provision of services but rather advice and consultancy as well as dissemination and policy analysis.

Alongside and often coexisting quite uneasily with an array of initiatives which are designed to be voluntary in nature has been the emergence of parenting initiatives under the Crime and Disorder Act 1998. As part of a series of changes in the youth justice system in England and Wales, a new disposal, the parenting order, was introduced for parents of children who are at risk of or known to be engaged in offending, or who are failing to attend school. Under the terms of this order, parents must engage with a parenting support and education service in a form directed by the court or their local multi-agency Youth Offending Teams. Failure to comply with the terms of the order can result in criminal 'breach' proceedings, a return to court, and potentially a fine or a further order being made. A range of services have thus been set up across England and Wales (see Ghate and Ramalla, 2002, for discussion and evaluation of such services; and discussion below).

In terms of concrete service provision, aside from the small if significant services developed under the Family Support Grant, there have been other key developments with significant amounts of funding attached. New services such as Sure Start and Connexions have been developed and a third, the Children's Fund, has emerged to provide streams of funding. These are considered in more detail in the next chapter but a brief outline is offered here.

Sure Start was initially targeted at children under four and their families in specific geographical areas defined as deprived. It was conceived as part of an overall strategy to tackle social exclusion and improve the life chances of younger children through better access to education and play, health services and family support (Glass, 1999). It is based upon local partnerships and core services are: outreach services and home visiting; support for parents; good quality play; learning and childcare; primary and community health care and advice about child development and health; support for those with special needs. There are now over 500 such programmes in England and Wales. A Children's Fund has been introduced to facilitate work with families and children over the age of four and Connexions has been introduced as a service to assist young people and their families with the transition from school to work or training or further education.

The social investment state

As I argued above, whilst there are also considerable tensions and instabilities there are also important tendencies which link parental responsibility within a project which invests in children. Welfare reform is recognised as central to this.

As Tony Blair (1999) argues, there has been a redrawing of the welfare contract around the notion of 'work for those who can: security for those who can't'. He argues that this means

> refocusing dramatically the objectives and operation of the welfare state. If the knowledge economy is an aim, then work, skill and above all *investing* in children become essential aims of welfare . . . a welfare state that is just about 'social security' is inadequate. It is passive where we now need it to be active. It encourages dependency where we need to encourage independence, initiative, enterprise for all. (My emphasis)

A key theme here is the importance of *investing* in children. A further theme is the importance of all those who can engaging in paid work and it is apparent that the boundaries in relation to those who are considered capable have been extended often controversially (for example, in relation to lone parents and those registered disabled). A further key theme is the formulation of a knowledge economy as the aim.

For some observers such themes exemplify the emergence of what has been called 'the social investment state'. This term was coined by Giddens (1998) in his articulation of the Third Way. He argued that in place of 'the welfare state' we should put in place 'the social investment state' and advocated a number of consequent strategies in relation to social security. The key guideline is 'investment in *human capital* wherever possible, rather than the direct provision of economic maintenance (Giddens, 1998, p. 117; emphasis in original). Jenson and Saint-Martin (2001), from Canada, have developed Giddens's ideas further in an analysis which explores developments in a range of Western countries. They argue that terms such as the social investment state have begun to circulate as a new design for successfully linking social and economic concerns in a paradigm shift away from the postwar welfare state.

The key elements of a discourse around social investment appear to be that the old welfare state sought to protect people from the market whereas a social investment state would seek to facilitate the integration of people into the market. People's security therefore comes from their capacity to change: thus the emphasis on investing in human capital and lifelong learning as the surest form of security:

> The notion is that such investments will be more suited to the labour markets of global capitalism, in which job security is rare, and flexibility is highly valued. For its part, social policy should be 'productivist' and investment oriented, rather than distributive and consumption oriented. The emphasis in social policy should shift from consumption and income maintenance-programs to those that invest in people and enhance their capacity to participate in the productive economy. (Jenson and Saint-Martin, 2001, p. 4)

This builds on a controversial discourse from economics which has promoted constructions of people, crucially children, as wealth that can be augmented by investment. This discourse supports an associated image of a businesslike, market-friendly entrepreneurial state and fits well with a discourse around management which has emerged since the 1980s (see Clarke and Newman, 1997; Newman, 2001; Lister, 2002a; and discussion in Chapter 5).

Jenson and Saint-Martin (2001) explore the notion of *time* which underpins the social investment approach to the role of the state. The results produced by an investment are located in the *future*, whereas consumption is something that occurs in the *present*. For state spending to be effective and worthwhile it must not simply be consumed in the present but must be an investment that will pay off and reap rewards in the future. Thus spending may legitimately be directed: to supporting and educating children because they hold the promise of the future; to promoting health and healthy populations because they pay off in lower future costs; to reducing the probability of future costs of school failure and crime with a heavy emphasis on children; and to fostering employability so as to increase future labour force participation rates.

Spending for current needs, by contrast, must be cautious and targeted and is motivated not just by reasons of social justice but also to reduce the threat to social cohesion posed by those who are at the margins. Inclusion of the marginalised is a necessary current expenditure.

Jenson and Saint-Martin compare what they call the citizenship regime associated with the postwar welfare state and its social rights with the social investment regime they see as currently under construction. Whilst it is beyond the scope of this chapter to explore this fully there are a number of key points which are pertinent to contemporary discussions. Social rights postwar accrued to the model citizen who was the waged – usually male – worker. Full employment policies responded to his primary interest as did the politics of workplace representation and a range of social rights to protect against the risks of life in an industrial society. The other social rights were to meet the needs of non-participants in the workforce who, apart from women and children, were expected to be few in number.

Clearly this shifted as economies became more open with the shifts to a global market (see Jordan with Jordan, 2000). The shift was from the state seeking to maintain stable employment in a relatively closed national economy to the need to enhance competitiveness through increasing flexibility and permanent socioeconomic innovation in open economies by intervening mainly on the supply side. There was also a shift away from a focus on redistribution in terms of welfare policies on fostering equality in the here and now to the fostering of equality of life chances. This involves distribution and redistribution of opportunities and capabilities more than resources.

High rates of inequality, low wages and poor jobs are not serious problems in themselves in a social investment approach; they are only problems if people become trapped and if they affect future life chances or social cohesion in the present. State actions are therefore preventive – catch the problem early on rather than attempting to cure it later. One key implication is that the social investment state spends on children.

It is legitimate also to help parents, not because they need help in themselves but because they are crucial to the project of realising children as investments for the future. All parents in this approach are responsible for themselves and for earning their own living by their own labour. Gone is the option of full-time parenting except for those who can afford it. There is an emphasis also on the employability of parents in order to prevent children's poverty. There is, therefore, a need for a new partnership with parents generally in order to support their employability.

Partnerships with parents are not just promoted because of the importance of investing in children in terms of some future pay-off. As indicated previously the threat to social cohesion is seen as something to be managed now and to focus expenditure on. Divided and unequal societies cannot guarantee stability but the solutions proposed are usually to identify and target pockets of need or particular categories of people without tackling social structures. Parents of particular groups of children or particular kinds of parents or both become targeted for special measures.

Lister (2002a) argues that Jenson and Saint-Martin's elaboration of the social investment state does indeed help to understand key aspects of social policy developments under New Labour, noting that there has been 'a genuine, unprecedented attempt to shift the social priorities of the state and nation to investing in children' (p. 11). There has been a redistribution of resources 'by stealth' as well as a redistribution of opportunities in particular to enable the taking up of paid work by parents.

Lister argues that the discourse of social investment in children is neither a new one (see Daniel and Ivatts, 1998) nor necessarily retrogressive. It has proved useful, particularly given what a difficult place Britain proved to be for children in comparison with the rest of Europe, as it supports a case for better state help and services. However, it has a range of difficulties. If we only see the case for investing in children in instrumental terms there is no room for expenditure which contributes to their well-being or enjoyment as children. Moreover there is a danger that if there is seen to be no pay-off then the expenditure may cease. The child becomes a cipher for future economic prosperity, overshadowing the child as child–citizen and limiting discussion of their own needs, voices and quality of life issues in the here and now.

Moreover, Jenson warns that neglect of gender equality is one consequence of the future-oriented investment state as 'questions of gender power are more and more difficult to raise as adults are left to take responsibility for their own lives' (quoted in Lister, 2002a, p. 13). The issue of children's poverty is divorced from that of their parents, often with particular consequences for their mothers.

Feminist critiques

A range of commentators have expressed the view that feminism has appeared a dirty word in New Labour circles (see Franks, 1999; Coote, 2001). However, this does not mean that it has not appealed to women (McRobbie, 2000), or that it has not taken on some issues which have been highlighted over the years by feminists, such as domestic violence.

There are a number of concerns raised by feminists, however. One is the avoidance of a language around gender and an associated reluctance to acknowledge the complex structural inequalities and conflicts of interests between women and men (Franklin, 2000). The avoidance of a language explicitly indebted to feminism is understandable given New Labour's adherence to a populist project which seeks to woo rather than lead (see Lister, 2001). Feminism is a term which could be seen to be alienating, certainly to men.

Fairclough (2000) writes of the importance of language to New Labour which uses language very carefully. In a range of arenas 'tough', for example, is one of its keywords and appears part of its project of populist wooing (Lister, 2001). In *Supporting Families* the language used is instructive. In its attempt to navigate the tricky political waters which can accompany either state intervention or prescription in relation to family life, a construction of 'families under stress' is used. This is used in other key documents which develop guidelines in relation to ensuring children's welfare and safety such as the *Framework for the Assessment of Children in Need and their Families* (Department of Health, Department for Education and Employment and Home Office, 2000) and *Working Together to Safeguard Children: A Guide to Interagency Working to Safeguard and Promote the Welfare of Children* (Department of Health, Home Office and Department for Education and Employment, 1999). The difficulties with the notion of stress are returned to in the next chapter, particularly in relation to its mobilisation as an explanation for child abuse. Here its more general limitations are addressed.

The construction 'families under stress' has benign connotations and legitimises the development of support strategies. However, it is not mobilised in a way which clarifies what is going on in family life and why. For example, although the menu of issues thrown into the 'families under stress' basket varies in the three documents mentioned above, 'family breakdown' is mentioned in at least two as an indicator of the stress families are under. However, there is no analysis in any of the documents of what might be going on in relation to 'family breakdown'. One factor, for example, in the growth of divorce would appear to be the unwillingness of women to put up with unsatisfying emotional relationships with men (Beck and Beck-Gernsheim, 1995). Another factor for at least one in four women petitioning for divorce would appear to be the violence they experience from male partners (Cockett and Tripp, 1994; Humphreys, 2001). Interrelationships between what are identified as 'bads' in the 'families under stress' basket, such as domestic violence and family breakdown, are not explored, which leads to tensions in the policy agenda. Domestic violence is to be tackled but there is little recognition that this may lead to family breakdown. Father involvement is to be promoted particularly, it would appear, to facilitate good outcomes for their sons, but there is little recognition that some of these fathers may be those involved in domestic violence (Featherstone, 2003).

Of particular concern to feminists have been two related policy issues: how the emphasis on involvement in paid work can be balanced with caring responsibilities, and a challenging of the priority given to paid work. In relation to the first, concerns have been raised about the timidity and motivation of many of the proposals such as the childcare strategy and so on. Furthermore the emphasis attached to paid work by New Labour runs the danger of equating work with paid work, elevating all paid work over other forms of citizenship responsibility and devaluing caring and volunteering (Lister, 2001, 2002a, 2002b; Rake, 2001; Williams, 2001).

Feminist calls, such as those from Seventuijsen (2000), for a more rounded conception of citizenship to underpin policy which would acknowledge other forms of work as an expression of citizenship responsibilities and the importance of care as an activity and orientation, are very important and have led to a range of developments at theoretical, research and campaigning levels (see Williams, 1999, 2001). However, according to Lister (2002b), given the importance historically which feminists attached to women's involvement in paid work as a means of reducing their dependence upon men, there is a fine line to be trodden here. She alerts us to the dangers which can be associated with a project which emphasises care and women's right to stay at home to provide care. There may be a danger in reacting very understandably to the valorisation of paid work which is occurring, that in an overemphasis on care, sight is lost of the social, economic and psychological value of paid work for many women in a range of jobs. Lister argues for the 'universal caregiver' model of citizenship. At the heart of this model are the normative and transformative aims of making men more like women in terms of doing primary care work. This would bear women's needs in relation to paid work in mind as well as offer opportunities to men to become more involved in the work of care. Priority would be given to adequately paid parental leave incorporating what has been called a 'daddy quota', a month reserved for fathers. Time policies are also important, including the stricter regulation of working hours, greater flexibility under the control of employees, and the goal of a shorter working day. Lister argues that fewer hours in paid work should be the norm which would enable men and women to lead more balanced lives with time *to be* as well as to care and take part in voluntary work.

The implications of New Labour's policies in relation to lone parents, which in practice usually means lone mothers in receipt of state benefits, have been the focus of feminist concern. Whilst avoiding the compulsion which has attended compatible developments, for example in the USA, the proposals here alarmed feminists on a range of levels. It has been argued that the valorisation of paid work rides roughshod over many lone mothers' own beliefs about how they should act (Duncan and Edwards, 1999). Furthermore, there has been concern that proposals ignore gendered inequalities in the labour market which would restrict the kinds of jobs available, and moreover the importance of crucial compensatory proposals so that lone mothers do not get stuck in poorly paid, dead-end jobs has not been adequately recognised (McRobbie, 2000). Finally, there has been considerable anxiety about the childcare infrastructure in terms of quality and adequacy of cover.

Lister (2002b), whilst fully endorsing the above concerns, argues that there is a case to be made by feminists for supporting the involvement of lone mothers of older children in paid work without falling into the trap of seeing such work as 'more important' than their caring work. She argues that we should not forget that for some mothers paid work is central to their definition of being a 'good mother' and this appears particularly apparent for African-Caribbean women (Duncan and Edwards, 1999). Whilst issues around training and childcare are crucial, she also points out that there could be policy calls to protect mothers who are newly separated or bereaved or where they are struggling with particular issues such as truancy or children's behavioural problems. A compatible point to be added here which is not often addressed in the wider social policy arguments but would have resonance for workers with families is that there could be exemptions for those who are dealing with violence from ex-partners or the consequences for themselves and their children of violent and sexually abusive behaviour (see Brandwein's edited collection, 1999; and Chapter 8 in this book).

Overall, the election of New Labour opened up possibilities for a reenergised engagement by a range of feminists with issues which were often screened out by the Conservatives in relation to developing a supportive infrastructure around the balancing of care and work. However, developments have been timid and appear motivated more by concerns to reform welfare and economic practices in order to compete more successfully in a global market and invest in children as a key means to this than by gender equity and/or gender change.

At the same time as involvement in paid work appears to have become a central means by which people take responsibility for their own welfare – an agenda which displaces the historic ambivalence about mothers being involved in paid work (Land, 1999) – there is another agenda which emphasises the importance of parents taking responsibility for their children's behaviour in the here and now. Whilst this agenda has received some attention from feminists, it has not been the focus of extensive scrutiny although the gendered implications are considerable.

Creating responsible parents

The current picture in relation to developments in polices relating to parents, parenting and parental responsibilities reflects the concerns of a range of diverse and conflicting constituencies. In the early 1990s politicians such as Jack Straw, who on election became responsible for law and order issues as Home Secretary, became influenced by arguments from research studies which argued that parenting practices (for example, lack of supervision) led to the involvement of children in criminality. There was also, as Etzioni

(1993) argued, a broader set of arguments which located parents' own choices in relation, for example, to divorce and investment in paid work as central to the emergence of a range of poor outcomes for children. Parents' actions or inactions thus became the target of inquiry. These agendas often coalesced uneasily with the concerns of those who had been arguing without being heard throughout much of Conservative rule for the urgency of offering support services to parents struggling to bring up their children (Coleman, 2001). Thus, as Henricson *et al.* (2001) note, it is possible to find diverse agendas within what has become a growing parenting movement post-1997. There are those who argue that parents have value in their own right and deserve support and those who argue that they should be intervened with in order to ensure good outcomes for children, and/or because they are responsible for what children do and do not do. The elaboration of a discourse around the need to improve 'parenting skills' has coalesced with concerns to rethink notions of responsibility more widely and a mix of strategies on the support/control continuum have emerged.

As Chapter 3 highlighted, a preoccupation with 'parental responsibility' found legislative expression in key pieces of legislation under the Conservatives. This legislative infrastructure has been revised but not changed fundamentally in terms of its underlying principle in relation to the Child Support Act. It has not changed in relation to the Children Act. In relation to offending the notion has been extended and Muncie (1999) argues that the development of the parenting order in the Crime and Disorder Act 1998 is a logical extension of Conservative initiatives which emerged throughout the 1980s and 1990s. As Fox Harding (1999) notes, the emphasis on parental responsibility in the Child Support Act seemed designed to reinforce paternal responsibility explicitly and to control both men and women. The other two Acts and subsequent legislation in relation to offending enacted under New Labour (the Crime and Disorder Act 1998) pose parental responsibility in gender-neutral terms which does not mean that they do not have gendered implications (see Williams, 1998).

The national evaluation of parenting programmes carried out under the 1998 legislation offers some insights into such implications (Ghate and Ramalla, 2002). As the national evaluation points out, the programmes involved both those on orders and those 'referred' although there appeared to be a preference on the part of programme workers to avoid the compulsory route. However, the distinction between voluntary attendees and those on orders was recognised as misleading as many parents appeared to be 'persuaded' to go on programmes, with the alternative being to receive an order. General information was gathered on 800 parents and 500 young people. Most (96 per cent) who actually attended by whatever route were white British, 81 per cent were women and half were lone parents. They reported very high levels of need, ranging from problems with debt to health and relationship problems and more than eight in ten said they wanted help in managing a difficult child, the majority of whom were male. Staff noted among a range of training needs the need for help in working with child protection, family violence and substance misuse issues.

The gendered implications of developing parenting programmes which appeared to cater in the main for women, a half of whom were lone mothers, who were struggling with parenting their sons are not drawn out by Ghate and Ramalla. Moreover, whilst the context in which such mothers parented, that of poverty and high levels of need, is alluded to, these too are not addressed in any depth.

Williams (1998) argued that a language around parenting and parental responsibility holds considerable dangers in that it obscures what would appear to be happening in terms of material practices. It treats gender equality as a *given* rather than a *goal*. Whilst it has an inclusive ring to it, she argued that in practice it would impact disproportionately upon women and this is indeed what appears to have happened in these particular programmes.

The evidence that it is largely women who are involved as participants, whether on a voluntary or compulsory basis (this distinction is however problematic), would support a straightforward reading that the programmes are an oppressive top-down attempt to render women personally responsible for their sons' behaviour and this 'reality' is obscured within a gender-neutral rhetoric.

Such a reading offers possibilities for understanding what is going on – possibilities which are screened out currently by the predominant use of gender-neutral language. However, it is also important to locate such a reading within an acknowledgement that these programmes were by no means all bad news for women. There is ample evidence in the evaluation of the programmes of women feeling supported, listened to and helped and gaining a great deal indeed from the programmes. Moreover, it is important to note Ferguson's (2003) comments, that men's reluctance to avail themselves of services does not always work to their advantage in that it allows their needs to continue to go unmet. Such remarks will be considered further in Chapters 7 and 8 where practice issues in relation to working with men and women are considered more fully.

Freely (2000), too, in her account of one programme where she talked to women workers and service users, found considerable benefits being experienced by those who participated. But they and she explicitly alluded to gender issues in a way which was missing from the much more extensive evaluation documented above. A number of issues emerged: men would sabotage the implementation of the insights women gained from the programmes; and there were high levels of violence between men and women which workers were having to engage with.

Whilst parenting programmes in this arena, and in the particular evaluation considered above, do not appear to be addressing gender issues, New Labour are making 'masculinity policy' in their appeals to men as fathers in some arenas (Scourfield and Drakeford, 2002). However, the unevenness of developments would indicate that the agenda is not about reconstructing gender relations or facilitating the normative project outlined above of encouraging men to take on primary care work but primarily about targeting poor fathers who are considered problematic.

Bringing daddy back – but not for everyone?

Developments in relation to fathers have their roots in the 1990s (Williams, 1998). A diverse and contradictory constituency of forces put fathers and fatherhood onto the agendas of think tanks, cultural commentators and academics. Many of these commentators were concerned primarily with the 'absent father' and indeed primarily with those who did not reside with their children. Murray (1990) in particular linked such concerns to the rise of an underclass, a class characterised by fecklessness and irresponsibility whose selfish lifestyles were subsidised by the welfare state. In these arguments women were often seen as individualists who jeopardised the well-being of their children, particularly their sons, in order to fulfil their own desires and they were supported in this by the welfare state. However, concerns were not limited to those on the political right. From the left, in the UK, writers such as Dennis and Erdos (1992) linked social unrest in the North-East of England to the decline in marriage and the rise of absent fathers.

Another set of constituencies emerged concerned with the 'distant father'. He was prevented from taking on active fathering to the detriment of himself, his children and his partner by employment patterns and cultural barriers. This approach argued for the importance of tackling such barriers and for the need for more positive representations of fathers (Burgess, 1997).

A limited rationale for developments in relation to service provision for men as fathers was outlined in *Supporting Families: A Consultation Document* (Home Office, 1998). It argued that research shows that father involvement, which is not defined in terms of what it should consist of, is good for children and that boys particularly benefit. It promotes a shopping list of difficulties boys are facing, such as the decline in traditional jobs, but does not adequately address why or how father involvement could engage with such difficulties.

Developments in relation to service provision have been pioneered by the Home Office where under the Family Support Programme, funding has been made available to encourage both new and established initiatives to develop practice skills in 'engaging fathers'. Other provision such as Sure Start is also being encouraged to take the needs of fathers and male carers seriously and tailor services in ways which are deemed to be attractive to them. The national evaluation of Sure Start has begun a specific evaluation of how fathers are being engaged with in Sure Start provision. Not only have specialist initiatives been funded, but there is also a push in relation to more generic services. Developments in relation to service provision across government are uneven, however. The Department of Health commissioned research into how statutory services worked with fathers (Ryan, 2000), but has not developed any ongoing work in this area. There are initiatives in the childcare and education sectors to recruit more male staff at every stage of children's lives, from early years to formal schooling. However, these are pursued in the absence of wider engagement with the low status and renumeration attached to such work.

Whilst Chapter 7 will document some of the positives that have accrued to individual fathers in some of the initiatives developed under New Labour, this must be located within a wider policy and legislative context, many elements of which were identified above, which offers little concrete support to restructure the gendered division of labour in relation to childcare responsibilities. Furthermore, there has been little attempt to develop a more wide-ranging debate about what constructions of fathering are to be supported or proscribed. There has been, as indicated, a mobilisation of a discourse around fathers being important for their sons which feeds into traditional assumptions which are not borne out by research evidence (Lamb, 1997) but also indicates that much of what motivates this agenda are concerns about the employability of boys and the threat they are perceived to pose to social cohesion. For example, young unemployed fathers appear to have been a specific target certainly in early funding streams.

Service provision is focused, therefore, on those perceived as deviant whilst the wider structural changes necessary are not adequately addressed. It is possible to see a form of social engineering occurring here which does not engage with either the complexities of men's lives, the differences between them or gender relations.

Concluding remarks

This chapter has traced the contours of the policy climate ushered in by New Labour which marks a break with the assumptions which underpinned the postwar welfare state and is argued to be consistent with the emergence of a social investment state. Considerable attention is being paid in this policy context to investing in children and constructing responsible parents, and a bewildering array of developments have emerged at a range of levels to support such aims. It is therefore possible to see a new approach to 'family support' as part of this agenda. The emergence of parenting orders under the Crime and Disorder Act 1998 is a clear example of family support activities being inserted within the youth justice system. Other initiatives such as Sure Start, which are discussed in more detail in the next chapter, tie family support into goals in relation to the future employability of children and the present employability of parents. There is little evidence of overt attempts to engage with the gendered implications of such policies although they do have gendered impacts, as the research into parenting orders indicates.

Feminist critiques have emerged in relation to specific policy measures such as the inadequacy of the childcare strategy or the timidity of family-friendly policies and have also often located themselves within approaches around 'care' which call for a more thoroughgoing transformation of underpinning values as well as the articulation of new policy possibilities.

CHAPTER 5

Family Support: Diversity, Contradictions and Gaps

In 2001 the National Family and Parenting Institute published what they argued were the results of the first ever mapping exercise of family support and parenting services conducted throughout England and Wales (Henricson *et al.*, 2001). Other more specific mapping exercises have also emerged, either in relation to the activities of a specific organisation (Gardner, 2002a), a geographical area (Penn and Gough, 2002), or areas such as those characterised as rural (Frost, 2002). A mapping exercise of family support services in relation to domestic violence has been undertaken (Humphreys *et al.*, 2000).

An obvious feature of the contemporary landscape is that a range of activities called family support may be carried out in a variety of organisational settings with very differing histories or lack of histories in relation to the meaning of 'family support'. This is not new but the scale of such activities is perhaps unprecedented. For example, Henricson *et al.* (2001) noted that 40 per cent of the developments surveyed had emerged in the previous five years. There would appear to be a postcode lottery in relation to provision with many projects relying on short-term sources of funding. A high proportion of family support provision is offered by voluntary organisations.

The various mapping exercises contribute to building up a picture of what is being offered, where and by whom, and they also identify varying gaps. It is not the purpose of this chapter to repeat their efforts, although key aspects of the current contexts in which provision is delivered will be reflected upon.

This chapter looks initially at how family support in a range of settings, 'new' and 'old', is being configured under New Labour. It will argue that for New Labour family support and the allied term 'prevention' have been mobilised within a project which is concerned with investing in children, in particular those who are poor, and a corresponding focus on the development of preventive strategies to end poverty through fostering employability. It is also concerned with reducing threats to social cohesion through a focus on preventing criminality, as we saw in Chapter 4 in the discussion on parenting orders which involve the insertion of family support activities within youth justice settings. This is accompanied by a focus on expanding the responsibilities of parents in relation to their children via strategies which can be controlling and supportive. However, 'older' understandings and practices of family support exist, most obviously embodied in the Children Act 1989. As we saw in Chapter 3, this links family support into a history of debates and developments in relation to preventing children being removed from their families (although short-term care can be provided), and debates and developments in relation to the protection of children from harm.

New Labour's primary concern has been in relation to the first project explored above, although this does not mean that initiatives explicitly directed at the protection of children have not emerged (see, for example, the Protection of Children Act 1999).

Over the years, as we saw in Chapter 3, an important concern which motivated and linked advocates of prevention such as Bob Holman (1988) or family support such as Tunstill (1997) was evidence that so many poor children were being removed from their families and placed in state care. There have also been longstanding concerns among such advocates about the deleterious impact of poverty on the ability of parents to offer children what they need to flourish within their own families. Therefore, New Labour's concern to abolish child poverty maps to a great extent onto their long-standing concerns, although Tunstill (2000) expresses her doubts about the emphasis on parental employability in pursuit of this goal.

There are other less well-rehearsed concerns about New Labour's agenda. In starting from a top-down agenda which is predominantly about employability and social cohesion, I would argue that there appears to be discomfort about addressing the kinds of issues which are thrown up by the older discourses in relation to family support. In particular, although this is not the only gap, there seems to be a lack of thinking about the *range* of harms children can suffer, including as a result of the inactions/actions of their parents.

There can therefore be a lack of joined-up thinking evidenced in the splits between older and newer understandings of family support. Prevention and support activities are mobilised in relation to different aims, and some issues, such as sexual abuse, which were often very uneasily situated on the agenda of 'older' understandings, do not appear part of the remit of the 'newer' understandings at all.

Prevention and support – new services for a new approach

Sure Start would appear to be a classic example of a social investment approach and I will explore this first. In launching Sure Start, the then Secretary of State for Education spoke of wanting to do 'something that would be entirely new and innovative from the word go, to get to the core of the difficulties facing families and communities' (Blunkett, 1999, quoted in Gardner, 2002a, p. 135). He also argued that one of the difficulties was the deep cynicism about professionalism, about government in all its guises, about agencies and departments. It has also become apparent to me in forums where national figures involved with Sure Start have spoken that there is a view among at least some of them that Sure Start was a necessary development in view of the 'failure' of social services departments particularly, although the exact nature of that 'failure' has not been specified. At other times, for example, in the service-level agreement between the national Sure Start unit and each programme, it is argued that Sure Start will provide 'important learning' for the mainstream services (http://www.ness.bbk.ac.uk).

Whilst the newness of Sure Start can be overstated in the sense that it has been inspired by developments such as Head Start in the USA, and is compatible with developments in Canada, such as the Aboriginal Head Start programmes, it is new in the UK context. Until December 2002 the term Sure Start was generally associated with local programmes which were expected to reach 500 in number by March 2004, covering 400,000 children and around one-third of children living in poverty (HM Treasury, 2002, para. 5.27). (In fact there are 522 programmes either in place or planned at the time of writing.) These are directed at children up to the age of four and their parents. An allied development was Sure Start Plus which was aimed at tackling teenage pregnancy. However, since December 2002, Sure Start Plus has been combined with early years education and childcare within a single interdepartmental unit called Sure Start. This unit is designed to promote a joined-up approach to childcare, early years education and family and health support in England and spans three departments, education, health, and work and pensions. It is aimed at helping families access flexible childcare, early learning and family and health support where possible through a single point of contact. It also has a remit to cover families from pregnancy until children are 14 or 16 when they have special educational needs. Funding will be available to achieve nursery provision for all 3- and 4-year-olds by 2004 and a statutory duty will be placed on LEAs to secure sufficient education provision for all 3-year-olds by April 2004. It is also planned to set up children's centres in the council wards scoring highest on official indices of deprivation which would combine nursery classes for pre-schoolers with childcare, family support and clinics for young children.

At the time of writing it is the Sure Start local programmes set up on a rolling basis which have the most obvious implications in terms of the actual delivery of family support services. All local programmes are provided by partnerships which have a very explicit emphasis on the participation of parents at every level of the programme from management onwards. Partnership is of course not a new idea and was indeed a key theme of the Children Act 1989 in the sense that workers were expected to work in partnership with parents, although the emphasis on parental involvement at every level of service operation is new (see Newman, 2001, for a discussion of the importance of partnerships to New Labour's governance agenda).

Sure Start partnerships comprise a mix dependent upon locality of agencies with one agency taking the lead. Funding for each programme is tied to the meeting of a set of objectives to which there are attached specific targets. The Sure Start Service Level Agreement between the unit and local programmes specifies the exact targets (see below) within an overall discussion (http://www.ness.bbk.ac.uk). It notes, for example, that the gains from Sure Start are expected to be long-term and lasting, and most will not be measurable during the period of the agreement. The targets outlined in the service-level agreement are those that every local programme should work towards. At the time of writing they are the measures of the progress that programmes are expected to achieve between 2001/2 and 2003/4. Apart from such measures outlined below, local programmes are also expected to keep information about other factors in the area, which over the longer term will be important in judging the success of the programme such as: the number of children excluded at primary school; the rate of juvenile contact with the criminal justice system; and adult literacy and numeracy. Allocation of the Sure Start grant is dependent on local Sure Start programmes demonstrating how they intend to reach the national targets and fulfil the national objectives. Local programmes produce their own milestones for each of the national targets, with output-related milestones for the end of each financial year of the programme, and with process-related milestones for each quarter of the first financial year. Progress against these milestones is assessed by the Sure Start unit at regular intervals, and continuing payment of the grant is linked to the milestones.

Sure Start's aim and objectives

The overall aim is to work with parents to be, parents and children to promote the physical, intellectual and social development of babies and young children – particularly those who are disadvantaged – so that they can flourish at home and when they get to school, and thereby break the cycle of disadvantage for the current generation of young children. (http://www.ness.bbk.ac.uk)

A range of targets have been set for each programme which have changed over the years in relation to four objectives which contribute to the above overall aim: improving social and emotional development; improving health; improving the ability to learn; strengthening families and communities.

Key targets for programmes up to press are as follows:

- To reduce the proportion of children aged 0–3 in the 500 Sure Start areas who are reregistered within the space of twelve months on the child protection register by 20 per cent by 2004;
- To achieve by 2004 in the 500 Sure Start areas a 10 per cent reduction in mothers who smoke in pregnancy;
- To achieve by 2004 for children aged 0–3 in the 500 Sure Start areas a reduction of five percentage points in the number of children with speech and language problems requiring specialist intervention by the age of four;
- To reduce the number of 0–3-year-old children in Sure Start areas living in households where no one is working by at least 12 per cent by 2004.

The targets selected represent a particular construction of the causes and consequences of poverty (see Glass, 1999, for an exploration of the thinking behind the setting up of Sure Start). They emerged from an extensive consultation process between different government departments and 'childcare experts'.

The targets selected have continued to evolve from the onset and at the time of writing it appears they are being changed again. However, for most programmes the targets set out above have been the ones worked towards. They have tended to tie programmes and by implication family support approaches very obviously to the pursuit of particular policy goals, for example, parental involvement in paid work, and in seeking to eliminate smoking through pregnancy also tie programmes very firmly to behaviour control.

The Sure Start programmes represent a considerable investment on the part of the state in poor children and their families. They exhibit strong features of New Labour's approach in terms of targeting and using targets. Moreover, Sure Start itself is an example of New Labour's tendency to target specific geographical areas (Toynbee and Walker, 2001) and neither they nor the planned children's centres are universally available across the country.

A comprehensive system of monitoring and evaluation has been set up at a local and national level. The first results in relation to 118 programmes were published in 2002 (http://www.ness.bbk.ac.uk). These were concerned primarily with the implementation process, including an evaluation of the extent of parental involvement at all levels of the programmes. The national evaluation of Sure Start has placed considerable emphasis on monitoring and supporting the involvement of fathers within Sure Start, although in general it has little to say about gender relations. There are no targets in relation to domestic violence, for example, although there are projects developing initiatives in relation to domestic violence and there seems to be considerable involvement by organisations such as Women's Aid as part of local partnerships.

Sure Start programmes have shared one common target with local authorities in relation to reducing the proportion of children aged 0–3 on the child protection register reregistered within a year – this could be seen to tie Sure Start programmes to some extent into an overt child protection agenda, although in practice this is not considered a meaningful target given that in many areas I am aware of reregistration is a very uncommon practice anyway. Furthermore, as Jeffery (2003) notes, the target assumes that reregistration is necessarily a negative activity to be proscribed, whereas it may be a very necessary response to a change in a child's circumstance which necessitates protective action, such as the introduction of a man convicted of sexual offences into the child's life.

There does not appear to be a national strategy in relation to training Sure Start workers around child protection issues or developing coherent approaches to working with the kinds of child protection issues which can emerge in community settings. Finally, little attention appears to be paid in national guidance to addressing the kinds of dilemmas which can emerge when workers work *alongside* parents and issues concerning the safety of their children emerge.

Overall, Sure Start fits within an agenda in which prevention and family support are tied to the prevention of unemployment, in the sense of equipping individuals to be employable, and to preventing early difficulties either escalating into threats to social cohesion or trapping people in cycles of disadvantage.

Other initiatives

Other initiatives which link with this agenda include the following: the Children's Fund; programmes funded under the Family Support Grant; and Connexions. The Children's Fund is intended to provide a 'flexible and responsive approach of meeting needs and developing good practice for services for vulnerable children, supporting them and their families in breaking the cycle of poverty and disadvantage. Its overarching objective will be to provide additional resources over and above those provided through mainstream and specific programmes' (http://www.nya.org.uk). It is designed to complement and bridge the gap in preventive services between Sure Start and Early Years programmes and the development of the Connexions service for the 13-plus age group. It has established 'local networks' which should by April 2004 consist of around fifty local funds. Each fund will be administered by a local voluntary sector grant-giving body which builds on existing voluntary sector networks.

Its remit is clearly preventive: to develop services to identify children who are showing early signs of difficulty; to provide them and their families with the support they need to enable them to overcome barriers and disadvantage; and also to reach those children who are perceived as below the threshold of statutory services and so are often not identified and do not receive support until they hit a crisis. Services will need to be put in place which identify children showing early signs of difficulty and refer them to support for them and their families in overcoming difficulties through activities such as mentoring, counselling and advice. The Children's Fund is a funding stream rather than a service provider itself. It too is subject to national and local evaluation.

Alongside these substantial developments have emerged the much smaller family support initiatives outlined in the last chapter from the Home Office under its Family Support Programme which represent a tiny proportion of the overall budget (Dean, 2002). These are typically three years in duration and themes are set annually for each funding programme. These appear to have focused on what appear to be gaps in existing services – minority ethnic families or 'hard to reach' groups, such as fathers.

A further development has been the emergence of Connexions which is supposed to provide a universal service dispensing information, advice and guidance to all 13–19-year-olds, or for those with learning difficulties and disabilities until they reach 25. Garrett (2002) provides an account of the emergence of this service and critically discusses one of its key implications which has been the development of a 'new' group of workers, personal advisers. These personal advisers have as their chief role the provision of one-to-one support, information, advice and guidance to young people and their families or carers in negotiating the transition from school to further education, training or paid work. Garrett notes they will be trained to seek transformation in the young people as well as in other services. It is crucial to ensure that young people are prepared for the world of work as it is today: 'if we are to succeed as a nation and if our young people are to succeed as individuals in the knowledge economy of the 21st century, we must provide all teenagers with the opportunity and support they need to make the transition to adulthood' (Department for Education and Employment, quoted in Garrett, 2002, p. 608).

It would appear that new family support activities are located within sites of practice informed by a narrative which is concerned with promoting employability and responsible parenting as key to ensuring the welfare of children. These can be inserted therefore in a range of contexts and in the pursuit of a range of policy goals. However, family support and prevention activities have a different history and set of meanings, particularly but *by no means exclusively* in the statutory sector. I will now explore how and whether such meanings are being reconfigured under New Labour.

Statutory settings and family support

Lister (2002a) argues that a strong element of scepticism charac-
terises New Labour's attitudes to the 'state' generally and locates
this scepticism historically. Under Margaret Thatcher, the Conservatives had set out to challenge the model of the state indebted
to the ideas of Beveridge and Keynes: provision and funding of
welfare on a more or less universal basis and the maintenance of
full male employment. 'Central to the assault was a determination
(not totally successful in execution) to cut public expenditure and
taxation and "to roll back the state" or at least the welfare arms
of it' (Lister, 2002a, p. 4). The ambition became increasingly to
turn the provider state into a regulatory state operating in certain
spheres through quasi markets. This was strongly influenced by
public choice theory which insisted that private was good and
public bad. By the end of the Conservative era, a target-setting, per-
formance-centred managerial state had emerged whose users were
constructed as consumers or customers or welfare dependants/
scroungers (Clarke, 1997; Lister, 2002a).

Whilst not as anti-state as the new right, New Labour is scepti-
cal about the state in a way that distinguishes it from traditional
social democratic thinking. In Chapter 4 we have already seen the
emergence of 'the social investment state' which is a reformulation
of the role of the welfare state. In terms of 'how' policies are imple-
mented there has been a continuation from the Conservatives of
what has become known as 'the managerial partnership state'.
Enabling, brokerage and regulating are emphasised over providing. Where the state does provide this is both targeted and subject
to target-setting. The setting of targets is a clear expression of New
Labour's inheritance in relation to managerialism. This involves
the tying of public spending to an emphasis on value for money,
reform, audits and targets. Quality Protects (explored below) is one
example of this agenda and is a good example of the increased tendency by politicians, particularly New Labour, to engage in 'micro
management' (McTiernan, 2002).

However, clearly, as we have seen, the setting of targets is by no
means restricted to old state institutions; it is an important aspect
of Sure Start, but there does seem to be a scepticism about the
ability of the old state to deliver what New Labour wants, as we
have seen in the comments made by Mr Blunkett in relation to Sure
Start.

Since New Labour came to power there appears to be no desire
to change the legislative basis for practice in the statutory sector in

terms of either massively revising or abandoning the Children Act. However, the development of an array of centrally funded service initiatives with a preventive and support remit working in partnership with local authorities, including social services departments but not under their control, has opened up considerable debate about what New Labour's intentions are in relation to the roles and functions of social services departments and/or social workers (Jordan with Jordan, 2000; Garrett, 2002).

There are indications that in terms of work with children and families, local authorities have been offered a highly restricted and monitored role. Gardner (2002a) argues that under New Labour 'refocusing' has come to mean reinforcing the tendency in many departments to concentrate on children already in the child protection and accommodation systems and on providing an assessment service, and therefore leaving family support activities to the new initiatives. She offers as evidence here the emergence of Quality Protects initiatives (see also Tunstill, 2000).

The distinctive features of Quality Protects include a detailed statement of national objectives for children's services, broken down into those which are child or family outcome-related and those which are service-related. Local authorities are required to provide action plans to address the centrally developed objectives and key tasks and funding is attached to both implementation and delivery. As Mitchell (2000) notes, from 1999 onwards the Department of Health was positioned 'squarely at the head of a programme of social services reform with clearly defined intended outcomes in an almost unprecedented way' (p. 191).

Tunstill argues that linked to the restriction of the local government and social services role in relation to family support has been the emergence of a range of service developments, particularly Sure Start, which are being promoted as the key sites for the development of 'family support'. It is indeed possible to see what is happening as a way of institutionalising an extra-organisational split between child protection activities and family support activities, although this is by no means clear-cut or overt. It is also possible to see the mobilising of notions of 'family support' in support of two quite different agendas in different sites of practice (although these sites are not always distinct as social services departments are stakeholders in Sure Start projects, for example). There has been a call to institute an organisational split between 'child protection' and 'family support' by the Institute for Public Policy Research (Harker and Kendall, 2002). They argue that there is a need for a mechanism to separate out child protection work 'to enable the rest of social care to shift its focus towards empowering vulnerable people, mobilising communities and promoting well-being and prevention' (p. 11).

Whilst such a call is explicable given the argument in Chapter 3 that *Messages from Research* (Department of Health, 1995) legitimated such split thinking, it is important to note that this call has been strongly challenged by a range of childcare constituencies. For example, research on the implementation of the Children Act (Department of Health, 2001) indicated concern that the system of separating child protection inquiries and family support assessment which the Children Act can be seen to promote has been both ineffective and counterproductive to meeting the needs of children and families and reinforces the importance of not splitting such systems. A key event was the report published by Lord Laming at the beginning of 2003 after an inquiry into the death of Victoria Climbié (Laming, 2003). This inquiry was carried out in two phases. Phase 1 inquired into the circumstances surrounding the death of Victoria. Phase 2 was concerned to look at broader questions around how systems were working more generally in relation to safeguarding children for the future. A series of seminars was held with a wide range of invited participants. In Seminar 3 the question of how cases become categorised as either Section 47 or Section 17 and the implications were raised explicitly, although this was raised throughout the inquiry. Whilst a range of views were expressed in relation to the desirability or otherwise of current practices, there seemed to be considerable consensus reflected in the report complied by Lord Laming that protective and supportive activities needed integrating and resourcing. He located his remarks in the context of opposition to any suggestion that a separate Child Protection Agency should be established.

At the time of writing the government has indicated that it intends to incorporate its response to his report within a Green Paper on preventive services which had been planned prior to his report. This may pose considerable difficulties for a government which has seemed comfortable with developing a coherent narrative based upon a social investment state approach to children and parents but has seemed less certain about addressing why children are harmed in a variety of ways. However, it does pose opportunities also for developing a more integrated agenda in relation both to family support and to child protection, and to the relationship between them. It is a key argument of this book that feminist insights could play an important role here.

Before turning to address this it is important to note that as Henricson *et al.*'s mapping exercise demonstrates there are a wide variety of family support projects in existence outside the statutory sector and initiatives developed by New Labour. As Chapter 3 noted, Holman (1988) documents the historical backdrop for many of these. In Chapters 6 and 7 I will be exploring examples of such provision. Funding comes from a range of sources which can allow providers some freedom to decide on what they wish to offer, which may not link in with dominant policy narratives. This is especially true of the larger charities (see Gardner, 2002a, for an exploration of the range of provision offered by the NSPCC in relation to family support). However, in a competitive landscape many projects need to gear their applications to the priorities of their local Children's Fund, for example. Therefore the dominant policy context is extremely important in influencing the priorities of a diverse range of family support provision, although it should not be seen as hegemonic. Part II of this book, in exploring the issues in relation to practice delivery, will highlight some of the diversities which can be apparent on the ground.

Why feminism? How can it help?

There is a clear and laudable attempt under New Labour to locate children's well-being within the context of tackling child poverty. This is crucial and cannot be welcomed enough after decades of inattention on the part of successive governments. However, how does this fit exactly with preventing the range of harms children can suffer, for example, as a result of parental actions/inactions? Well, in many ways it is absolutely crucial. Poverty can itself be constructed as a harm or abuse and can appear to lead to other forms of abuse although there have been ongoing debates about this (Parton, 1985, 1990).

However, there is little developed thinking beyond the need to counteract poverty and New Labour explanations for what might lead parents to cause harm seem rather undeveloped. In various publications the language of 'stress' has emerged to hang diverse issues together (see Home Office, 1998; Department of Health, Home Office and Department for Education and Employment,

1999; and Department of Health, Department of Education and Employment and Home Office, 2000). For example,

> Many of the families who become the subject of child protection suffer from multiple disadvantages. Providing services and support to children and families under stress may strengthen the capacity of parents to respond to the needs of their children before problems develop into abuse. (DOH, HO and DFEE, 1999, p. 2)

Areas of stress highlighted in this document include the following: social exclusion; domestic violence; the mental illness of a parent or carer; and drug and alcohol misuse. The latter three are argued to emerge from a strong evidence base (Cleaver *et al.*, 1999).

However, the mobilisation of a language around 'stress' may obscure as much as it illuminates. Stress is a notoriously imprecise and slippery term as Busfield (1996) argues in her interrogation of its use in understanding mental health difficulties. There is a need to distinguish between the way the concept of stress is used to refer to certain features of an individual's social situation – 'stressful situations' or 'stressors' (p. 191) – and to refer to the physical or psychological responses to difficulties – 'stress responses'. Busfield argues that even if we only use the term to refer to stressful situations rather than stress responses we still have to identify 'the domain of the stressful' – which features are considered to be likely to prove stressful. 'Potentially, the domain is infinite; in practice researchers limit the range quite considerably, incorporating varying assumptions as to what is stressful in their research' (p. 191). Divorce and unemployment are usually included but not war or sexual abuse. Exclusion of issues such as childhood sexual abuse from the list is not only a matter of the presumed exceptional nature of the occurrence, according to Busfield, but also because of another common limitation on the domain of the stressful. It is usually restricted to recent occurrences – usually the previous year or six months – rather than to more distant events. Furthermore, the domain of the stressful tends to focus on *events* such as marital breakdown rather than ongoing difficulties or 'chronic hassles'. When the focus is only on events, then becoming unemployed during the period in question is included while being unemployed throughout the period is not. This distinction is also relevant to many features of the situation of women which may only feature as stressors if ongoing difficulties are included. This applies not only to the possible ongoing stress of domestic labour and child care or managing household tasks alongside full-time work outside the home. It also applies to the quality of relations within the home . . . and to the experience of discrimination' (p. 192).

There are important issues, therefore, involved in what is selected as a stressor and by whom. Moreover, it is important to try and think through what is a source and what is a response. Is domestic violence, for example, a source of stress or a response to stress or both?

Busfield agrees that there is empirical support for the existence of a link between stressful events and psychological distress, but there is a need for complex models which account for the ways in which individuals express inner tension and stress at a number of levels. She also argues most importantly that we need to account for the differences in Western societies in how men and women handle psychological distress, with women commonly displaying depression and men directing their feelings outwards in violence or aggression.

However, two key documents directed at practitioners, the *Framework for the Assessment of Children in Need and their Families* (DOH, 2000) and *Working Together to Safeguard Children: A Guide to Interagency Working to Safeguard and Promote the Welfare of Children* (DOH, 1999), make no overt references to gender at all and the use of the gender-neutral term 'parent' recurs throughout. There is no attempt therefore to explore whether and how men or women might experience different stressors and/or respond differently and whether there might be gendered dimensions to both.

If we take an area such as mental health, there is a considerable scholarship which would indicate that men and women in general can have quite different life experiences and different psychological responses to such experiences, and be constructed in quite different ways by mental health systems (Busfield, 1996). Women who kill their children, for example, are much more likely to be constructed as mentally ill than men who do so. Moreover, both women's and men's motivations for doing so would appear to reflect wider gendered processes in terms of how they are constructed and construct themselves. Women are more likely to do so because they do not feel good enough or fear for their child's future whereas men are more likely to do so because of jealousy and a desire to retain control (Wilczynski, 1995).

Domestic violence is highlighted in a range of government publications as impeding the capacity of parents to respond to the needs of their children. The term is not explored either in terms of the debates that surround its usage (see Mullender, 1996) or in terms of its gendered dimensions. One background study informing government thinking does acknowledge gender issues (Cleaver *et al.*, 1999). Here, whilst there is an explicit recognition that it is mainly about men's violence to women, the reasons for such violence are not explored. Moreover, whilst this study does quite appropriately acknowledge that women can also be violent to men, there is no analysis of whether this might be motivated by differing factors or differ in terms of its impact and seriousness. As explored in Chapter 2, for example, Smart and Neale's (1999) study did indicate that both women and men might be violent to each other at a point of particular difficulty around their separation (see also Johnston and Campbell, 1993; Featherstone and Trinder, 1997). But they drew a distinction between this 'one off' violence and more sustained psychologically injurious as well as physically serious violence which was predominantly a male phenomenon. Currently, for example, it would appear that women are far more likely to be killed or seriously injured by such violence than men are by women's violence. Moreover, men who are violent to women exhibit an increased likelihood of being violent in a range of ways to children, whereas there seems little empirical research to support a link between women's violence to men and their abuse of children.

The failure to engage with a gendered analysis or to employ a language informed by a gender analysis is particularly sharply posed when considering sexual abuse. Frosh (2002, p. 85), in exploring the research literature dealing with the characteristics of sexual abusers and the causes of sexual offending, offers the following observations: sexual abusers are an extremely heterogeneous group; they are prone to abuse in multiple and repetitive ways; they are mostly male, though not exclusively; many abusers are very young themselves and the sources of abusive behaviour lie in a mixture of individual history and shared socialisation processes.

He argues that although it is important to acknowledge that women do abuse sexually, the evidence would suggest that there may be systematic features of masculine sexuality that contribute to sexual abuse. He further argues that although the situation in relation to empirical data continues to be unsatisfactory, the finding that 'most abusers are men seems a secure one, requiring explanation' (p. 85). He argues for an explanation that explores masculine sexual socialisation. The implication, however, from government documents is that it is a response to stress on the part of 'parents'.

Given the overall focus on prevention, the neglect of overt strategies to prevent men's violence, including sexual abuse, generally seems a curious omission. This does not of course mean that some of what is being advocated under the prevention agenda may not be of relevance here. For example, there have long been concerns among feminist and pro-feminist commentators about the difficulties for marginalised men who do not have access to sources of belonging and legitimation, such as employment, and the links between such difficulties and their involvement in some forms of violent behaviour (Segal, 1990), and initiatives both to help men currently in such situations and to prevent young men growing up into such situations are important developments. Moreover, anti-poverty strategies generally may help considerably in relation to certain types of violence. However, they are much less relevant to others, such as sexual violence to children, and they must be complemented by strategies which tackle gendered assumptions about rights and entitlements and offer men spaces to explore complex issues in relation to power and powerlessness. Moreover, currently when men engage in violent behaviour of whatever kind there are limited resources available for working with them around changing their behaviour, and there appear to be few ongoing resources to support more democratic practices on the part of such men (Chapter 8).

As indicated above there is an opportunity for the government to develop an integrated strategy in its Green Paper. This could look at questions such as the following, and *these are just a sample*. Why are men so much more likely to engage in the sexual abuse of children? What sense are men making of a landscape where traditional sources of legitimation at economic, social and cultural levels are questioned or unavailable? What positive sources of identity can they draw upon or be supported to develop?

More generally Ferguson (2001a), writing from an Irish context, has explored the practice implications of bringing in gender-informed insights to contemporary practices in child protection and family support. He offers examples from his research to argue that, at its best, practice incorporating a number of dimensions in terms of practical and therapeutic supports can assist men, women and children to move beyond traditional hierarchical forms of patriarchal relationships towards the creation of democratic families. Such families are those where children are heard as well as seen and feel safe, women as well as men are treated with respect, and men as well as women are enabled to have expressive emotional lives and relationships. In a late-modern context, promoting self actualization and equality for all family members is central to the achievement of effective child protection, welfare and healing and essentially defines what child care and protection work needs to be all about. (Ferguson, 2001a, p. 8)

Ferguson argues against the counterposing of supportive and protective activities. The project of building democratic families needs both. His accounts of practice demonstrate a commitment on the part of practitioners to engage in dialogue about such strategies with those they work with and this commitment seems key, particularly as we shall see in Chapter 9 in relation to children and young people.

Ferguson explicitly brings in a language which seems missing from most contemporary discussions of family support within a wide array of literature from government guidance to research, a language around men, women and democracy. In Part II of this book I address the implications of Ferguson's approach, directly identifying sites of practice where I think helpful developments are occurring in relation to work with 'families', men, women and children and identifying some of the barriers to further development.

In moving to Part II of this book which is concerned with day-to-day practices, this seems an apt place to make some general reflections on the contexts in which such practices are being carried out. Such reflections merit much more consideration than I can offer here but the key features are identified. The report by Lord Laming drew attention to issues which have been of concern for some time in relation to difficulties in recruiting and retaining social workers in the statutory sector (see Garrett, 2002, for some indicators of the scale of the 'crisis'). The development of initiatives such as those outlined above like Sure Start may be exacerbating such difficulties in that there is a movement of staff out of statutory social work into such initiatives. Moreover, there have been ongoing concerns about the emphasis on target-setting and managerialism which have come to dominate the organisational regimes most obviously in the statutory sector although, as noted, the emphasis on target-setting has been extended into the initiatives set up under New Labour. A key concern here is that 'reflection' on process and wider questions in relation to why particular kinds of activities are being carried out can be a casualty of such target-setting regimes. Moreover, the emphasis on 'what works' in the comprehensive evaluative processes set up in a variety of settings may also impede such considerations.

In Part II issues such as *time* and *space* for reflection recur consistently as themes in a variety of ways and evidence will be offered of the possibilities and constraints which are apparent to me both from the literature and from the work I have undertaken in a variety of roles as an evaluator and as a volunteer. Suffice it to say here that time and space for reflection are obvious casualties in a landscape which is characterised by staff shortages and/or target setting regimes where sources of funding are time-limited.

Concluding remarks

This chapter has explored 'new' developments under New Labour which locate family support activities within a concern to promote employability and reduce threats to social cohesion. It argues that 'old' developments, particularly within statutory settings, seem less securely anchored partly because of a scepticism about the ability of the state to deliver and partly because they sharply focus issues about the gendered dimensions of abusive activity which New Labour seem less happy to engage with. It argues that there is a need to continue to think about such dimensions, however, and the next four chapters offer not only compelling evidence for the urgency of such thinking but also pointers towards what is happening in particular sites of practice.

PART II

Delivering Family Support

CHAPTER 6

Working with 'Families'

In Chapters 1 and 2, it was argued that contemporary family life was characterised by tendencies towards diversity in terms of family forms and that furthermore the term 'family' was being used to cover a wide spectrum of family forms. It was also noted, however, that a focus on diversity could obscure the degree to which in a range of forms there was considerable convergence around 'working things out' in the absence of fixed markers relating to what it means to be a man or woman, mother or father, and children's expectations. Such 'working out' moreover seemed characterised by increased tendencies or aspirations towards 'democratisation' and it was argued that feminism had played an important role in both documenting and supporting such tendencies.

This chapter concentrates specifically on some of the general issues raised for practitioners by the increased diversity in family forms. Subsequent chapters focus on more specific issues in relation to men, women and children. Structuring the discussion in this way is problematic as it is important to explore the interrelationships between men, women and children but has been judged necessary in order to give some coherence. At various points throughout these chapters I draw on some small pieces of research conducted in the last period (Featherstone, unpublished; Featherstone, 2001; Featherstone and Manby, 2002) to illustrate my arguments.

Working with complexity and diversity

Chapter 1 offered evidence of the complex links between poverty and family form. It is therefore not that surprising to find that in many family support settings directed at those in poverty, workers are encountering quite complex arrangements. For example, in an evaluation of a small family support project, run by a charity based in a school setting on a deprived estate in the North of England, it became clear to the evaluators in their interviews with service users and service providers that the term 'family' covered a variety of situations and relationships (Featherstone and Manby, 2002). It also became clear that it was extremely difficult for workers on a small project to engage with the complexities of the arrangements encountered for a range of reasons linked to time, resources and their perceived lack of skills. However, they were well aware that by not doing so they were often not tackling key factors which impacted upon children's welfare.

For example, in interviews with two children about their views of the service provided, the evaluator found that the children expressed considerable distress about their stepmother which seemed to be primarily linked to the problems they had with her, but also symbolised a wider distress about having moved geographically away from their birth mother. In a subsequent interview with one of the evaluators the project worker mentioned a specific visit to the home where she had walked in on an argument between the father and stepmother in this family. The incident had left her feeling very upset because of the nature of the argument and because it made her realise the difficulties impacting upon the children – difficulties she did not feel able to address.

This example not only brought home to the evaluator the issues which were raised by the children about loss and transition, which seems important in terms of understanding what may be going on in stepfamilies, but it also raised a key issue around how equipped workers may feel at a range of levels including emotionally in engaging with adults and with conflict between adults in couples.

It also provoked some reflection on the widespread evidence that it is often women who are worked with by women workers in the delivery of family support (Gilligan, 2000) and that the 'family' in family support is frequently defined in practice as the mother and children. Whilst this does reflect gendered assumptions about women's roles it may also reflect the lack of confidence workers can feel not only in working with men, but also in working with men and women together. To add into the equation more than two adult partners, as in a stepfamily or other situations post-divorce/separation, can further compound the difficulties.

Freely (2000), writing of her own situation, paints a vivid picture of what may be involved:

> My two stepchildren have always resided with their mother, and my two older children from my first marriage spent most of their childhood living with me. But my stepchildren spent a lot of time with me too, and my children spent a lot of time with their father. And the arrangements have changed many, many times over the last ten years. This means that any researcher trying to get to grips with the problems in my household would have to look at two other households with which it has been closely linked, and also examine the erratic quality of cooperation between our households and the others, not to mention the changing relationships between the two sets of stepchildren, and between all four stepchildren and the two 'new' children to whom they are all related. (p. 102)

Not only does the above pose difficulties for researchers, it also poses difficulties for practitioners.

Batchelor (2003) explores the issues for practitioners in relation to stepfamilies. Such families are explored here in order to give some sense of the complexities of what can be involved.

Batchelor argues that the issues raised by step-parenting or step-family life are often not addressed in policy and practice despite the evidence that one in five children may be involved in stepfamily life. Legally the reality of step-parenting can be acknowledged, as step-parents can achieve parental responsibility under the Children Act 1989 through the making of a residence order, although there is a presumption of ongoing contact if not co-parenting on the part of both biological parents. There has been a decline in step-parent adoptions which was one way in which step-parents, usually stepfathers, achieved legal status although they continue to account for over half the adoption orders made in England and Wales (Department of Health, 1999; Batchelor, 2003). The continuing use of adoption may be related to a number of factors such as the desire for a 'new start' as well as a reflection of the level of stigma attached to and felt by stepfamilies (Batchelor, 2003).

As with lone mothers (see Chapter 1) there are a number of routes into stepfamilies – they are formed as a result of varying circumstances. As with lone parents there are issues in relation to material disadvantage to be addressed. Research has indicated that it may be harder to meet the material needs of all dependent children and that there are often very complex financial arrangements with child support money going in and out of the same household. Indeed the increased incidence of separation has been related to this.

Stepfamilies are not the same as nuclear families and they differ from each other in terms of histories and everyday lives. Pre-separation conflict will leave its mark on children. Roles will need renegotiation – attachments have been disrupted. From a gender perspective it is important to be aware of the amount of work women may need to do in relation to such renegotiations and the anxieties that may be posed for men who do not 'feel in charge', especially if this is combined with increased financial difficulties.

Freely notes the ongoing everyday challenges of step-parenting and the differential gender issues. Very often it is the relationship between the adults which is formed first – adults form relationships with other adults and then agree to parent the children. She argues that it is a position that is riddled with difficulties:

> If the children are very, very young when you take them on, you might just be able to forge a 'real' relationship with them. But even if you are replacing a parent who has died, older children tend to resent any effort on your part to assume parental authority. If you and your partner have differing ideas about child-rearing, you can expect him or her to undermine you too, which means you have even less to go on when trying to create a positive relationship with them . . . if you have experience with children, you can sometimes find a way around these obstacles – with time. According to the National Step Family Association, it takes between 2 and 10 years for the relationships to settle. If you are a woman who has often had to make the best of situations in which you do not have as much power as you might like, you might be able to make the best of this one too. You will not, in any event, feel even less of a 'woman' because of it. For a man who associates dominance with masculinity, the constraints of step-parenthood are likely to be more problematic, however. (Freely, 2000, pp. 103–4)

There is some contested evidence that children with step-parents are at increased risk of abuse compared to those living with birth parents. However, there are considerable methodological difficulties here. There is a lack of consistency not only in definitions of abuse but also in definitions of a stepfamily. As Sternberg (1997) notes in relation to violence, we simply do not know enough about the differences between stepfathers in terms of degrees of transience and attachment to families. Batchelor explores the importance of addressing, when abuse is attributed to a step-parent, whether he or she was a long-standing member of the child's household or one of several transient adults in that child's life. There may be a variety of scenarios here. Paedophiles may attach themselves deliberately to lone mothers, or men who have a history of violence may have a series of relationships with vulnerable lone mothers. These men may abuse children all of whom may be classified as his stepchildren regardless of how much of a parent or how involved he may have been. Thus it is possible to see the issue of men's sexual violence being obscured within a language which locates abuse within particular family forms.

There is some evidence to suggest that children are more likely to test out stepfathers (Brannen *et al.*, 2000) and that stepfathers need to work at establishing their position in ways that birth fathers may not do, though as we saw in Chapter 1 some authors argue that increased voluntarism is apparent in parent/child relationships generally.

There is evidence of complex gendered dynamics in how men negotiate their relationships with their 'own' children post-divorce, never mind other men's children in a stepfamily. In observations on post-divorce parenting, Smart (1999) expands upon the implications of earlier research by Backett (1987). Smart argues that the emphasis within legislation such as the Children Act on ongoing contact if not co-parenting in a context where the relationship between the adults as marital partners has changed definitively assumes that distinction can be made between the adult/adult relationship and adult/child relationship. However, parents do not simply relate to children, they relate to one another as parents and not simply as spouses. The dynamics are complex and multidimensional rather than unidirectional. Crucially, Backett's work indicates that fatherhood has often largely been mediated through the behaviour of the mother and has not operated as an independent relationship with the mother. Simply put, the father has often relied on the mother to have a relationship with the children. This of course needs renegotiating when the relationship with the mother changes. Entry into post-divorce family life poses problems for the father as he has to form a direct relationship with the children and needs the support of his former wife to do so. The mother must also rethink and redo her relationship – her status as a primary caretaker is challenged alongside her renegotiation of her role generally.

Batchelor explores how an understanding of the issues for stepfamilies could be used to inform assessment practices carried out under the *Framework for the Assessment of Children in Need and their Families* (Department of Health, Department for Education and Employment and Home Office, 2000), and offers some practice guidance here. She suggests the use of a range of techniques in order to map out patterns of contact, links and transitions. Obvious issues to consider are where children spend their time and how they negotiate living in a number of households if that is part of the arrangement. Her chapters offers important guidance on the kinds of issues which may be faced by stepfamilies and also some practice guidance for workers.

However, it is not immediately evident that there are either the resources or the supports available to undertake the kinds of work which may be required either at an assessment stage or in ongoing work. This is especially posed in climates where there are staff shortages or poorly funded projects with low staffing levels. For example, in the project alluded to above, one worker operated on her own for considerable periods of time, due to staffing difficulties.

Stepfamilies are but one family form, if potentially the more complex type of arrangement which practitioners may encounter. One practice development which has emerged in the 1990s is the family group conference which has offered some supports in particular settings for working with expanded understandings of family generally.

Family group conferences

The origins of family group conferences lie in New Zealand in the early 1980s. Here, they represented a response to the concerns of Maori people about the disproportionately high number of Maori children in the care system, the need to challenge the appropriateness of placing Maori children with white families and the lack of Maori social workers (Marsh and Crow, 1998). The issues which motivated their emergence in New Zealand converged with concerns in other countries and were to lead to interest and take-up more widely. From a UK perspective, Marsh and Crow (1998) argue they chimed with 'positive elements regarding the role of children and families, and more negative ones regarding the relative failure of existing services and the approach underlying them' (p. 37).

Marsh and Crow identify the Children Act 1989 as key in providing an impetus for the development of family group conferences in the UK. They argued that the Act provided such impetus in its emphasis on the following: the need for careful consideration of children's voices; the increased emphasis on race, religion and culture; the focus on links between children and their families; and the overall emphasis on partnership between families and services.

The family group conference appears to be primarily a 'method' used in order to plan for children which mobilises the child's network as a key aspect of such planning and decision-making. Marsh and Crow, in their research on its implementation in the UK, locate the method within an exploration of family change and diversity. They argue that a flexible definition of family is needed to encourage inclusive, culture-sensitive alliances to work in the best interests of the child. 'Such a definition needs to work from the family's perspective, rather than being based on the assumptions or knowledge base of the professional' (1998, p. 29). They further note that it is 'the psychosocial' influence a particular person exerts on the family which is important and alerts practitioners to the range of significant others who may need to be considered, who may or may not be kin. 'It is only the individuals within the family group itself who can define the circle of people who have significance and who can therefore be described as part of the family group. To work with the family, we have to ask the family who the family is' (p. 30).

There are a host of issues which emerge from Marsh and Crow's research into the implementation of family group conferences, in particular child welfare settings which cannot, for reasons of space, be dealt with fully here. Of key relevance is that although clearly linked into a process of ongoing work, the conference is an event or events that an independent coordinator needs to spend a considerable amount of time planning for. This kind of time is often quite simply not available to workers on an ongoing basis.

A considerable amount of that time is spent on negotiations over who should be invited. Whilst there was considerable variation in the projects researched by Marsh and Crow, the invitees included parents, step-parents and cohabitees, ex-step-parents and ex-cohabitees, grandparents, step-grandparents, aunts, uncles, siblings, half-siblings, step-siblings, siblings' partners and ex-partners, cousins, great-aunts, parents' friends, neighbours, peers and peers' parents. This represented, according to Marsh and Crow, 'the whole range of possible family structures and cultures from the close knit to the loose knit, and from kin to friends' (1998, p. 100). They comment that in the context of debates about *who* is family in over a quarter a friend or neighbour was present, and in 15 per cent the young person had a peer supporter attending.

Meetings were often experienced as emotional and stressful by family members, although the majority would choose to deal with future issues similarly. Coordinators found the process of setting up meetings, in particular, practically and emotionally demanding and the social workers often worried about whether the process would raise expectations in terms of resourcing and ongoing work (worries that the researchers felt were unfounded). Conferences nearly always resulted in agreed workable plans which appeared to reduce demands for expensive services such as state care, court procedures and child protection processes.

A key part of the process involves offering separate time to families without professionals to sort out a plan. Marsh and Crow do not have an extended discussion about power relations within families although they are clear that the coordinator needs to be very sensitive to the needs of those who are less powerful and needs to ensure full participation. Decisions around whom to exclude were partly about the possibility of intimidation. Furthermore, one of the key principles relates to the practising of respect. It is advocated that coordinators should encourage 'decent behaviour, and that they should firmly oppose behaviour which would be against equal opportunities or race relations legislation, but within these boundaries respecting the family's own way of working is vital. Co-ordinators should treat families with respect, and not impose their own views' (1998, p. 57). There is indeed some evidence from the research accounts garnered from social workers in the evaluation that fears that the conference would provide opportunities for mother-blaming proved unfounded although mothers' views on this specifically did not seem to be elicited.

McKenzie (2000), discussing the New Zealand experience, argues that power relations within families need more attention than they are receiving in the literature and in practice. She argues from her own experience that there are a range of often quite subtle ways in which such power relations can operate. Whilst there is considerable concern generally to ensure that children are involved and not silenced this does not extend to sustained discussions in the literature about gender relations. As the research by Smart and

Neale (1999) explored in Chapter 2 indicates, we cannot assume how power relations between the genders will operate. However, we cannot assume that they are irrelevant either. For example, there is some evidence to suggest that post-separation/divorce men translate feelings of powerlessness and vulnerability into angry appeals around rights to contact with children, appeals which are likely to be socially legitimated. By contrast, women's desires for space and independence are less likely to be recognised unless there has been violence and even then that is not always acknowledged as a legitimate reason for stopping contact. Gendered dynamics may operate between the professionals and family members with complex dynamics circulating around collusion and/or avoidance.

Moreover, it is unclear in the absence of empirical investigation *who* within the family takes on concrete responsibilities for *what* afterwards, an important point given the emphasis on the family taking more responsibility for their difficulties, although it is important to add here that Marsh and Crow found that in 92 per cent of cases specific services were requested by the families to support their efforts.

Family group conferences are not widespread practice (Petrie, 2003). The small summary here attests to the possibilities they offer for developing and working with inclusive notions of family. The amount of time and skills coordinators are judged to need alerts us, however, to the considerable difficulties this might pose for more ongoing work. More work is required to assess how gendered processes operate in relation to who is heard and what family responsibility can mean in practice.

As indicated, central to the development of family group conferences in New Zealand were demands by Maori people for child welfare agencies to develop methods of working which worked *with* their practices of decision-making and problem-solving, and their understandings of family which were seen as much wider than those of white New Zealanders of European descent. Moreover, this was promoted as crucial in reducing the disproportionate numbers of Maori children in state care.

Working with minority ethnic families

What has happened in the UK in terms of the opportunities and difficulties for practitioners to work with multiple understandings of family in relation to ethnicity? Specific guidance has been developed in association with the *Framework for the Assessment of Children in Need and their Families* (Dutt and Phillips, 2000). This highlights the importance for practitioners both of recognising that differing minority ethnic groups may have differing patterns of family formation and to be wary of 'stereotypical thinking' in this respect. For example, it highlights the importance of assuming that African-Caribbean women will not have men involved in their lives, at the same time as recognising that they tend to be heads of households.

It also warns against equating diversity with pathology, a point which would have been much more sharply underlined if the document did not appear premised upon assumptions that diversity was solely a feature of minority ethnic families. There is a tendency therefore to assume homogeneity in the wider community which is of course misleading and can lead to the very pathologising the document wishes to avoid.

Guidance is offered to practitioners in relation to understanding the impact of material disadvantage and recognising the specificities of such material disadvantage. For example, Pakistani and Bangladeshi families appear particularly vulnerable here (Butt and Box, 1998; see also Frost and Featherstone, 2003, for an analysis of the statistical evidence in relation to ethnicity and poverty).

This guidance developed by Dutt and Phillips underscores the tensions and dilemmas which have attended state intervention in minority ethnic families. Statutory interventions in relation to such families have evinced considerable concerns. The practice of placing mainly African-Caribbean children transracially and their disproportionate representation in state care generated considerable critique in the 1980s. The further evidence of their marginalisation in supportive services added force to such critiques (Barn, 1993). More recent research has explored the specific needs and difficulties of South Asian families in relation to the availability of and access to family support services (Quereshi *et al.*, 2000).

As Dutt and Phillips (2000) note, many parents from minority ethnic families can feel profoundly uneasy about what they perceive as tendencies within the wider society to undermine their ability to bring up their children in ways they consider appropriate to survive and prosper in a hostile environment. However, there are concerns from those such as Singh (1999) that such legitimate concerns are not mobilised by 'community leaders' in ways which legitimate oppressive and abusive gendered and generational relations.

Within wider feminist debates and campaigning, black women have been at the forefront in developing organisations such as the Organisation of Women of African and Asian Descent (OWAAD) to campaign against injustices facing the black community at large as well as issues facing black women generally. In so doing they have operated on a range of complex levels but crucial has been the refusal to remain silent about 'awkward family secrets' such as violence and abuse (Sudbury, 1998). Southall Black Sisters have carved out a distinctive role in terms of campaigning on behalf of and offering services to those women and children suffering the consequences of such 'awkward family secrets'.

Clearly, the complexities here are considerable, particularly but not exclusively for white state-employed workers in a post-Stephen Lawrence context, where 'institutionalised racism' has become recognised as part of the UK landscape (McLaughlin and Murji, 1999). The dangers of emphasising support and decrying control are particularly seductive if control is located within a negative framework which furthermore is mapped onto discrimination. However, there is ample evidence that eschewing control and leaving children unprotected can also be discriminatory as Dutt and Phillips (2000) note.

Deconstructing the needs and interests of differing family members and refusing assumptions that communities and families are homogeneous is not easy, as feminist organisations such as OWAAD and Southall Black Sisters have found, and such issues will continue to test practitioners.

Working with 'couples': the possibilities

In its mapping of family services Henricson *et al.* (2001) noted the need for and paucity of what they called 'couples work', by which they appeared to mean work with heterosexual parents in differing types of relationships. They argued that such work was a 'Cinderella activity'. The need for such work flowed from their acceptance that 'parental conflict' is a major source of distress to children whatever the family form and whether parents live separately or together (see also Chapter 1).

My own experiences from a variety of research projects would indicate that 'couples work' is often vital, if neglected, and can very sharply pose conflicts between men and women which are often gendered in two senses. First, they can be overtly about gendered expectations of each other and/or, second, they can reflect changes in gender relations where gendered expectations seem highly precarious if not irrelevant. For example, in relation to the first issue, in a small piece of research carried out some years ago with women who had physically abused their children, I found some evidence from mothers' narratives that conflicts arose because they and their partners when living together were unable to work out a mutually agreed way of caring for and particularly disciplining their children (see Featherstone, 2000, for a brief outline of this research). I called such conflicts gendered because they were based upon a belief by at least one party (usually but not always the man) that certain rights and behaviours were automatically attached to their gender. They had a certain role which was fixed and they were practically able to invest in that role (that is, by being economic providers). Such conflicts are, according to Sure Start workers I have talked to, quite common, and raise considerable anxieties particularly for women workers. Are they going to be seen as ganging up on the woman's side? How do they engage the man? Is it part of their role? Few workers I have met feel confident about doing this work although in the next chapter I document the evidence from some projects working with men around fathering which provided supports for compatible initiatives.

One reason for a lack of confidence seems to be the lack of certainty over whether there is a particular model of family life to be promoted by workers in relation to what men and women should or should not do. Whilst there is often considerable confidence on their part about what adults should do for their children, and they often experience little difficulty in articulating this, such confidence deserts them when it comes to looking at men and women's relationships. Whilst this is linked to the difficulties posed in the next chapter in relation to women practitioners engaging men and these are important, it does seem that clarifying the contours of a project which opened up a dialogue in relation to building democratic families or promoting democratic practices could offer some help in facilitating work in this area.

What such a project signals is not that there is a clear model in terms, for example, of who does what to be imposed, but the importance of all concerned being able in an uncoerced way to express their views and negotiate settlements which are based upon give and take rather than fixed beliefs. This does not mean that the aim is 'equality' of a predetermined kind where an accounting mentality measures who does what. But it does mean that it is possible for fixed beliefs about roles and behaviours to be challenged and that recourse to notions of tradition as in 'this is the way things have always been' are open to challenge rather than simply accepted.

The second kind of conflict which is often linked can appear less overtly gendered and is explored in the next chapter. This relates to questions around how men and women negotiate with each other from positions of considerable uncertainty. Young unemployed men who are non-resident fathers are a clear example here. Such men have few opportunities to draw on discourses about rights or to invest in discourses which provide them with something to offer.

Concluding remarks

Engaging with the complexity of family life offers considerable opportunities and challenges for practitioners (Pinkerton, 2000). Marsh and Crow (1998) highlight the opportunities to mobilise a broader range of resources to support children as well as reducing the need for expensive state resources. Adopting an inclusive notion of family also encourages attention to participants' own understandings rather than professional definitions. It can offer possibilities to reduce the tendency to focus on mothers and to develop culturally sensitive more inclusive practice.

However, the challenges are considerable. Resourcing of projects is an issue, as are issues around how equipped emotionally workers feel. There are considerable and understandable attractions in focusing narrowly either on the mother or children or both. In the next chapter on working with men I argue that the difficulties this work can pose are highly relevant to understanding why broader, more inclusive approaches are not often employed. I also highlight, however, the possibilities that are emerging for working both with men and with men and women together. They offer opportunities to men but also are important in the wider project around building 'democratic' families (Ferguson, 2001a). Such possibilities are embryonic and poorly funded but they do exist.

CHAPTER 7

Working with Men in a Changing World

The topic of men and the associated concept of masculinity have to a certain extent emerged onto policy and political agendas. This marks the explicit naming of men and masculinities as an object of concern, 'as something that needs to be attended to, to be dealt with, to be treated as a problem, to be changed, defended or even just to be talked about and debated' (Hearn, 1998, p. 37). Men and masculinities have also emerged as objects of theoretical exploration and critique in what has been called 'Critical Studies of Men'. Such studies are more likely to question men's practices, particularly those which are premised upon traditional models of authority and power relations. They have fostered the study of such practices in a diverse array of arenas including that of welfare, thus looking at men's variable locations as policy-makers, managers, providers and recipients of welfare (see Hearn, 1998, for a summary). A key theme in many of these explorations, according to Hearn, has been the urgency of recognising and addressing the social problem of men's violence and abuse to women, children and other men.

Lupton and Barclay argued in 1997 that there was little attention being paid within the literature on men and masculinities to looking at men's practices as fathers. However, partly in response to the ways in which fatherhood has moved onto the policy agenda in many countries since the 1990s, this has changed (Popay *et al.*, 1998; Williams, 1998; Hearn, 2002; Hobson, 2002).

Within this literature, for example, can now be found analyses which have sought to explore why fatherhood emerged as an issue of concern in the 1990s in the UK, and to analyse what models were being promoted and by whom (Williams, 1998). Of crucial concern here has been the importance of ascertaining how far such models were attempts to reestablish men's power over women and children or support more democratic settlements.

Since Williams's account in 1998 developments in the UK have moved on. New service initiatives aimed at 'engaging fathers' have emerged, funded by central government, which, whilst they are limited and short-term, mark a departure on the part of government. The emergence of organisations like Fathers Direct has meant that a national campaigning voice is to be found intervening in debates about employment policies, for example. Moreover, service providers such as Sure Start are explicitly addressing how fathers are being engaged with as part of their national evaluation. All of this of course must be located within a backdrop sketched out in Chapter 4 of limited supports for all parents in balancing paid work responsibilities with caring responsibilities. Moreover the mobilisation of a language around *fathers* may be both unhelpful and exclusionary given the diversity there may be in family forms.

This chapter explores the opportunities and difficulties posed by a climate which urges service providers to 'engage' fathers. It argues that there are opportunities to offer men who are often excluded such as young unemployed men, a voice as fathers. Furthermore, there are also opportunities to develop practices which engage their partners or ex-partners and children, which can contribute to the development of more inclusive understandings of family and the building of more democratic families. However, there would appear to be difficulties also, difficulties which are linked to the need to engage with the complexities of men's behaviour as fathers and men and the diverse ways in which they appear to be responding to their changing circumstances. There can also be difficulties in particular practice settings, such as those which were formerly women-only, or for women practitioners in being able to engage fathers for a variety of reasons.

This chapter explores some of the opportunities and difficulties. It begins by outlining briefly some of the key aspects of the demographic, social and cultural context.

Locating 'fathers'

Burghes *et al.*'s (1997) research was an important study of the demographic profile of fathers. It indicated that most fathering took place in intact two-parent first families. Whilst only a minority had very complicated family histories, 13 per cent did not live with any of their children and 23 per cent lived with some of their children. It would also appear that fathers of dependent children, particularly young children, tend to be strongly represented in labour force participation rates (Clarke, 1997). However, there have been important shifts as indicated in Chapter 1 and these appear particularly pronounced amongst those who are poor.

There is a dispersal of 'fathering' practices across households with the emergence of a range of living situations including post-divorce parenting, stepfamilies and lone-mother households, where men's degree of involvement varies. There has also been a rupturing of what often in dominant discourses appeared to be fixed aspects of a father's identity which were inscribed in assumptions about both the universality and desirability of a particular family form. Biology mapped onto residence and these were linked with a circumscribed set of practices, particularly in relation to the father as economic provider.

A range of research accounts marking out key features of fathers' lives and exploring the range of situations in which men 'father' has emerged in recent decades (Lamb, 1997; Burghes *et al.*, 1997; Warin *et al.*, 1999, are just some examples here). Lamb's edited collection provides detailed accounts which reflect diversity on a range of dimensions such as diversity within the category *fathers* along the lines of age, sexuality, 'race' and residence, and diversity linked to the situations in which fathering practices are carried out by those who are not biological fathers.

This diversity therefore obliges attention to language and to interrogating the term 'father' in terms of its exclusionary potential. Whilst I use the term 'father' in this chapter, this is for the sake of convenience and I will attempt to indicate the diversity and complexity which may be around in specific situations.

As has been pointed out in Chapter 1, the emphasis on diversity can obscure the degree of convergence which may be emerging across a range of living situations. For example, there are important trends in intimate relations already discussed at varying points in this book, trends which are applicable to employed fathers in intact two-parent married families as well as the minorities who are living apart from their children or fathering other men's children and those who are unable for whatever reason to access the economic provider role. No longer are intimate relationships fixed as previously, bringing new possibilities as well as dangers. No longer is it straightforwardly possible for men to say, for example, 'this is the way men are or indeed I refuse to discuss things further'.

There is a questioning of behaviour and expectations by adult women in relation to being able to discuss and negotiate which some men may be finding difficult (Ferguson, 2001a).

These trends coexist with small but discernible shifts in the opportunities offered some children at least, particularly older children, to evaluate paternal behaviour and/or misbehaviour. Milligan and Dowie's (1998) study into children's perceptions of what they needed from their fathers indicated that older children held sophisticated views about the importance of being able to respect their fathers. Such respect was not granted automatically on the basis of status or tradition, but on the basis of what fathers did or did not do. The evidence from a much wider study of just under 3,000 young people asked to reflect on their experiences of family life found that a fifth were sometimes really afraid of their fathers or stepfathers. This would lend support to the view that many men may be struggling to develop the kinds of relationships either they or their children may wish for (Cawson *et al.*, 2000). For whilst being afraid of one's father can be seen as desirable in more traditional discourses, it is unlikely to be considered so in the twenty-first century. The differences between birth fathers and men who are fathering children not biologically theirs may, however, continue to need attention here. There is some evidence to suggest that there is more confusion all round in relation to what a stepfather, for example, is expected to do and be.

It is possible to discern wider cultural shifts in expectations about how fathers can and should act, particularly when compared to previous decades. In recent years government ministers have both embraced such shifts and found themselves the victims of such shifts, for example when Tony Blair found himself subject to a certain level of scrutiny for not taking paternity leave when his son Leo was born (see Freely, 2000, for a discussion of how politicians have positioned themselves both as fathers and politicians).

A study by Henwood (2002) of first-time fathers from a range of backgrounds notes the considerable anxieties such men expressed in terms of being able to live up to the expectations they had of themselves and their perceptions of wider expectations. In subscribing to an 'involved father' model they worried about their ability to balance the demands of work and home.

A growing amount of research accounts which are disseminated more widely contribute to the construction of discourses around fathers which may be experienced as both supportive and constraining. For example, many non-resident fathers may take comfort from findings which indicate that good outcomes for children are not necessarily dependent on their physical residence in the home, but they remain subject to another set of prescriptions when such accounts stress that it is the absence of conflict between them and their ex-partners which is a key factor in ensuring good outcomes for children. Moreover, there is a clear presumption at the legislative level that ongoing contact between children and both their parents acting non-conflictually is the best way of ensuring good outcomes for children. This poses difficulties and opportunities for both men and women.

Thus whilst current developments can offer in theory at least a range of possibilities to men in terms of how they do fathering, old constraints remain and new ones have emerged. A range of developments at a collective level have become apparent which both attempt to help individual men deal with the opportunities and difficulties they experience and articulate rights and needs claims on behalf of men as fathers in relation to the law and service provision.

Men speak out as fathers

Attending one of the many conferences on providing services for fathers, which have started to become an increasingly regular feature of the landscape for practitioners since the late 1990s, offers a useful insight into the differing agendas which may mobilise men to claim an identity as fathers and to argue for rights and recognition claims in relation to that identity (see also Freely, 2000). An important constituency is those who seek to have contact or extend their contact with their children and are often highly critical of professional and judicial practices. A further grouping can be those who wish to challenge the array of barriers which impede them being more fully involved with their children whether they are living with them or not. These constituencies are of course neither counterposed nor necessarily distinct, although they can be. The distinctions here can map onto another distinction between those who wish to cooperate with women in caring for children and those who can appear to see women as part of the problem. For example, in my experience, some of the stronger advocates of fathers' rights to contact can express hostility to women whom they see as being favoured in the court setting particularly. This can map onto hostility to feminism which is constructed as having established a climate in which men are now victims.

Not surprisingly such conferences, particularly when the purpose is to encourage service providers to work with fathers, can be tense affairs where women workers can feel silenced. This can key into quite complex feelings about being silenced if not abused by men in other settings. In my experience they can capture in a stark form some of the tensions which can emerge in particular practice settings and this will be returned to below.

Lloyd's (2001) review of ten projects offering services to men as fathers offers useful and considered insights into why men may wish to claim an identity as fathers and make demands on a range of services. He shows, for example, how young fathers can be offered or can claim the space to contest both how they have been constructed and to articulate needs and rights claims on their behalf. Such young fathers are often either invisible or constructed as irresponsible in influential discourses (see, for example, Speak *et al.*, 1997). Lloyd's account of a young fathers' project in Norfolk explored how a project which was initiated by young fathers themselves over a period of seven years engaged in a range of activities, including individual and group support, as well as campaigning around the representation of young fathers and the rights of unmarried fathers.

A project evaluated by the author (Featherstone, unpublished), which emerged from workers' initiatives, and was supported by money available under the Family Support Grant from the Home Office, offered compatible supports to young men particularly in relation to individual support and advice about contact issues (although the remit of the project was not limited age-wise). However, as it did not emerge from any initiatives by men themselves and because of its location within a resource which offered training to unemployed men, there was considerable work to be done in gaining the trust of many of the men. Many expressed suspicion about being approached by workers and asked about their status as fathers. To claim an identity as a father is to open oneself up to child support demands and it is therefore an identity which offers constraints and opportunities. That a considerable number of men did engage with the project would appear to indicate that they felt it was worth it.

Lloyd explores a range of other projects where men of all ages became involved for a variety of reasons. For some men particular changes or crises provoked involvement: a relationship breaking up; taking on full-time care of children; or the mother taking on full-time work. For other men, it was where a woman was struggling as a result of either a difficult childbirth or post-natal depression. Here men could be stepping in because of a problem in relation to the mother, rather than any independent desire on their part. Women also played a role in encouraging male involvement, particularly, it appeared, in encouraging men to attend groups to learn appropriate ways of disciplining children and 'managing their anger'. Although I did not interview female partners about male involvement in the project I evaluated, I found from discussions with workers that women were often reassured by and supported male involvement in the project as they felt it would help the men cope better with access visits. However, there is also important evidence that in established projects which have in practice provided a service to women and children, establishing services for men can elicit hostility from women, both service users and practitioners (Draper, 2001; Ghate *et al.*, 2000). Draper notes, for example, that a day trip organised for men and their children as part of an initiative to encourage the service to become more attractive to fathers left lone mothers feeling discriminated against. In a quite well-resourced project established over a long period working with women and children, the introduction of work with men provoked anxieties about safety and protection issues (Lloyd, 2001).

A range of complex processes may be at play in terms of what motivates men's engagements with projects which appeal to them as fathers. The articulation of needs and rights claims can be linked with men's wishes to share responsibility with women for family life, challenge women's sole caretaker status and take on sole caretaking. Women too may see such projects as supporting them to change or improve men's behaviour towards children. But where male involvement is either not prompted by women or emerges in what have been predominantly women's and children's spaces, there can be difficulties which practitioners may have to deal with. These will be returned to below.

Working with men: the issues which emerge

In the project I evaluated (Featherstone, unpublished), a key issue which emerged was the necessity for the project worker to engage directly with the negotiations between men and women which arose from men's claims for contact with their children. This was both time-consuming and anxiety-provoking, particularly for a lone female worker. However, she judged that it was necessary and, of course, it was because for many of these unmarried non-resident fathers, the mother's role as gatekeeper in relation to access was central.

Many of the men could not locate themselves within a legal discourse around rights because they were unmarried. At an individual level this was often distressing as I watched vulnerable young men clearly desperate for contact with few avenues to pursue such claims. On the other hand, it has been argued that men hide their vulnerability by appeals to rights in ways which do not help them seek respectful solutions (Day Sclater and Yates, 1999). Certainly, the emphasis on negotiation which became necessary seemed to encourage moves towards more holistic understandings on the part of all involved. It would support the view that if negotiations between men and women are conducted solely within a rights discourse and accompanied by a sense of entitlement on the part of men, they can be highly problematic if not dangerous for women and children. They can also leave men stuck in a discourse which offers them few opportunities to develop the negotiating skills they require to engage respectfully on an ongoing basis with women and children.

The difficulties of this work should not be underestimated however. Feelings of adult vulnerability were played out in conflicts over children which could lead to painful exchanges. However, as indicated above, it was difficult to avoid doing this work in a project aimed at fathers as if it was not done the fathers could have no children to father and the project would lose its *raison d'être*. It is much easier to avoid doing this work in more general projects as mothers' involvement with children is not mediated through fathers.

Accounts from some of the younger men in the project seemed, at a verbal level, accepting of the changes they perceived in men and women's lives over the last decades. For example, in interviews with six young men which I conducted, it was notable how often they mentioned that 'things had changed' in a way which emphasised the positives of such changes, not least the positives it offered them in terms of being more involved with their children. A number mentioned the public visibility of 'men pushing prams' over the last ten years as an indicator here. They often emphasised their desire to father differently from how they had been fathered. Doing it differently seemed to encompass a range of features from physical caretaking to feeling that they could talk to and be talked to by their children.

This is not to paint an unduly rosy picture – confusion, anxiety and anger were apparent. Vulnerable young men desperate for contact might desire to sort out the issues respectfully at one point, but at another could feel compelled to go and hammer on their ex-partner's door in a threatening fashion late at night.

However, the project worker's view that many of the young men often lacked the ability but not the desire to engage in respectful communications with adult women they were no longer partners with, while being in loving relationships with their children, did appear valid much of the time. Her work around improving their emotional literacy seemed crucial (see Ferguson, 1998, 2001a, for a discussion of this in relation to work with fathers).

However, it is important to note that in many of the projects set up to work specifically with men around fathering, violence by men to women is not usually considered to be an issue that is dealt with as workers do not feel equipped to do so. Given that work with men who are violent may not explicitly address their role as fathers (Peled, 2000), there is an important gap here which can be particularly sharply posed in working with men in family support work. This is a gap which is replicated at the level of government policy under New Labour. For example, the agenda in relation to tackling domestic violence has appeared to proceed alongside injunctions to 'engage fathers' without any joined-up thinking about the need to develop services for violent men who are fathers (Featherstone, 2003).

Working with men in family support: the barriers and the possibilities for workers

As Gilligan (2000) acknowledges, men are not worked with often in a range of projects which call themselves family support and this needs to change, he argues, if family support is to engage adequately with gender issues. I would also add that this is essential to developing practices which adopt inclusive notions of family and build democratic families. But which men are to be engaged with? Well, to a large extent we do not know because they have been invisible.

Ryan (2000) analyses the position of fathers within families who come to the attention of social services, through an exploration of the studies disseminated through *Child Protection: Messages from Research* (Department of Health, 1995). She found that the structure of families involved in the child protection process at all stages of the process differed from the overall sociodemographic picture in that fewer children lived with both their parents and more lived with lone mothers or in a range of stepfamily settings. This finding must be set alongside the evidence of high levels of unemployment and poverty, with 57 per cent of the families lacking a wage earner. As we saw in Chapter 1, poverty and family structure are complexly related.

The picture that emerges from Ryan's analysis indicates a considerable number of absent fathers and the need for children to come to terms with and negotiate with 'father figures'. This also occurred in contexts where high levels of conflict including violence were ongoing features of the adult relationships. Moreover, a small but significant number of men were described as having mental and physical health problems and/or had been abused in their own childhoods.

Ryan's analysis, which is a secondary analysis of a very diverse range of research projects into social work practices, must be treated with caution in that the very 'realities' uncovered by the researchers for a range of diverse research purposes and then reconstructed by Ryan may themselves reproduce rather than interrogate complex social processes in relation to who gets constructed as problematic and in need of intervention.

Her analysis is important, however, particularly given the dearth of information in this area. It would appear that men may be involved variously in a number of households with a range of attachments of varying degrees of depth and they may struggle with negotiating relationships with women and children in ways which do not involve violence, although there is an urgent need to explore more carefully what is meant by conflict and violence here. Furthermore, she draws attention to the considerable amount of unmet need on the part of the men themselves.

Currently, although this is too simple, Ryan's analysis in conjunction with some of the analyses emerging from men's projects can help practitioners to see fathers and male carers falling into three categories to whom opportunities and constraints are variously attached.

There are, as work in the projects outlined above has demonstrated, numbers of men who wish to work alongside women and/or substitute for women if circumstances demand it, including taking on full-time care of children in certain circumstances (Featherstone, 2003). Such men can be constructed as *resources* for women and children.

There is another category whose own needs in relation to health, mental and physical, and/or past experiences may preclude their being able to develop mutually agreed working parental partnerships and/or offer much to children. These I will call *vulnerable* men – a term I have borrowed from Ferguson (1998), although I am using it more broadly than he does. Ferguson has argued, for example, that there are particular issues posed for older men who have sought meaning through traditional identities such as employment and who are thrown into turmoil through long-term unemployment. He argues that such men can get stuck in grief, mourning the loss of the productive self, and experience major problems in finding meaning in domestic roles and intimacy. He does argue that such men can be engaged with but that their vulnerability must be acknowledged. Indeed, he argues that constructing such men as vulnerable is important in order to both understand their experiences and feelings and establish their entitlement to services.

Finally, there is another category whose involvement in violent or abusive behaviour poses considerable difficulties not only for women and children but also for service providers. Currently, apart from court-mandated programmes which work with men around their offending behaviour there appear to be hardly any service initiatives which work with such men, particularly in relation to fathering issues. Such men can be categorised as *risks*.

The advantages of deconstructing men and fathers as resources, vulnerable and risks are considerable. The key advantage is that it challenges a very influential construction within statutory social work of men as risks (Scourfield, 2003). Furthermore, it can serve to remove some of the fear which it is argued can imbue engaging with men generally (Milner, 1996; Scourfield, 2003). It can support the observations of Daniel and Taylor (2001) that men are important attachment figures for children. It can also offer important supports to ensuring that the needs of vulnerable men do not go unmet.

However, there are also dangers in categorisations of this kind in that they can obscure the complexities of men's lives and reinforce already existing tendencies not to engage with those who are risks. For example, in relation to the first point, I have interviewed men on parenting orders under the Crime and Disorder Act 1998 with considerable unmet needs, whom I would categorise as vulnerable but who were offering a resource to women and children. However, what emerged was that that such resources in the form of placements for children were precarious if attention was not paid to the men's needs and vulnerabilities (Featherstone, 2001).

Furthermore, the distinction between men who are vulnerable and those who are violent may be too simple, implying that vulnerability is never a factor in violence. Indeed Frosh (1994) argues the opposite in that he sees male vulnerability particularly in contemporary conditions as key to understanding their violent behaviour:

> Men's domination has always been supported by violence; this violence is no less present as domination is called into question. It is observable all the time, particularly as sexual violence, but also in other paranoid exchanges within family life. It arises from a mixture of rage at the dissolution of the fantasy of masculine rationality and of employment as a strategy to hold onto this power. (p. 230)

In relation to the second point, Peled (2000) argues for the importance of engaging violent men as fathers and working with children around their feelings, noting that this can not only promote positive outcomes for children, but also contribute to a project around gender equity. There is a clear gap in provision at the moment, however, in relation to working with men's violence. There seems little provision to take on work with them as fathers rather than as offenders, work which can also engage with the needs of the women and children concerned. In advising one Sure Start project considering taking on such work, it became apparent to me and the workers concerned that considerable resources would be needed at a range of levels to undertake such work. It would involve multi-agency coordination to ensure safety and appropriate training, for example, and would involve a considerable input of time and resources which, given that engaging with such violence was not a target set for the Sure Start project, could jeopardise other work which had targets attached.

Discussion

The mere introduction of a different language in relation to men may, however, fail to address the complex feelings women practitioners may have about engaging with men. Although fear of violence is the most commonly acknowledged barrier, less well-articulated is a phenomenon I have observed which is women practitioners' own sense of anger/disappointment with men – the hostility noted above in relation to women service users can also be replicated at practitioner levels. My own experience of teaching a range of very experienced practitioners as well as attending conferences for practitioners over the years has alerted me to the possibility of the above. The majority of men and women react with interest and sympathy to the idea that men should be engaged with in terms of providing supports for children particularly. A further point often made is that in the context of concerns about young men's well-being, encouraging active fatherhood might be a positive. However, they also acknowledge that young women may not always want them involved and the difficulties this can pose.

There is a much smaller group of women (mainly but not exclusively), however, who express antagonism. Their expressed concerns coalesce round the following: men are being reproduced as victims when in reality they are often victimisers and it is dangerous to encourage their involvement in family life; scarce resources are being taken away from women once again; if such work is to be done then men should take responsibility for such work as women have been taking responsibility for trying to change men's behaviour for too long. These discussions where antagonism is expressed are often the liveliest and stand out in teaching terms as the times when I feel there has been a very genuine interaction within the class with ideas and emotions being freely expressed.

It would be unwise to see complex feelings in relation to such issues as solely the province of women. Men too may struggle as the topic involves them in engaging with complex feelings around the commonalities and differences between men. It necessitates engaging specifically with questions which can arouse defensiveness, guilt and anxiety.

An interesting point here is that different versions of feminism can be mobilised to support the importance of both engaging men as fathers and not doing so. Why men should be engaged with can be located within discourses around gender equity in a liberal sense – men and women should be treated equally – alongside discourses which seek to challenge gender inequity. In relation to the latter, engaging men is seen as part of a project which resists mother-blaming or reinforcing women's responsibilities and facilitates the development of strategies which challenge men's behaviour from their non-participation in childcare through to their abusive behaviour. However, there are other strands within feminism which emphasise the dangers and link this with a concern that attempts to engage men as fathers as part of wider attempts to reinstate men's control over women and children in families (see Segal, 1995, for a summary). This is not surprising given the tensions within feminism over the role of men in family life noted in Chapter 2.

In my experience the debates over *why engage fathers* can overshadow *how to engage fathers*, although it is also apparent that sometimes questioning *why* can itself be seen as offensive by both men and women. This has led me to the conclusion that engaging with *how* without engaging with *why* can be problematic. The two must be interlinked and the difficulties and anxieties of all concerned explored. Such difficulties and anxieties are linked to complex gendered debates and struggles in wider society. Furthermore, there would appear to be a need for a range of strategies dependent upon setting. As I will discuss in the next chapter, women-only spaces continue to be important and the introduction of men into such settings should be considered cautiously. Separate provision within an integrated approach is one possibility here. Whatever strategies are developed these must be accompanied by considerable attention to process issues. Cameron *et al.* (1999) have noted in their study of men working in nurseries that the introduction of men in whatever role into what have often been women-only settings needs to be located within a commitment by all involved, including management, to what they call 'reflexivity'. They see this as offering spaces for the 'opening up' of gender, crucially through offering time and space to discuss and reflect. My own experience of 'opening up' gender is that it can involve engaging with complex emotions, which motivate the quite complex and diverse positions which can be taken.

Concluding remarks

This chapter has located the differing situations in which men father today and has outlined some of the issues emerging from a range of projects working with such men. It is argued that in order to develop thinking and practice, the deconstruction of men as fathers into resources, vulnerable and risks, whilst carrying dangers, has some merit in trying to capture the complexities of fathers' situations. However, it cautions against developing projects which are solely focused on the *how* to and which fail to engage with *why* issues. Engaging with *why* involves engaging with the complexities of gender relations in a changing world – such complexities impact on all of us as gendered beings.

CHAPTER 8

Working with Women

The previous chapters explored some of the possibilities and barriers to developing practices which involved wider understandings of family and work with men, and argued that it is important to continue developments in these areas in order to offer services which engage with the complexities of service users' lives and attachments. It has also been argued that it is crucial not to focus service provision exclusively on women in order to advance gender equity, increase children's sources of attachment and offer opportunities to men to engage in family life and get their needs met.

However, it is also important to acknowledge that working exclusively with women may be necessary in particular situations and settings. There is a need for safe spaces for women in order to give them the resources to escape violent partnerships, engage in healing, negotiate different settlements with men, and so on. It can therefore play a very important role in women's ability to 'life plan' (Ferguson, 2001a).

Whilst there is evidence that family support activities can play important roles here there is also evidence to suggest that family support activities can increase the burden of responsibility that is placed upon women as mothers, particularly in the new initiatives set up under New Labour. Moreover, whilst there is a discourse around 'needs' which can be mobilised in relation to mothers rather than reserved exclusively for children, its mobilisation is precarious and not widely legitimated. This is further exacerbated by an overall context which can offer little support to notions that parents have needs and which sees them simply as conduits for the promotion of children's welfare. Furthermore, there would appear to be a need to offer more attention to dialogue that engages with women around *their* concerns and self-understandings about their needs and rights as mothers and as women. An interesting feature of the last chapter was, for example, the emergence of men's voices articulating their rights and needs as fathers and of attempts to communicate with service providers around such needs and rights. Whilst this chapter documents an example of a compatible initiative in relation to mothers of children who have been sexually abused, there is much less evidence of such developments by women as mothers more generally.

The chapter starts with a brief attempt to locate women in the twenty-first century.

Locating women today

The lack of fixity apparent in relation to what it means to be a woman today is both the result of and feeds into changed material practices. For substantial periods of the twentieth century, woman equated with wife and mother for the majority of the population and norms about the incompatibility of either wifehood or mothering with paid work were widely invested in if not practically possible for many women to act out. Today, paid work is at least part of the landscape for most women including mothers and is increasingly an expectation on the part of the state in relation to women who may otherwise seek state support.

Becoming a mother or a wife is not an inevitable part of women's landscape today and there has been a growth in the numbers of women choosing not to have children, as well as delaying childbearing. For numbers of the population, taking on a previously silenced identity such as lesbianism and combining it with motherhood has become achievable (Kershaw, 2001).

What is also apparent is that both becoming a mother and the contexts in which mothering is carried out continue to be shot through with both old as well as new disparities/inequalities. Becoming a mother is more likely for women who are poor and/or with low educational attainments and it is also more likely that such women will become mothers at a younger age (Walkerdine *et al.*, 2001). Poorer women are more likely to mother alone for periods. Mothering alone also increases the chances of poverty (Frost and Featherstone, 2003). There are complex issues in relation to choice to be considered here. Whilst there may be some evidence to support Mann and Roseneil's (1999) arguments that lone motherhood can be a conscious choice for young poor women, as it appears to be for some educated and financially secure women, it is also probable that some 'choose' it because poor men have little to offer them, or do not wish to offer what little they have, in terms of either material or emotional resources (Franks, 1999).

However, the picture is shot through with complexity. Bangladeshi women are unlikely to mother outside marriage or be in the paid labour force but are likely to be in poverty. African-Caribbean women are more likely to be in full-time paid employment, registered as the head of household and have a range of relationships with the father/s of their children, and the research on African-Caribbean children would indicate that considerable numbers live in poverty (Frost and Featherstone, 2003; Platt, 2003).

A complex feature of today which is engaged with variously by women is that a discourse which offers women access to notions of *self* has emerged (Kaplan, 1992). This can vary considerably in terms of the meanings attached and the implications. At the risk of oversimplifying, it is now possible to say that many women operate within understandings that 'they have needs too' – in what can often be a defensive reaction to attempts to restrict them to meeting the needs of others as well as springing from positive impulses towards self-actualisation. This has had an obvious impact upon how mothering is thought about and done. For example, Kaplan (1992) argues that a discourse around the seeking of self-fulfilment has emerged, a discourse which is unprecedented in the context of a dominance of notions of duty and self-sacrifice and which is leading women to varying degrees to seek the fulfilment of self through mothering as well as in an array of other arenas (see Beck and Beck-Gernsheim, 1995, on the emergence of 'the female biography'). However, coexisting with this are societal discourses which mothers, workers and service users alike invest in, which can allow little space for mothers to articulate their needs and which in prioritising the meeting of children's needs can act to restrict mothers' talk (Lawler, 1999).

How are family support developments engaging with what appears to be happening? One trend does appear to affirm the importance of supporting women as mothers in taking up a range of roles alongside mothering and this is having both welcome and unwelcome consequences.

Family support: expanding mothers' identities or a new form of regulation?

Gilligan (2000) argues for the importance of affirming the multiple identities of those who use family support services. For example,

he argues that developing strengths in one area such as community involvement can encourage a mother to feel more confident
about other roles. There is indeed evidence that projects can do this.
For example, the project explored in Chapter 6 which was developed from a school setting offered a range of opportunities and
identities to both mothers and fathers, although in practice it was
mothers in the main who took up these opportunities. Many of the
mothers I interviewed moved from seeking individual support for
their own or their children's difficulties to volunteering in the classroom or undertaking accredited training as classroom assistants.
The benefits of such a flexible approach were that the women were
able both to see themselves and be seen as resources for their children and the school generally. An important offshoot was that their
ability to provide for themselves economically through seeking
paid work was increased.

Gardner (2002a) noted that compatible opportunities were provided in some family support projects run by the NSPCC. She also
noted that such activities coexisted with important opportunities
to engage in healing work in relation to past and ongoing traumas
and abuses and offered a range of emotional and practical supports
to develop more positive and multiple identities.

There is often an explicit awareness within such projects that the
impacts of past or ongoing abusive experiences can militate against
moving on and indeed that pressure to move on, for example, into
paid work can cause considerable difficulties. For example, women
can and do use the benefit systems as a way to remove themselves
and their children from abusive relationships and a period on
benefits can be a lifeline for those wishing to reconstruct their lives.
Any compulsion in relation to taking on paid work within a fixed
period of time is therefore problematic and, moreover, would take
little account of the kinds of jobs available and the adequacy of the
infrastructure to support good quality childcare.

Many contemporary developments, particularly in the voluntary sector, in relation to family support are premised upon varying
assumptions, which may be more or less negotiated with all concerned, about what parents, mothers and fathers alike, need *for
themselves* and in order *to parent children well* and do not involve
compulsion in relation, for example, to taking up training or paid
work.

Compatible *activities* can be carried out in the initiatives specifically developed under New Labour, although such projects are
linked to differing and more explicit policy objectives. I will explore

Sure Start here as this is the initiative set up under New Labour with which I am most familiar. The observations are based upon wide-ranging discussions with people involved with Sure Start projects in a range of capacities and do not refer specifically to any of the projects I am currently involved in evaluating, as permission has not been received to do so. Sure Start projects are based upon local partnerships and there is a clear emphasis upon parental involvement at all levels from the management of the project to taking on pieces of paid work, running groups and so on. Although generally framed in gender-neutral terms, the involvement of men/fathers is being monitored by the national evaluation team and indeed their first report into implementation issues noted that 50 per cent of Sure Start management boards had a male parent involved (http://www.ness.bbk.ac.uk).

The overall emphasis on developing a partnership approach to the delivery of services in New Labour's agenda has led to concerns from observers for a range of reasons (see Newman, 2001). One concern that has been raised is that it involves a diverse range of constituencies in delivering a policy agenda that they have not themselves been involved in developing.

However, implementation on the ground reveals a more complex picture. My own observations would indicate that Sure Start projects offer opportunities for the exercising of voice on the part of adult service users. Indeed this appears to be one of its attractions for them and for workers who, in my experience, are leaving the statutory sector partly to engage in what they see as more democratic working practices. It is apparent that many workers are deliberately fashioning a style of work which is characterised by working alongside service users and developing supportive trusting partnerships. One former social worker described this to me as going back to her community development days.

However, the exercising of voice on the part of service users and workers does indeed operate within clear constraints. Targets are set centrally in relation to the overall work, targets which have not been developed in consultation with either parents who use services or with children. Some targets directly require parents to change their behaviour in order to ensure better outcomes for children and whilst they are accompanied by supportive strategies, there are tensions here in terms of the implications of such targets for the welfare of the adults themselves. Specific targets in relation to women, such as a reduction in the numbers smoking throughout pregnancy, have aroused concern that there is an underlying failure to appreciate the meanings which can be attached to smoking by poor women. Increasingly, it would appear that smoking is a marker of poverty and can also have a gendered dimension – women use it as a way of having time out, something for themselves, managing their weight and managing anger and distress. Whilst workers can make room for incorporating such understandings into their support strategies, they are still bound to achieve the targets within a specified timescale.

Moreover, there can be considerable tensions which reflect un-resolved issues in government policies, for example, between re-ducing jobless households (see Chapter 5 for the targets here), engaging parents with their children and being involved in initia-tives such as Sure Start. My own observations of a number of pro-jects would indicate that considerable opportunities are being made available and taken up by mothers in the main. These involve attending and speaking at conferences and training events, and developing a range of skills such as being involved in local evalu-ative activities. However, these are time-consuming in themselves and if accompanied by specific injunctions to seek any paid work of whatever kind can lead to difficulties.

It would appear that in some settings which term themselves family support, there can be explicit commitment for a variety of reasons to affirming and supporting mothers in a range of identi-ties, although there is evidence of tensions within the newer initiatives because of the targets they are obliged to meet. More-over, these newer initiatives can evidence what Scourfield and Drakeford (2002) have identified under New Labour as 'pessimistic policies on parenting that have a greater impact on women because of the gendered division of child care' (p. 627). They instance the development of parenting orders developed under the Crime and Disorder Act 1998 as an example here. Such orders, whilst framed in gender-neutral terms, do indeed appear to have impacted directly upon women although I have also argued that such de-velopments do not have uniformly pessimistic implications for women (see Chapter 4).

There are also projects which do not explicitly term themselves 'family support' which have merged in a bottom-up way from women themselves in their capacities as mothers. These offer important insights about identity and space, insights which are not always available to or recognised fully by either the more estab-lished projects (although they can be – see Gardner, 2002a) or those developed under New Labour.

My involvement for over six years with one such project, a project for mothers known as MOSAIC, is offered as an illustration here. Initially developed for and by mothers whose children have been sexually abused and who wished to be and indeed considered themselves to be protective mothers, this has worked with a dynamic bottom-up approach to needs. This has meant that services have been developed, changed and rethought in an ongoing way.

The mothers come from a range of class and occupational backgrounds and the overwhelming majority are white British. They are involved at different points with the project, such as immediately after discovery of the abuse to years afterwards. The process requires quite profound rethinking in relation to their identities. For example, many become lone mothers immediately with many of the attendant practical consequences, including applying for benefits maybe for the first time. The issues identified in Chapter 1 in relation to the kinds of difficulties a lone mother may face generally are writ large in such circumstances. Alongside practical needs are emotional issues in relation to mourning the loss of a partner, if he was the abuser, which he often is. Divorce/separation can involve the rethinking of past, present and future identities with considerable emotional consequences and these can be particularly traumatic in situations where a partner has sexually abused their child.

What happens impacts upon women in relation to a variety of identities – as wives, mothers and women. They are forced to develop new narratives which involve integrating past pain into more hopeful stories for the future as well as dealing with what are often considerable current difficulties. MOSAIC engages with and offers services to such women to meet a diversity of needs – services as varied as benefits and housing advice, counselling, massage and 'runaway' days based upon the articulation of what they feel they need. It offers spaces for the 'healing and self definition' which Ferguson (2001a) argues is fundamental to good practice in family support and child protection work. Such spaces require practical as well as emotional underpinnings. The question of time is important in the sense of offering services which can be accessed for as long as women need them. The question of time is also posed in relation to tendencies in the current policy context. Whilst most mothers will wish to work and many continue to do so, and indeed it is often their lifeline, others need time away from such pressures and considerations. Discussing the current policy context with such mothers has led me to really appreciate the fear that compulsion in relation to paid work can evoke. Moreover, an important aspect of MOSAIC is the involvement of mothers themselves in the project in a variety of roles, most of which are unpaid but are essential to the running and ongoing development of MOSAIC. It is important to note that this offers concrete support to the concerns of those who, whilst broadly welcoming the promotion of paid work for women, do see that it could militate against their involvement in a host of activities within specific communities which actively contribute to social capital (Lister, 2001).

MOSAIC's experience would indicate a complex picture in relation to statutory services in the part of England where it is located. At a range of forums where dialogue between women involved with MOSAIC and a range of service providers has taken place, the following seems evident to me. Women's stories in all their complexities can be heard by workers, even those in the statutory sector who are often the target of MOSAIC's criticisms. It is often felt by the women coming to MOSAIC that such workers are only concerned with securing the safety of the child and that they are constructed solely as conduits for children's safety. They also often feel very judged by workers in the sense that it is assumed they should have known that the abuse was happening and that it is therefore a reflection on their lack of attention to their children. This can often key very painfully into their own feelings that they have let the child/children down and reflects wider discourses around femininity and mothering in relation to self-blame and maternal perfectibility which both workers and service users invest in. Dialogue can, however, take place as indicated and can open up horizons on both sides. Connections can be made, although there exist real limitations on the room for manoeuvre that statutory workers have in relation to offering the kind of resources women need.

Ferguson (2001a) is much more confident that such services can be offered by statutory services although his research evidence to support this, it is important to note, does come from the Republic of Ireland. The experience of MOSAIC would indicate that the pessimistic picture painted by Farmer and Owen (1995) still has considerable resonance in the part of England MOSAIC covers. Indeed research being conducted by myself at the time of writing would suggest that a considerable degree of pessimism is in order. For example, a focus group with six female carers as part of such research revealed considerable levels of dissatisfaction on the part of the carers with the support provided by social services in particular (Featherstone *et al.*, forthcoming).

Whilst there is evidence of family support projects, particularly in the voluntary sector, taking on work with mothers in these situations is usually very focused, time-limited work often directed specifically at helping mothers manage the difficult behaviour of their children. Gardner (2002a) does offer important evidence that strict time limits are not adhered to by some projects operating open-door policies and services. However, in a discussion about such projects at a conference, it became very apparent to me that the majority of participants from a range of organisations were unanimous that this was not common practice in a climate dominated by an emphasis on a quick throughput of work (Gardner, 2002b).

Engaging with mothers today appears premised in some settings within family support at least upon a recognition that they inhabit a number of identities and working with them flexibly in relation to how they see these at particular stages of their lives. This is to be welcomed although there can be a tendency to premise services around mothers taking on additional activities which have either the explicit aim of improving their 'parenting' or longer-term goals such as improving their employability. Respite for mothers can be offered but is often attached to conditions, however, such as attending a parenting group.

There is less space to hear women who to varying degrees refuse or resist key aspects of the mothering role. I interviewed Edie as part of a small research project which was aimed at exploring issues of physical violence towards children by their mothers (see Featherstone, 2000). Edie asked to be interviewed in order that her story might be heard by other mothers. Her experience of mothering two small children obliged her to confront a range of processes at both an emotional and social level which became unmanageable and not only resulted in physical violence towards one child, but also obliged her to leave her children in the care of their father and to live elsewhere whilst retaining contact with the children. Mothering, she concluded, obliged a sacrifice of 'self' that she was ultimately unable to deal with by remaining in a full-time maternal role.

Such mothers appear to be in the minority. But they do alert us to an ongoing process evident in contemporary developments more widely. They confirm a rupturing of assumptions about the following: all women want to be mothers; all mothers love their children; all mothers who love their children want to care for them. Accounts from mothers who leave indicate that they can make a distinction between loving their children and caring for them and indeed for some, their love was a key factor motivating their decision to 'leave' (Jackson, 1994).

Discussions around the variations in women's desires in relation to mothering are difficult to raise, however. Feminist insights are helpful in understanding such difficulties but have also contributed to such difficulties themselves.

Feminist social work – opportunities and constraints

As Chapter 3 briefly outlined, there is a considerable history of attempts to elaborate something called feminist social work (see, for example, Brook and Davis, 1985; Hanmer and Statham, 1988; Dominelli and McLeod, 1989; Langan and Day, 1992; Featherstone, 1997, 1999). This had links with the wider feminist movement but also with other social movements in the 1960s and 1970s which have had a range of impacts upon social welfare. There are now clear strands of research and campaigning activities committed to exploring welfare subjects as historically constructed through a complex web of social relations rather than through class, which was the primary concern of critics of welfare hitherto. This thinking is not just about 'adding in' other forms of oppression but exploring the complexities of multiply positioned subjects who are both active and acted upon. It has been about recognising and giving voice to bottom-up challenges by service users to how they are constructed by policy-makers and engaged with by professional workers (see, for example, Croft and Beresford, 1996; Taylor, 1998; Williams, 1999).

Feminist social work, in its early emphasis on women workers identifying with women service users around a shared gender identity in order to develop transformative practices, held some potential to and indeed did allow for more democratising practices between workers and service users in my own experience. It was a brave attempt to put women's needs on the social work map, to argue that they should not be considered solely as wives and mothers, and it was also an attempt to construct working relationships which were characterised by sharing and mutuality.

However, it ran aground quite quickly, particularly in its early manifestations in the work of those such as Brook and Davis (1985). Here it was promoted as a project essentially concerned with women workers working with women service users in order to challenge the ways they were defined and treated. This was a project which used language to challenge women's confinement to the maternal and the marital – women were not just wives and mothers. It also highlighted the similarities between workers and service users as women who were oppressed by the same forces and saw such similarities as resources to be used to understand and challenge oppressive definitions and practices.

Such understandings were quickly challenged by the contexts in which workers operated. Many early feminists moved to a pragmatic recognition that there was limited room for manoeuvre in services organised around ensuring the welfare of children for arguing for services which took women's needs seriously. Violence to women would only be taken seriously, for example, if the links between such violence and harm to children was emphasised (see Mullender and Morley's book in 1994 whose very title *Putting the Abuse of Women on the Child Care Agenda* seemed to signal this recognition).

This led to an attempt, which was successful but had clear limitations, to argue for the coincidence of women's interests as mothers with their children's. Supporting children meant supporting mothers. However, whilst there is clearly an overlap between the welfare of children and that of their mothers, this does not mean there is coincidence. To sustain such a position would mean erasing children's agency and restricting women to a particular model of motherhood which ironed out considerations around subjectivity.

However, feminists did get associated with rather sanitised notions of motherhood which in the context of child welfare debates constructed mothers as automatically on the side of their children in joint battles against powerful and/or violent men. This has changed as feminists have become more involved in research into what children's own understandings are (for example, in relation to domestic violence, see Peled, 2000). At a research level this has meant that it is less and less acceptable to elicit children's perspectives from mothers (see Featherstone and Trinder, 1997, for a discussion of past feminist practice here).

The assumption that women's shared gender identity could form the basis for working relationships foundered on the growing realisation that differences between women were complex and mattered. Women's organisational identity mattered and often overrode whatever similarities there were between them and the women they worked with (Wise, 1995).

A feminist critique informed by psychoanalytic understandings emerged which has sought to explore why encounters between women workers and service users which are centrally about mothering can evoke difficult emotions for both parties (Lawrence, 1992; Featherstone, 1997). This is indebted to more general feminist understandings about mothering and motherhood and relationships between mothers. Parker (1995, 1997) has developed an analysis, for example, which explores the function of ambivalence (feelings of love and hate) in mothers' lives. She further explores how difficult it is for mothers to express their ambivalence and indeed how other mothers can censor such expressions. Coward (1993) has explored how relationships between mothers can become imbued with feelings of competition and anxiety in relation to each other about not being good enough. Such feelings can become sharply posed when one party is in effect paid to engage with the other around her mothering practices.

In many settings, I have observed that there can often be few spaces to deal with the difficult emotions which can be evoked by such work for all concerned. I have also observed how the introduction of such feminist insights as those of Parker can strike a chord in a way which earlier feminist insights simply do not (Featherstone, 1999). Whilst feminist insights about fear of men do strike a chord and appear widely available, more complex insights about the difficulties which can arise in women's work with other women are less well-known though welcomed when introduced.

Women workers' feelings of anger, disappointment and indeed envy of women service users can be conveniently displaced onto concern for the welfare of the child and thus obscured from more complex interrogation. For example, in my previous work I explored how and why a woman worker could not bear to hear a woman who repeatedly said she did not want to care for her child, and noted that one of the factors was that she repressed such feelings in herself and was therefore unable to hear them expressed by another (Featherstone, 1997).

Difficult feelings are particularly sharply posed in my view where workers are committed to developing supportive relationships but women resist or contest workers' definitions particularly of what their children need. Such battles can be essentially political battles – in relation to needs definition and indeed crucially resources.

Where projects are premised upon voluntary involvement, such mothers can simply not be dealt with, although clearly if this became a widespread phenomenon projects such as Sure Start would have to justify why they were not working with anyone! Statutory workers in situations where a child's welfare is considered to be endangered of course do not have this option (see Featherstone, 1997).

In such settings, while certain situations can more easily lead themselves to a degree of certainty about what should be done, many do not and my own impression is that women workers can find themselves mediating the consequences of a limited repertoire of resources which are premised upon mothers being physically and emotionally available to their children at all times. Such mediation can involve the deployment of distancing techniques in order not to appreciate the full range of needs a mother has which are simply not able to be met by a limited repertoire of resources. Such distancing techniques can be interrupted by the introduction of feminist insights which may not lend themselves to any easy resolution of the difficulties but do allow for more thoughtful discussions about the multiple meanings of mothering for women.

Concluding remarks

There is evidence that many family support projects in a range of settings can support mothers taking on expanded roles and identities. However, there is also evidence to suggest that this can be at a price and increase their burdens as well as expanding their horizons and options. There seems to be less space for more fundamental discussions about the difficult feelings that motherhood can evoke and/or allow mothers legitimacy in rethinking 'how they want to be mothers'. Whilst there has been a tendency for feminist writings to reproduce sanitised accounts of mothers and mothering, there are also writings available which, in my experience, are helpful to workers in trying to reflect on the complexities of the situations they encounter and the difficult feelings which can be evoked for them.

CHAPTER 9

Children, Young People, Gender and Family Support

In the early 1980s I worked with young offenders as a statutory social worker. The majority of such offenders were male from a range of ethnic backgrounds, although a small number were female. The project in common with many at that time was underpinned by a strong set of beliefs about the nature of offending and there was a very clear associated direction laid out in relation to policies and practices. Basically, it was believed that offending was a 'normal' feature of adolescent (male) development and that the majority would grow out of such behaviour as they acquired a stake in society, crucially through gaining employment and developing stable adult family relationships. However, young people could be launched onto 'criminal careers' by professional and legal interventions which labelled them and/or institutionalised them as criminals.

The main purpose of professional intervention was to avert such labelling and criminalisation and the focus of much of my work was working with other professionals to stop them recommending to the courts that the young people receive either residential or custodial outcomes.

Looking back on this work it is impossible not to be struck by the naivety of our assumptions in relation to both work and adult relationships and how little prepared we were for the changes which were to transform profoundly the economic and social landscapes of young men in the 1980s. But it also strikes me in retrospect that such work generally was located in an approach to young people that was premised upon notions of 'becoming' rather than 'being'. Lee (2001) has explored this more widely and argues that approaches to childhood generally have been skewed towards 'becoming' and the 'future' which are problematic in terms of appreciating the diversities and complexities of children's actual lives in the here and now. They are also premised upon adulthood being a 'final' stage of development:

> As long as adulthood could be treated as a fixed point that everybody understood, childhood could be defined in relation to this certainty. Thus children were often defined as whatever adults were *not*. Where adults were stable and mostly unchanging over time, children, as they grew up, were going through many changes. This made them, by nature, unstable and incomplete . . . the clear contrast between adulthood and childhood, between beings and becomings, meant that it was hard to understand children as persons in their own right. But now the permanent jobs and permanent relationships that made adulthood look like a state of stability are not so widely available . . . one of the main bases for the clear contrast between adulthood and childhood is being eroded. (Lee, 2001, p. 8; emphasis in original)

Consequently, it would seem that although a key aspect of work needs to be premised upon enabling young people generally to develop flexible and open ways of thinking about what their 'futures' might hold, this work needs locating too within understandings that their 'presents' may be comprised of a multiplicity of attachments and challenges. Such presents contain adults who are continuing to 'become' as well as to 'be'.

Thinking about the 'here and now'

There has been a considerable increase in research generally with children and young people in recent years which has been given added impetus by the Economic and Social Research Council (ESRC) Children 5–16 programme which explored children's perspectives on what they needed in a range of situations, such as where domestic violence was occurring and when their parents were divorcing (see Prout, 2001, for an overview). This research programme was premised upon a basic belief in the importance of eliciting children's and young people's accounts of what mattered to them and how they made sense of their social worlds.

One particular piece of research within the ESRC programme conducted by Frosh *et al.* (2002) offers valuable insights into the views of boys at age 11–14. This research indicated the policing role boys play in relation to each other, generally linked to notions of masculinity. Popular masculinity was associated with being hard, good at sport, wearing designer clothes, not being seen to get on with schoolwork and not doing anything that could be construed as girlish. Boys who could not claim to be tough and/or good at sport and wished to get on with schoolwork were called names, including homophobic names, and sometimes bullied. Boys of African-Caribbean descent were seen as particularly masculine and those of Asian or directly African descent were not considered very masculine.

The research provided support for the existence of hegemonic masculinity as a powerful idea that regulates boys' behaviour. However, most boys did not feel that they themselves possessed the characteristics of 'proper' masculinity. This meant that they had to put considerable work into accounting for themselves to other boys in order to produce themselves as acceptably masculine. They did this in a number of ways. They disparaged those whom they said were just pretending to be hard and reproduced themselves as 'at least real' and they talked themselves up the hierarchy of hardness. Some, a minority, tried to subvert it by considering themselves above it. Some managed to do well at school and be good at sport.

Boys policed their identities by identifying as effeminate or gay those boys they saw as transgressing gender boundaries. They also commonly contrasted the characteristics they considered masculine with those they considered feminine. Several described girls as more mature, serious about schoolwork, having close friendships and able to keep emotional confidences. A number of boys seemed to project onto girls a capacity for closeness and sympathy which they denied in boys. The researchers also found that the construction of heterosexual desire seemed to involve a positive affirmation of these gendered oppositions: that is, gender difference was eroticised.

Frosh *et al.* also interviewed a number of girls of the same age in this study in order to ascertain their views on boys, masculinity and gendered relations. The girls constructed similar kinds of gendered dichotomies as the boys, although they attached different meanings to these, and differently evaluated the feminine and masculine components. Almost all the girls were very critical of boys for being immature, irresponsible and troublesome and they constructed themselves by contrast as mature, sensible and conscientious with a wider range of interests. However this cannot be reduced to straightforward divisions between 'good girls' and 'bad boys'. The girls did see exceptions and they did emphasise context – often attributing boys' 'bad behaviour' to peer pressure, thus implying that when they were on their own boys were not bad. Furthermore, the girls also tended to eroticise gendered differences: they did not want 'nice' boys as boyfriends but boys who were funny and sporty.

In general, most boys constructed their mothers as more sensitive and emotionally closer to them than their fathers who were seen to be more jokey, but also more distant and detached. 'Twenty-three boys (out of 78) indicated that their fathers were much less available to them than their mothers; only two said it was the other way around, and many boys wished they could see more of their fathers, with some indicating that fathers did not respond adequately to their needs for help' (Frosh *et al.*, 2002, p. 13). Nineteen boys specifically mentioned turning to their mothers when things went wrong, compared to four who turned to their fathers. Many communicated a strong sense of loss when talking about their relationships, particularly with fathers. They sometimes idealised the ways in which girls interacted or how they saw other boys engage with their fathers.

The researchers found that generally, even at age 11, the boys were often capable of reflecting in a complex way on how their actual lives were at odds with what they would wish them to be, and even how constraining certain aspects of masculinity might be. 'They often spoke particularly poignantly about losses in their lives and also the value they placed upon parents who attended to them sensitively and seriously – and how disappointed they were by parents who did not' (ibid., p. 256).

A lesson the researchers drew from their work is that part of the 'problem' of young masculinities is its very construction as a problem. The boys were very aware that they were constructed as a problem societally and that they struggled to be heard by adults partly because of this construction. However, when engaged with by adult researchers who worked hard to hear them, they were well able to engage and reflect on their lives. This led the researchers to speculate that they commonly experienced a lack of 'recognition' as subjects. 'This kind of recognition is thought within some psychoanalytic theories to be a basic necessity for the emergence of psychological well-being . . . that is, seriously acknowledging the existence of others as subjects is a crucial element in producing people who have confidence in their worth and their own capacity for thoughtfulness and positive relationships' (ibid., p. 257).

Although it was not the primary purpose of the research, Frosh *et al.* did identify some possibilities in terms of doing 'boys' work'. They found that the research format adopted, which involved open group discussions with an adult other than a teacher, was effective. It required patience to get past the teasing and 'cussing' but it did allow new avenues for boys to think about redressing the distortions produced by the constraints of hegemonic masculinity. They suggest that this method should be employed more widely and reflect on the merits and otherwise of boys-only groups. They argue that it is important not to preclude the possibility of boys in boys-only groups being sensitive with each other, and of not reproducing self-fulfilling prophecies in relation to boys in boys-only groups being problematic, but they also do acknowledge the difficulties that can arise in such groups.

They challenge what they see as a tendency of projects to focus on activities such as football in order to engage boys. Whilst 'this has an obvious rationale in building group solidarity and indeed making the project acceptable to boys . . . our view is that too much emphasis on what are taken to be "natural" boys' activities feeds into the discourse of a narrowly exclusionary "hegemonic" masculinity and thus makes the constructions of alternatives more difficult' (ibid., p. 261). From a perspective concerned to develop explicit work with fathers, it is important to note Lloyd's (2001) observations that Dads and Lads projects which use football and other sports to engage fathers have had difficulties in making the transition from a sports and activity focus to a more explicit fathers' programme which looks at issues around fathering.

Frosh *et al.* found that there did seem to be an embargo on close, dependent contact between boys and their fathers which fed into an idealisation of girls and women that itself was stereotyped and alternated with overt misogyny. Many boys seemed to be asking their fathers to change here and Frosh *et al.* note the possibilities of getting parents of both genders involved in the discussions they advocate. They do not discuss this in any detail, however, and it does raise quite complex issues. There is considerable evidence that initiatives introduced by adults and premised upon 'correct' understandings of how children should be will be resisted (see, for example, Rattansi, 1992, on the lessons which emerged from some anti-racist initiatives in schools in the 1980s). This is an area of work, however, in which practice wisdom is currently being developed on an ongoing basis, particularly pioneered by Fathers Direct (see www.fathersdirect.co.uk. for ongoing initiatives).

A further piece of research within the ESRC Children 5–16 programme, conducted by Hallett *et al.* (2003), looked at how young people coped with problems in their lives and to whom they turned for help and support. The most common response to problems was to tell someone, usually best friends, parents or siblings, or for those living in residential care their key worker. However, a third said they would not tell anyone and boys were more likely to keep their problems to themselves. In support of this, analyses of calls to ChildLine have found boys use their services less than girls (MacLeod, 1999). Friendship characteristics differed between boys and girls. Amongst girls, friends were an important source of social support. Indeed some of the boys recognised that the support girls offered each other might enable them to cope better with their problems (although this may reflect the idealisation noted by Frosh *et al.*). Within the family setting boys seeking help with issues such as bullying could find that fathers put pressure on them to stand up for themselves. There is some evidence that anti-bullying strategies in school may be jeopardised by the attitudes of teachers who see boys who complain as wimps (Katz, 2001). Thus boys may experience difficulties in getting help as a result of a variety of factors including peer relations as well as adult reactions.

Although there are particular difficulties for boys in terms of their relationships with each other it would be unwise to assume that all is well for girls. There is long-standing evidence that girls police each other, particularly in relation to sexual behaviour (see, for example Lees, 1999), and it would be unhelpful to see girls' relationships with each other as in some way 'better' than boys'. Indeed, Cawson *et al.* (2000) found excluding behaviour was a feature of girls' relationships and was a form of bullying.

A prevalence study into young people's experiences of family life and maltreatment opened up questions not only about the importance of young people's relationships with each other but also about the difficulties such relationships can often pose (Cawson *et al.*, 2000). Bullying emerged as by far the most common abusive experience for young people throughout their childhoods. According to the researchers this reinforced the importance of developing strategies which engage with young people's lives in the multiplicity of contexts in which they live their lives. Moreover, the levels of sexual violence between young people led the researchers to refine the above critique further and to call for practice strategies which incorporated an understanding of gender relationships. Such violence was largely by older boys against younger girls.

There is important evidence, however, to suggest that whilst bullying is an important and significant problem, children and young people act as important sources of support for each other. Friends, siblings and to a lesser extent cousins – those closer in age – were seen by young people as more likely than adults to understand their problems in Hallett *et al.*'s (2003) study. Lack of empathy from adults was a dominant theme throughout the study. Young people felt that it was important that they could help each other with their worries in contrast to the one-sided problem-solving which typified dealings with adults. They also gave more instances of negative than positive adult responses to their problems. They feared that adults would take over their problems, and insist they do something about it against their will. Adults' responses might exacerbate the problem, cause embarrassment or be moralistic. Adults were also felt to trivialise children and young people's problems.

It is important to recognise that young people act both as resources and risks for each other and that young people negotiate whom they discuss things with. Parents are not necessarily the first port of call although there is considerable evidence to suggest that where parents are unable to offer what is required, this is mourned by children.

Relationships between young people themselves are complex and constitute a key feature of their everyday lives.

Working with boys and girls around their futures

> Everything is presented as a possibility today. But this also means that individuals are increasingly held accountable for their own fate . . . The necessity for self invention is imposed in extremely contradictory, economic, social and individual landscapes where everything is open to change but at the same time older patterns of gender practices remain firmly entrenched. (Walkerdine *et al.*, 2001, p. 81)

Walkerdine *et al.* explore the complexities of gender and class as exemplified in the lives of a number of girls growing up in the 1980s. They argue that girls face the labour market of the future deeply regulated and divided by class. They therefore criticise the simplicities of popular cultural constructions of 'girl power' and point out the substantial costs which can be borne by young women of differing classes in planning for futures which call for a considerable degree of self-invention on their part. They argue from their research that middle-class girls often appear deeply anxiety-ridden about the importance of working hard and achieving success. For working-class girls, however, success could signify distance from their families and peers and involve paying a considerable price in terms of psychological security in order to enter an unfriendly and strange world. However, a key issue for all was their recognition of the juggling that so many of their mothers appeared to engage in across the classes to manage work and home. Whilst Walkerdine *et al.* (2001) stress the difficulties in order, as indicated, to counter current simplicities in relation to girl power, they also recognise the possibilities open to girls today.

Lees (1999) examined the oral testimonies of middle- and working-class young women interviewed in the early 1980s and 1990s in order to explore their views. She saw what she considered as a puzzling contradiction in the young women's views of marriage in the early 1980s; it was seen as anything but romantic and brought in its train subordination and loneliness. Yet most of them saw a future without marriage as unimaginable, with only three saying they did not want to get married. Despite their often vivid documentation of the violence and subordination they witnessed in adult relationships, they saw no realistic alternative: 'the choice of getting married became a negative one – of avoiding being left on the shelf. The young women saw this as carrying a stigma, a whole battery of neglect, suspicion and derision being directed at the non-married and the childless, who were stereotyped as shirking their duty, selfish, immature, lonely, bitter, abnormal or pathetic' (Lees, 1999, p. 65). However, they had quite negative views of marriage and were concerned to postpone it in order to have a life before.

Negative views of marriage on the part of girls became even more common in the 1990s. Sharpe updated her book *Just Like a Girl*, which was first published in 1976, by returning to the London schools where she had interviewed 200 15-year-old girls in the early 1990s and compared them. The most dramatic change she found in the oral testimonies related to the girls' changed views of marriage. Over three-quarters of the girls she interviewed had said yes to marriage in her previous study. By 1991 this had dropped to under half. Most did not want to get married and saw 'it as something to be approached with extreme caution' (Sharpe, 1994, p. 66).

However, other studies have found that although girls were not romantic about marriage and relationships with men, they saw marriage and child-rearing as an important feature of their future lives. Lees (1999) found important differences between cohorts of girls. She notes that ethnic differences are complex and polarised. Research which compared a group of young Irish with black African-Caribbean women found considerable differences in attitudes to marriage, the family and careers. Both groups were the children of immigrants who had moved to England in the 1950s. The Irish girls consistently expressed a desire for marriage and children which they saw as incompatible with a permanent commitment to the labour market; the young black women were committed to a full-time career, which they did not see as incompatible with children and relationships with men.

In terms of class, poor job prospects and rising unemployment among young men are factors which appear to be influencing girls' attitudes. Prendergast and Forrest (1997, quoted in Lees, 1999) undertook a pilot study of boys and girls at three secondary modern schools in areas of high unemployment and deprivation. All the girls had plans for the future but few spoke about marriage and children. The young women spoke of their peers as 'wasters' and predicted that they 'would let you down' and asked questions such as: why would any sensible woman have children with them?

However, it would appear that boys' attitudes to marriage have changed far less than girls'. Three-quarters uncritically assumed marriage would be part of their future lives and compared to half the girls researched, few boys thought it likely they would get divorced. A significant proportion, however, did think that men should be more involved in looking after children.

According to Lees (1999):

> The widening discrepancies between young men's own ideas and expectations and those of the young women they hope to marry do not bode well for the future of the two-parent nuclear family. Sam failed to see how the change in girls' attitudes would affect him when he commented: 'Sometimes feminism and women's equality is a load of rubbish, but mostly it's just important for women. It's their choice really, what they do with their lives. Men have got a little bit to do with it but not much.' (p. 71)

Lees argues that young women are becoming less prepared to accept what has been called the sexual contract and seem to be demanding a form of partnership with young men in which they are no longer prepared to take on a subservient role and are less prepared to put up with unsatisfactory and sometimes violent relationships.

However, it is quite a complex picture if one looks at the research into sexual behaviour and the use of contraception and safe-sex practices. For example, Holland (1998, p. 6) argues that 'To be conventionally feminine is to appear sexually unknowing, to aspire to a relationship, to let sex "happen", to trust to love, and to make men happy'. This can make it difficult to negotiate the use of contraception and safe sex. Walkerdine *et al.* (2001) found in their research that many young working-class women felt considerable anxiety about being seen as a 'slag' or a 'tart' and carrying contraception could support such name-calling. Their analysis would suggest, however, that becoming pregnant and having a child at a young age, which was predominantly a working-class phenomenon, could be seen as linked to anxieties about class dislocation.

The implications for family support

Within social work there has been an increased recognition of the need to consult with children and young people, underpinned by the Children Act 1989, although there remain considerable concerns about how well this is happening (J. Roche, 2001). Much of the research, for example, on the formal child protection system in England and Wales has evinced concern about the low levels of referrals by children and young people themselves (Wattam, 2002). This has raised complex issues in relation to how well that system generally engages with the needs and wishes of children and young people. A review of the literature in relation to help-seeking which I conducted brought up a host of issues here. One was the fear on the part of many children and young people about how well they might be able to control who knew what, the timing and pace of events post-referral and what control they might have over what happened (Featherstone, 2001b). The experience of ChildLine, a telephone line set up by adults, which appears to engage seriously with their concerns, offers pointers towards their concerns and also to the thinking required to make other services more responsive to them (see MacLeod, 1999, for an account).

In relation to help-seeking more generally, the research above indicated that children and young people may struggle to be heard by adults in a range of settings and that boys may have particular barriers to overcome in relation to help-seeking. Frosh *et al.*'s research does point out, however, the importance of contesting and the inaccuracies which would be involved in constructing boys as a 'problem' here. What this research indicates is that there are possibilities for engagement with boys but such possibilities need to engage with wider considerations around how boys 'do gender' in an array of everyday settings. This is particularly highlighted when considering child sexual abuse. Whilst predominantly a male phenomenon in terms of causation, *both* boys and girls experience such abuse. A considerable literature attests to treatment and consequences which do not differentiate between genders (see, for example, Hanks and Stratton, 2002). However, not surprisingly, given what the above research indicated in relation to help-seeking more generally, there would appear to be particular difficulties for boys in relation to disclosing and reporting. As Bacon and Richardson (2000) note, worries about sexual orientation can prevent disclosure as the boy gets older. As Draucker (2000) notes, adult male survivors may be even more likely than females to avoid treatment or disclosure and to minimise their abuse experiences. Males also will often present with behavioural issues such as problems with aggression rather than complaints of depression as is more common with women. I am currently involved in discussions with a project beginning work with men who have been sexually abused who are fathers themselves and it is apparent that such men have considerable needs in relation to identity and parenting issues. Moreover, there are considerable gaps in terms of services for such men who are often fathering boys.

Important issues about adult/child relationships emerge from the literature on help-seeking. Whilst adult-run services such as ChildLine can be very important and highly appreciated by children and young people, there does seem to be a need to think about why children often find their concerns trivialised or magnified by adults. Of particular concern seem to be the difficulties fathers have in engaging with their children and acting as sources of support for them. Indeed, as we saw in Chapter 7, minorities of children and young people reported sometimes being really afraid of their fathers or stepfathers and levels of closeness were generally much less than for mothers and other children (Cawson *et al.*, 2000).

As Gilligan (2000) notes in his overview of family support developments, there is evidence of these engaging with the concerns expressed by children and young people themselves in relation to issues such as bullying. However, there seems little attempt within the family support literature to question the role adults, both men and women, can or should play and there has been little discussion about how gendered understandings could inform such work. This work is vital, if rife with dilemmas.

In particular, careful consideration has to be given to how gendered understandings are introduced in work with children and young people partly because it opens up issues about power relations between adults and children and partly because of linked issues about what the purpose of such work should or might be. In relation to the first point it has been argued that there is a need to interrogate the constructions of children and childhood which underpin policy and practice developments and which reflect wider adult agendas. Moss *et al.* (2000), for example, argue that the discourse around 'children in need' enshrined in the Children Act 1989 rests upon a deficit model of children and childhood which insists on children as incomplete, deficient and dependent upon adults to offer the right input in order to become complete. Not only does this preclude an appreciation of the strengths and capacities of the child, it can also reinforce the one-sided nature of relationships as identified by Hallett *et al.*'s research. Adults tell children what is best for them rather than engaging in dialogue around their understandings.

In Chapter 6 I argued that there were dangers in developing approaches with adult men and women which were premised upon top-down understandings of something called gender equality and that it was important to encourage practices which opened up the possibilities for such men and women to negotiate in an uncoerced way about their expectations in relation to each other. Whilst this lends itself to the setting down of guidelines in relation to the use of acts of violence (which is admittedly only one barometer of coercion), it can otherwise be an open project.

If adults are to introduce issues around gender in work with children and young people, one does need to be located within a project which is committed to dialogue with such children and young people, rather than premised upon top-down understanding of what they should or should not do, believe or say. Moreover, there is evidence from research such as Frosh *et al.*'s of the need to engage with the complexities and contradictions in children's and young people's positionings. The boys and girls interviewed gave accounts which resisted, condemned and eroticised gendered differences, for example. Whilst as in work with adults there are certain ground rules to be laid down in relation to violent and abusive behaviour, in general such work should be characterised by a commitment to openness and dialogue.

Concluding remarks

Boys and girls live within a world characterised by complexity, fixity and fluidity. If their welfare in the present and the welfare of children in the future is to be attended to fully, then understanding and engaging with their lived experiences as boys and girls seems imperative. The role of adults in such endeavours is not straightforward. Whilst there is evidence of adult-run services which offer them spaces to address their concerns in ways which allow them some control, there is evidence that many adults struggle to 'hear' children and young people in a range of formal and informal settings. There would appear to be specific concerns for boys in relation to help-seeking although there are also indicators from research about how they might be engaged with. Considerable challenges are posed for services here although as indicated there are considerable possibilities also.

Conclusion

In the Introduction to this book I highlighted four *linked* issues which feminist insights obliged us to engage with, which I felt were of considerable importance for family support. I argued that first they obliged attention to language. Second, they obliged us to think about family practices rather than the family as an institution. Third, through the concept of democratisation they underscored the continued importance of attending to issues such as violence which has a clear gendered dimension. Finally, the work on 'care' being undertaken by feminists amongst others contained important pointers for developing an infrastructure which supported both those doing family life in the twenty first century and the practitioners engaging with them.

In this Conclusion I return to these issues. However, I want to concentrate in the main on the fourth issue in relation to 'care' because it has become more and more apparent to me in writing this book that the work emerging here is of profound importance in a range of ways.

It's all in a name – the importance of language

At its simplest I hope the analysis developed here has reinforced the importance of interrogating what it is we mean when we talk of 'family'. This is immediately seen as relevant by practitioners, in my experience, although as we saw in Chapter 6 there are considerable difficulties involved in integrating this into everyday practices of engagement. Who is considered family and why are important questions and the feminist contribution here has been to both draw attention to the changes which have occurred and link such changes with important and desirable changes in women's ability to make their voices heard about power imbalances in particular family arrangements. In the process, they have aided a process of deconstruction of 'the family' as a specific model. This process opened up spaces for children also, although there have been tendencies at times for feminists to assume that women could speak for children. Many of the contemporary feminist approaches are, however, very firmly located within a project which explores children's perspectives in their own right. Moreover, work on gender has allowed the airing of important concerns about how boys and girls are engaging with the complexities of their social worlds and of crucial importance here are issues in relation to help-seeking.

I have argued throughout that the deployment of a language around gender offers important possibilities for opening up issues which can be obscured by gender-neutral terms such as 'parent'. Such issues concern who does what in concrete situations as well as offering pointers towards thinking about identities. What does it mean to be a woman and a mother today? What is a father for? How do I want to be a father? Whilst terms like 'parents' can indeed offer pointers towards settlements where binaries are overcome and such terms are embraced, sometimes for that very reason they also obscure and evade. Moreover, they can be used to avoid dealing with the structural barriers to overcoming differentiated practices in everyday lives. The deployment of the term 'gender' has immediate resonance for practitioners and indeed the introduction of an emphasis on engaging fathers in some family support initiatives has acted to focus attention here. As Chapter 7 has pointed out this work exposes as well as offers space for dealing with tensions around gender relations, which can remain invisible otherwise.

Family practices and democratisation

The emphasis on 'family practices', obvious in much of the research currently being undertaken (see Chapter 2), is particularly important as it focuses attention on what practices should be fostered. This sharply engages all concerned with issues to do with the *what* and the *how* of family life – what is done/not done and how. I argued in the Introduction that the rather ungainly concept of 'democratisation' had emerged to capture processes here. The term supports the exercising of 'voice' on the part of all concerned and represents a clear rejection of the privileging of male voice and authority relations which was to be found in more traditional arrangements.

In embracing a language of democracy, I have tried to underscore that at its heart must be a commitment to dialogue between all concerned, including workers. There are dangers which feminists have fallen into at various points of advancing prescriptive accounting-type approaches to what happens or does not happen between men and women particularly. This kind of prescription, according to Walter (1999), has meant that feminism has often been portrayed as and experienced as yet another form of disciplinary project. In my teaching and dialogue generally with practitioners and would-be practitioners, concerns in relation to a form of feminist authoritarianism do indeed emerge. However, apart from the issues involved in violence, which are explored below, it seems to me that the concept of 'democratisation' implies a journey rather than a destination. This journey involves a commitment to processes of negotiation and to being open. However, in order for those processes to operate, there are unavoidable prescriptions in relation to the use of violence of whatever type. This is where family support policies and practices cannot avoid engaging with issues around control and protection and where feminist understandings are crucial. Attempts by those such as Kendall and Harker (2002) to separate out child protection in order 'to enable the rest of social care to shift its focus towards empowering vulnerable people, mobilising communities and promoting well-being and prevention' (p. 11), are profoundly misconceived and fundamentally destabilised by feminist insights into the ubiquity of gendered violence and the importance of developing prevention strategies in relation to such violence. Moreover, the necessity of interweaving supportive and protective activities emerges from such insights.

The question of 'care'

Freely (2000) is only one of many to have noted their bemusement with the policy context ushered in by New Labour. As someone who had worked in the paid labour force all her adult life and brought up a number of children in a variety of arrangements she exhibits considerable awareness of how privatised and individualised issues around caring have been. Under the Conservatives, for example, record numbers of women including mothers entered the paid labour force and yet provision in relation to childcare remained an individual matter. Moreover, whilst there was plenty of rhetoric about poor parenting, there was no space to discuss what parents and children needed to sustain them. Under New Labour there has been an explosion of interest, initiatives and pronouncements on all aspects of family life. But much of it, she argues, appears to start from the wrong place in that it is not rooted in a consistent dialogue with those the policies and initiatives are designed to reach. An associated limitation which has become more and more apparent to me in my discussions with practitioners is how little space there is currently in their organisations for such dialogue or indeed for reflection on their work more generally.

In the work which is emerging from those concerned with articulating a new basis for policy and welfare measures which links them to 'practices of care', the need for such dialogue is becoming more and more highlighted. Williams (2001) challenges the values underpinning the welfare settlement being developed by New Labour when she calls for a new 'political ethics of care'. This starts from a commitment to understanding care as involving a complex set of practices which is often rendered natural, invisible or marginalised. Care of the self and care of others are meaningful activities *in their own right* and they involve us all as we are not just givers or receivers. In the right conditions, which material support and material respect are central to, we learn the civic duties of responsibility, trust, tolerance for human limitations and frailty and acceptance of diversity. Interdependence is the basis of human interaction and is expected and recognised rather than individual self-sufficiency. Moral worth is attributed to the fostering of dignity and good quality human interactions and the fostering of such dimensions can occur in a variety of arrangements whether based upon blood, kinship, sexual intimacy, friendship, collegiality, contract or service. The social process of care can therefore encompass plurality and diversity and this should be both respected and valued.

A key theme in the context of the concerns of this book seems to me the need to start from the basics as Williams does. We are interdependent so we all need care as well as give it. Currently, the giving and receiving of such care appears to be highly gendered in relation to families with dependent children at all levels from mothers through to those who work with them.

If we start generally from a different place in our reordering of the social relations of welfare – a place where care is valued properly – then this starts to open up different possibilities for the future, and Chapter 4 outlined some of the varying possibilities being advanced by feminists in relation to the kinds of policy measures which could be considered. This would involve challenging employment practices in particular which would have very clear implications for the possibilities open to fathers and male carers. It would also offer a profound challenge to the values underpinning the 'social investment state' and would displace paid work as the key organising principles around which daily lives are constructed.

It would also involve rethinking the balance of responsibility in relation to the care of children more broadly. New Labour have signalled a willingness to break with the past construction of such responsibility as a private matter for families through their commitment to a National Childcare Strategy. However, in practice developments have been patchy and piecemeal and we are a very long way away from having a well-resourced high quality service universally available to all carers and their children irrespective of income.

Ongoing dialogue in relation to these possibilities is important for those interested in making family support relevant to the challenges facing those doing family life in the twenty-first century. The work on care, as Williams notes, has implications for all, including those who work in a paid capacity who are involved in the giving and receiving of care in a variety of capacities and, at the front line, continue to be mainly women. The challenges involved in offering workers the supports they require are considerable. Brannen and Moss's (2003) edited collection is an important contribution from within the work around care to this project. It outlines the need for material respect – levels of pay are obviously crucial and the problems here have been well-rehearsed in relation to a range of settings – alongside calling for the need for democratic debate in relation to provision and practice. Care activities in a range of settings such as childminding, the nursery and social work offices 'need to be recognized for the complex, ambiguous and demanding activities that they are, with opportunities for carers to document, discuss and reflect upon their practice' (Brannen and Moss, 2003, p. 208). Brannen and Moss's call for opportunities for reflective practice seems crucial to me and the importance of such opportunities in 'opening up gender' seems vital as has been highlighted particularly in Part II of this book.

Concluding remarks

This book has tried to illuminate the complexities of the meanings and practices which can be attached to notions of family in the twenty-first century. It has explored why feminist understandings offer an important compass to understanding such meanings and practices, and in particular why the language of gender continues to be important in illuminating key aspects of such meanings and practices. It has explored the policy landscape within which a diverse set of complex activities called family support have come to be mobilised and it argues that feminist understandings can contribute to rethinking such policies and practices in ways which hold important possibilities for men, women and children as they negotiate a complex and changing world.

References

J. Aldgate and J. Tunstill, *Making Sense of Section 17* (London: The Stationery Office, 1996).

Audit Commission, *Seen But Not Heard: Co-ordinating Community Health and Social Services for Children in Need* (London: The Stationery Office, 1994).

K. Backett, 'The negotiation of fatherhood', in Lewis, C. and O'Brien, M. (eds) *Reassessing Fatherhood* (London: Sage, 1987).

H. Bacon and S. Richardson, 'Child sexual abuse and the continuum of victim disclosure: professionals working with children in Cleveland', in Itzin, C. (ed.) *Home Truths and Child Sexual Abuse: Influencing Policy and Practice, A Reader* (London: Routledge, 2000).

A. Bainham, S. Day Sclater and M. Richards (eds) *What is a Parent? A Socio-Legal Analysis* (Oxford: Hart Publishing, 1999).

A. Barlow and S. Duncan, 'Supporting families? New Labour's communitarianism and the "rationality mistake": Part 1', *Journal of Social Welfare and Family Law*, 22, 1 (2000) 23–42.

T. Bamford, *The Future of Social Work* (London: Macmillan – now Palgrave Macmillan, 1990).

R. Barn, *Black Children in the Public Care System* (London: Batsford, 1993).

M. Barrett and M. McIntosh, *The Anti-Social Family* (London: Verso, 1982).

J. Batchelor, 'Working with family change: repartnering and stepfamily life', in Bell, M. and Stewart, K. (eds) *The Practitioner's Guide to Working with Families* (Basingstoke: Palgrave Macmillan, 2003).

A. Bebbington and J. Miles, 'The background of children who enter local authority care', *British Journal of Social Work*, 19, 5 (1989) 249–269.

U. Beck and E. Beck-Gernsheim, *The Normal Chaos of Love* (Cambridge: Polity, 1995).

U. Beck and E. Beck-Gernsheim, *Individualization* (London: Sage, 2001).

M. Benn, *Madonna and Child: Towards a New Politics of Motherhood* (London: Jonathan Cape, 1998).

U. Björnberg, 'Ideology and choice between work and care', *Critical Social Policy*, 22, 1 (2002) 33–53.

T. Blair, Conference Speech to Annual Labour Party Conference, *Guardian*, 1 October 1997.

T. Blair, Beveridge Lecture, Toynbee Hall, London, 18 March 1999.

E. Blyth, Inaugural Lecture, University of Huddersfield, 3 April 2001.

J. Bowlby, *Child Care and the Growth of Love* (Harmondsworth: Penguin, 1953).

R. Brandwein (ed.), *Battered Women, Children and Welfare Reform* (London/ Thousand Oaks, Calif.: Sage, 1999).

J. Brannen and P. Moss (eds) *Rethinking Children's Care* (Buckingham: Open University Press, 2003).

J. Brannen and P. Moss, 'Some thoughts on rethinking children's care', in Brannen, J. and Moss, P. (eds) *Rethinking Children's Care* (Buckingham: Open University Press, 2003).

J. Brannen, E. Heptinstall and K. Bhopal, *Connecting Children: Care and Family Life in Later Childhood* (London: Routledge Falmer, 2000).

D. Braun, 'Perspectives on parenting', in Foley, P., Roche, J. and Tucker, S. (eds) *Children in Society: Contemporary Theory, Policy and Practice* (Basingstoke: Palgrave Macmillan in association with The Open University, 2001).

E. Brook and A. Davis (eds) *Women, the Family and Social Work* (London: Tavistock, 1985).

V. Bryson, *Feminist Debates: Issues of Theory and Political Practice* (Basingstoke: Palgrave Macmillan, 2002).

A. Burgess, *Fatherhood Reclaimed: The Making of the Modern Father* (London: Vermillion, 1997).

L. Burghes, L. Clarke and N. Cronin (eds) *Father and Fatherhood in Britain* (London: Family Policy Studies Centre, 1997).

J. Busfield, *Men, Women and Madness: Understanding Gender and Mental Disorder* (London: Macmillan – now Palgrave Macmillan, 1996).

J. Butt and L. Box, *Family Centre: A Study of the Use of Family Centres by Black Families* (London: Race Equality Unit, 1998).

C. Cameron, P. Moss and C. Owen, *Men in the Nursery* (London: Chapman, 1999).

J. Canavan, P. Dolan and J. Pinkerton, *Family Support: Direction from Diversity* (London: Jessica Kingsley, 2000).

P. Cawson, C. Wattam, C. Brooker and G. Kelly, *Child Maltreatment in the United Kingdom* (London: NSPCC, 2000).

D. Cheal, *Sociology of Family Life* (Basingstoke: Palgrave, Macmillan, 2002).

N. Chodorow, *The Reproduction of Mothering* (London: University of California Press, 1978).

N. Chodorow with S. Contratto, 'The fantasy of the perfect mother' in Thorne, B. and Yalom, M. (eds) *Rethinking the Family: Some Feminist Questions* (New York: Longman, 1982).

J. Clarke, 'Capturing the customer', *Self Agency and Society*, 1, 1 (1997) 55–73.

J. Clarke and J. Newman, *The Managerial State* (London: Sage, 1997).

J. Clarke, M. Langan and F. Williams, 'The construction of the British welfare state 1945–1975', in Cochrane, A., Clarke, J. and Gewirtz, S. (eds) *Comparing Welfare States*, 2nd edn (London: Sage in association with The Open University, 2000).

L. Clarke, 'Who are fathers? A socio-demographic profile', in Burghes, L., Clarke, L. and Cronin, N. (eds) *Fathers and Fatherhood in Britain* (London: Family Policy Studies Centre, 1997).

L. Clarke and M. O'Brien, 'Father involvement in Britain: the research and policy evidence', in Day, R.D. and Lamb, M.E. (eds) *Reconceptualising and Measuring Fatherhood* (New York: Lawrence Erlbaum, 2002).

H. Cleaver, L. Unell and J. Aldgate, *Children's Needs – Parenting Capacity: The Impact of Parental Mental Illness, Problem Alcohol and Drug Abuse, and Domestic Violence on Children's Development* (London: The Stationery Office, 1999).

M. Cockett and J. Tripp, *The Exeter Family Study: Family Breakdown and its Impact on Children* (Exeter: University of Exeter Press, 1994).

L. Colclough, N. Parton and M. Anslow, 'Family support', in Parton, N. and Wattam, C. (eds) *Child Sexual Abuse: Responding to the Experiences of Children* (Chichester: Wiley/NSPCC, 1999).

J. Coleman, Speech at Conference on Parenting and Diversity, Trust for the Study of Adolescence, York, 2001.

R. Connell, *Masculinities* (Cambridge: Polity, 1995).

A. Coote, 'Feminism and the Third Way: a call for dialogue', in White, S. (ed.) *New Labour. The Progessive Future?* (Basingstoke: Palgrave Macmillan, 2001).

B. Corby, 'Child abuse and child protection', in Goldson, B., Lavallete, M. and McKechnie, J. (eds) *Children, Welfare and the State* (London: Sage, 2002).

R. Coward, *Our Treacherous Hearts: Why Women Let Men Get Their Way* (London: Faber & Faber, 1993).

R. Coward, *Sacred Cows* (London: HarperCollins, 1999).

S. Croft and P. Beresford, 'The politics of participation', in Taylor, D. (ed.) *Critical Social Policy: A Reader* (London: Sage, 1996).

P. Daniel and J. Ivatts, *Children and Social Policy* (London: Macmillan – now Palgrave Macmillan, 1998).

B. Daniel and J. Taylor, *Engaging with Fathers: Practice Issues for Health and Social Care* (London: Jessica Kingsley, 2001).

S. Day Sclater, *Divorce: A Psychosocial Study* (Aldershot: Ashgate, 1999).

S. Day Sclater and C. Yates, 'The psycho-politics of post-divorce parenting', in Bainham, A., Day Sclater, S. and Richards, M. (eds) *What is a Parent? A Socio-Legal Analysis* (Oxford: Hart Publishing, 1999).

M. Dean, 'Don't ignore the flexible parent', *Guardian*, 11 December 2002.

N. Dennis and G. Erdos, *Families without Fatherhood* (London: IEA Health and Welfare Unit, 1992).

Department for Education and Employment, *Meeting the Childcare Challenge*, Green Paper (London: HMSO, 2000).

Department of Health, *The Children Act 1989 Guidance and Regulations: Volume 2, Family Support, Day Care and Educational Provision for Young Children* (London: HMSO, 1991).

Department of Health, *Child Protection: Messages from Research* (London: The Stationery Office, 1995).

Department of Health, *Children in Need: Report of an SSI National Inspection of Social Services Departments' Family Support Services, 1993–1995* (London: The Stationery Office, 1996).

Department of Health, *Getting Family Support Right* (London: The Stationery Office, 1999).

Department of Health, *The Children Act Now: Messages from Research* (London: The Stationery Office, 2001).

Department of Health, Department for Education and Employment and Home Office, *Framework for the Assessment of Children in Need and their Families* (London: The Stationery Office, 2000).

Department of Health, Home Office and Department for Education and Employment, *Working Together to Safeguard Children: A Guide to Interagency Working to Safeguard and Promote the Welfare of Children* (London: The Stationery Office, 1999).

Department of Health and Social Security, *Report of the Committee on One Parent Families* (Finer Report) (London: HMSO, 1974).

Department of Health and Social Security, *Report of the Inquiry into Child Abuse in Cleveland* (London: HMSO, 1988).

Department of Trade and Industry, *Work and Parents: Competitiveness and Choice* (London: The Stationery Office, 2001).

R. Dingwall, J. Eekelaar and T. Murray, *The Protection of Children: State Intervention and Family Life* (Oxford: Basil Blackwell, 1983).

D. Dinnerstein, *The Rocking of the Cradle and the Ruling of the World* (London: Souvenir Press, 1976).

L. Dominelli and E. McLeod, *Feminist Social Work* (London: Macmillan – now Palgrave Macmillan, 1989).

J. Donzelot, *The Policing of Families* (London: Hutchinson, 1980).

L. Draper, 'Being evaluated: a practitioner's view', *Children & Society*, 15 (2001) 46–52.

C.B. Draucker, *Counselling Survivors of Childhood Sexual Abuse*, 2nd edn (London: Sage, 2000).

S. Driver and L. Martell, 'New Labour's communitarianisms', *Critical Social Policy*, 17, 3 (1997) 27–46.

S. Duncan and R. Edwards, *Lone Mothers, Paid Work and Gendered Moral Rationalities* (London: Macmillan – now Palgrave Macmillan, 1999).

J. Dunn and K. Deater-Deckard, *Children's Views of their Changing Families* (York: Joseph Rowntree Foundation, 2001).

R. Dutt and M. Phillips, 'Assessing black children in need and their families', in *Department of Health, Assessing Children in Need and their Families* (London: The Stationery Office, 2000).

J. Eekelaar, 'Parental responsibility: state of nature or nature of the state?', *Journal of Social Welfare and Family Law*, 1 (1991) 37–50.

H. Eisenstein, *Contemporary Feminist Thought* (London: Unwin, 1984).

A. Etzioni, *The Parenting Deficit* (London: Demos, 1993).

N. Fairclough, *New Labour, New Language* (London: Routledge, 2000).

E. Farmer and M. Owen, *Child Protection Practice: Private Risks and Public Remedies* (London: HMSO, 1995).

B. Fawcett, B. Featherstone and J. Goddard, *Contemporary Child Care Policy* (Basingstoke: Palgrave Macmillan, forthcoming).

B. Featherstone, 'I wouldn't do your job: women, social work and child abuse', in Hollway, W. and Featherstone, B. (eds) *Mothering and Ambivalence* (London: Routledge, 1997).

B. Featherstone, 'Taking mothering seriously: the issues for child protection', *Child and Family Social Work*, 4 (1999) 43–53.

B. Featherstone, 'Evaluating a parenting programme for fathers', University of Huddersfield, Nationwide Children's Research Centre (unpublished).

B. Featherstone, 'Researching into mothers' violence: some thoughts on the process', in Fawcett, B., Featherstone, B., Fook, J. and Roissiter, A. (eds) *Practice and Research in Social Work: Feminist Postmodern Perspectives* (London: Routledge, 2000).

B. Featherstone, *An Evaluation of a Parenting Group for Fathers* (Huddersfield: Nationwide Children's Research Centre, 2001).

B. Featherstone, 'Children and telling', unpublished paper, 2001a.

B. Featherstone, 'Gender and child abuse', in Stewar, K. and James, A. (eds) *The Handbook of Child Protection*, 2nd edn (London: Baillière Tindall, 2002).

B. Featherstone, 'Taking fathers seriously', *British Journal of Social Work*, 33 (2003) 239–54.

B. Featherstone and M. Manby, *Working with Families. Evaluation Report* (Huddersfield: Nationwide Children's Research Centre/University of Huddersfield, 2002).

B. Featherstone and L. Trinder, 'Familiar subjects: domestic violence and child welfare', *Child and Family Social Work*, 2 (1997) 147–59.

H. Ferguson, 'State services and supports for fathers', in McKeown, K., Ferguson, H. and Rooney, D. (eds) *Changing Fathers?* (Cork: The Collins Press, 1998).

H. Ferguson, 'Promoting child protection, welfare and healing: the case for developing best practice', *Child and Family Social Work*, 6, 1 (2001a) 1–13.

H. Ferguson, 'Social work, individualization and life politics', *British Journal of Social Work*, 31 (2001b) 41–55.

H. Ferguson, 'Welfare, social exclusion and reflexivity: the case for woman and child protection', *Journal of Social Policy*, 32 (2003) 199–217.

E. Ferri, *Growing Up in a One Parent Family* (Slough: NFER, 1976).

J. Finch, *Family Obligation and Social Change* (Cambridge: Polity, 1989).

G. Finlayson, *Citizen, State and Social Welfare 1830–1990* (Oxford: Oxford University Press, 1994).

S. Firestone, *The Dialectic of Sex: The Case for Feminist Revolution* (New York: William Morrow, 1970).

L. Fox Harding, *Perspectives in Child Care Policy* (Harlow: Longman, 1991).

L. Fox Harding, *Family, State and Social Policy* (London: Macmillan – now Palgrave Macmillan, 1996a).

L. Fox Harding, ' "Parental responsibility": the reassertion of private patriarchy?', in Silva, E.B. (ed.) *Good Enough Mothering? Feminist Perspectives on Lone Motherhood* (London: Routledge, 1996b).

L. Fox Harding, ' "Family values" and Conservative government policy', in Jagger, G. and Wright, C. (eds) *Changing Family Values* (London: Routledge, 1999).

J. Franklin, 'What's wrong with New Labour politics?' *Feminist Review*, 66 (2000) 138–42.

S. Franks, *Having None of It: Women, Men and the Future of Work* (London: Granta, 1999).

E. Frazer, 'Unpicking political communitarianism: a critique of "the communitarian family" ', in Jagger, G. and Wright, C. (eds) *Changing Family Values* (London: Routledge, 1999).

M. Freely, *What About Us? An Open Letter to the Mothers Feminism Forgot* (London: Bloomsbury, 1996).

M. Freely, *The Parent Trap: Children, Families and the New Morality* (London: Virago, 2000).

B. Friedan, *The Feminine Mystique* (Harmondsworth: Penguin, 1963).

S. Frosh, *Sexual Difference, Masculinity and Psychoanalysis* (London: Routledge, 1994).

S. Frosh, 'Characteristics of sexual abusers', in Stewark, K. and James, A. (eds) *The Handbook of Child Protection*, 2nd edn (London: Baillière Tindall, 2002).

S. Frosh, A. Phoenix and R. Pattman, *Young Masculinities* (Basingstoke: Palgrave Macmillan, 2002).

N. Frost, *Family Support in Rural Areas* (Barkingside: Barnardos, 2002).

N. Frost, 'Understanding family support: theories, concepts and issues', in Frost, N., Lloyd, A. and Jeffrey, L. (eds) *The RHP Companion to Family Support* (Dorset: Russell House Publishing, 2003).

N. Frost and B. Featherstone, 'Families, social change and diversity', in Bell, M. and Stewart, K. (eds) *The Practitioner's Guide to Working with Families* (Basingstoke: Palgrave Macmillan, 2003).

N. Frost and M. Stein, *The Politics of Child Welfare* (London: Harvester Wheatsheaf, 1989).

N. Frost, A. Lloyd and L. Jeffrey (eds) *The RHP Companion to Family Support* (Dorset: Russell House Publishing, 2003).

R. Gardner, *Supporting Families: Protecting Children in the Community* (Chichester: Wiley/NSPCC, 2002a).

R. Gardner, 'New labour, child welfare and child protection', workshop at conference, University of Huddersfield, 19 September (2002b).

P. Garrett, 'Encounters in the new welfare domains of the Third Way: social work, the Connexions agency and personal advisers', *Critical Social Policy*, 22, 4 (2002) 596–619.

D. Ghate, D. Shaw and N. Hazel, *Fathers and Family Centres: Engaging Fathers in Preventive Services* (London: Policy Research Bureau/Joseph Rowntree Foundation, 2000).

H. Ghate and M. Ramalla, *Positive Parenting: The National Evaluation of the Youth Justice Board's Parenting Programme* (London: Policy Research Bureau, 2002).

P. Ghazi, *The 24 Hour Family: A Parent's Guide to the Work–Life Balance* (London: The Women's Press, 2003).

A. Giddens, *The Transformation of Intimacy* (Cambridge: Polity, 1992).

A. Giddens, *The Third Way: The Renewal of Social Democracy* (Cambridge: Polity, 1998).

A. Giddens, *The Third Way and Its Critics* (Cambridge: Polity, 2000).

R. Gilligan, 'Family support: issues and prospects', in Canavan, J., Dolan, P. and Pinkerton, J. (eds) *Family Support: Direction from Diversity* (London: Jessica Kingsley, 2000).

J. Gillis, *A World of Their Own Making: A History of Myth and Ritual in Family Life* (Oxford: Oxford University Press, 1996).

N. Glass, 'Sure Start: the development of an Early Intervention Programme for Young Children', *Children and Society*, 13, 4 (1999) 257–65.

J. Glover, 'The "balance model": theorising women's employment behaviour', in Carling, A., Duncan, S. and Edwards, R. (eds) *Analysing Families: Morality and Rationality in Family Policy* (London: Routledge, 2002).

S. Golombok, *Parenting: What Really Counts?* (London: Routledge, 2000).

S. Golombok, F. Tasker and C. Murray, 'Children raised in fatherless families from infancy: family relationships and the socio-emotional development of children of lesbian and single heterosexual mothers', *Journal of Child Psychology and Psychiatry*, 38, 7 (1997) 783–92.

L. Gordon, 'Feminism and social control: the case of child abuse and neglect', in Mitchell, J. and Oakley, A. (eds) *What is Feminism?* (Oxford: Blackwell, 1986).

L. Gordon, *Heroes of Their Own Lives, The Politics and History of Family Violence*, Boston 1880–1960 (New York: Viking, 1989).

D. Gough, *Child Abuse Interventions: A Review of the Research Literature* (London: HMSO, 1993).

J. Grier, 'A spirit of "friendly rivalry"? Voluntary societies and the formation of post-war child welfare legislation in Britain', in Lawrence, J. and Starkey, P. (eds) *Child Welfare and Social Action in the Nineteenth and Twentieth Centuries* (Liverpool: Liverpool University Press, 2001).

C. Hakim, 'Five feminist myths about female employment', *British Journal of Sociology*, 46, 3 (1996) 429–55.

C. Hallett, C. Murray and S. Punch, 'Young people and welfare: negotiating pathways', in Hallett, C. and Prout, A. (eds) *Hearing the Voices of Children: Social Policy for a New Century* (London: Routledge, 2003).

H. Hanks and P. Stratton, 'Consequences and indicators of child abuse', in Wilson, K. and James, A. (eds) *The Child Protection Handbook*, 2nd edn (London: Baillière Tindall, 2002).

J. Hanmer and D. Statham, *Women and Social Work: Towards a Woman-centred Practice* (Basingstoke: Macmillan – now Palgrave Macmillan, 1988).

J. Hearn, 'The welfare of men?', in Popay, J., Hearn, J. and Edwards, J. (eds) *Men, Gender Divisions and Welfare* (London: Routledge, 1998).

J. Hearn, 'Men, fathers and the state: national and global relations', in Hobson, B. (ed.) *Making Men into Fathers: Men, Masculinities and the Social Politics of Fatherhood* (Cambridge: Cambridge University Press, 2002).

H. Hendrick, *Child Welfare: 1870–1989* (London: Routledge, 1994).

C. Henricson, I. Katz, J. Mesie, M. Sandison and J. Tunstill, *National Mapping of Family Services in England and Wales: A Consultation Document* (London: National Family and Parenting Institute, 2001).

K. Henwood, 'Fatherhood and transition to parenthood: findings from a Norfolk study', ESRC Research Seminar Series, University of East Anglia, 12 April 2002.

M. Hetherington and M.M. Stanley-Hagan, 'Stepfamilies', in Lamb, M.E. (ed.) *Parenting and Child Development in 'Nontraditional' Families* (Hillsdale, NJ: Lawrence Erlbaum Associates, 1999).

HM Treasury, *Budget Report* (London: HM Treasury, 2002).

B. Hobson (ed.) *Making Men into Fathers: Men, Masculinities and the Social Politics of Fatherhood* (Cambridge: Cambridge University Press, 2002).

J. Holland, *The Male in the Head: Young Women, Heterosexuality and Power* (London: Tuffnell, 1998).

B. Holman, *Putting Families First* (London: Macmillan – new Palgrave Macmillan, 1988).

Home Office, *Supporting Families: A Consultation Document* (London: The Stationery Office, 1998).

b. hooks, *From the Margin to the Centre* (Boston, Mass.: South End Press, 1984).

C.-A. Hooper, *Mothers Surviving Child Sexual Abuse* (London: Routledge, 1992).

C. Humphreys, 'The impact of domestic violence on children', in Foley, P., Roche, J. and Tucker, S. (eds) *Children in Society: Contemporary Theory, Policy and Practice* (Basingstoke: Palgrave Macmillan in association with The Open University, 2001).

C. Humphreys, M. Hester, G. Hague, A. Mullender, H. Abrahams and P. Lowe, *From Good Intentions to Good Practice: Mapping Services with Families Where There is Domestic Violence* (Bristol: The Policy Press, 2000).

R. Jackson, *Mothers Who Leave* (London: Virago, 1994).

G. Jagger and C. Wright, 'Introduction: changing family values', in Jagger, G. and Wright, C. (eds) *Changing Family Values* (London: Routledge, 1999).

L. Jamieson, *Intimacy: Personal Relationships in Modern Society* (Cambridge: Polity, 1998).

L. Jeffery, 'New Labour, new initiatives: Sure Start and the Children's Fund', in N. Frost, A. Lloyd and L. Jeffery (eds) *The RHP Companion to Family Support* (Dorset, Russell House Publishing, 2003).

C. Jenks, *Childhood* (London: Routledge, 1996).

J. Jenson and D. Saint-Martin, 'Changing citizenship regimes: social policy strategies in the investment state', workshop on 'Fostering Social Cohesion: A Comparison of New Policy Strategies', Université de Montreal, 21–22 June 2001.

J. Johnston and L. Campbell, 'A clinical typology of interpersonal violence in disputed-custody divorces', *American Journal of Orthopsychiatry*, 63 (1993) 190–9.

B. Jordan with C. Jordan, *Social Work and the Third Way: Tough Love as Social Policy* (London: Sage, 2000).

H. Joshi, D. Wiggins and L. Clarke, *The Changing Home: Outcomes for Children*, ESRC Children 5–16 Research Programme (2000).

S. Kamerman and A. Kahn (eds) *Family Policy in Fourteen Countries* (New York: University of Columbia Press, 1978).

E.-A. Kaplan, *Motherhood and Representation: The Mother in Popular Culture and Melodrama* (London: Routledge, 1992).

A. Katz, *Bullying* (Surrey: Young Voice, 2001).

L. Kelly, *Surviving Sexual Violence* (Cambridge: Polity Press, 1988).

L. Kelly, L. Regan and S. Burton, *An Exploratory Study of the Prevalence of Sexual Abuse in a Sample of 16–21 Year Olds* (London: Child and Woman Abuse Studies Unit, University of North London, 1991).

L. Kendall and L. Harker, 'A vision for social care', in L. Kendall and L. Harker (eds) *From Welfare to Wellbeing* (London: IPPR, 2002).

S. Kershaw, 'Living in a lesbian household: the effects on children', *Child and Family Social Work*, 5, 4 (2001) 365–73.

M.E. Lamb, 'Fathers and child development: an introductory overview', in Lamb, M.E. (ed.) *The Role of the Father in Child Development*, 3rd edn (Chichester: Wiley, 1997).

M.E. Lamb (ed.) *Parenting and Child Development in 'Nontraditional' Families* (Hillsdale, NJ: Lawrence Erlbaum Associates, 1999).

M.E. Lamb, K. Sternberg and R. Thompson, 'The effects of divorce and custody arrangements on children's behaviour, development and adjustment', in Lamb, M.E. (ed.) *Parenting and Child Development in 'Nontraditional' Families* (Hillsdale, NJ: Lawrence Erlbaum Associates, 1999).

Lord Laming, *The Victoria Climbié Inquiry. Report* (London: The Stationery Office, 2003).

H. Land, 'New Labour, new families', in Dean, H. and Woods R. (eds) *Social Policy Review 11* (Luton: Social Policy Association, 1999).

H. Land, *Building on Sand. Facing the Future Policy Papers* (London: Day Care Trust, 2002).

H. Land and R. Parker, 'The hidden dimensions of family policy', in Kamerman, S. and Kahn, A. (eds) *Family Policy in Fourteen Countries* (New York: Columbia University Press, 1978).

M. Langan and L. Day (eds) *Women, Oppression and Social Work: Issues in Anti-Discriminatory Practice* (London: Routledge, 1992).

S. Lawler, 'Children need but mothers only want: the power of needs talk', in Seymour, J. and Bagguley, P. (eds) *Relating Intimacies: Power and Resistance* (London: Macmillan – now Palgrave Macmillan, 1999).

M. Lawrence, 'Women's psychology and feminist social work practice', in Langan, M. and Day, L. (eds) *Women, Oppression and Social Work: Issues in Anti-discriminatory Practice* (London: Routledge, 1992).

N. Lee, *Childhood and Society* (Buckingham: Open University Press, 2001).

S. Lees, 'Will boys be left on the shelf?', in Jagger, G. and Wright, C. (eds) *Changing Family Values* (London: Routledge, 1999).

G. Lewis, S. Gewirtz and J. Clarke (eds) *Rethinking Social Policy* (London: Sage in association with The Open University, 2000).

J. Lewis, 'Gender and welfare regimes', in Lewis, G., Gewirtz , S. and Clarke, J. (eds) *Rethinking Social Policy* (London: Sage in association with The Open University, 2000).

J. Lewis, *The End of Marriage? Individualism and Intimate Relations* (Cheltenham: Edward Elgar, 2001).

J. Lewis, 'The problem of fathers: policy and behaviour in Britain', in Hobson, B. (ed.) *Making Men into Fathers: Men, Masculinities and the Social Politics of Fatherhood* (Cambridge: Cambridge University Press, 2002).

R. Lister, *Citizenship: Feminist Perspectives* (London: Macmillan – now Palgrave Macmillan, 1997).

R. Lister, 'New Labour: a study in ambiguity from a position of ambivalence', *Critical Social Policy*, 21, 4, Issue 69 (2001) 425–49.

R. Lister, 'Investing in the citizen-workers of the future: New Labour's 'third way' in welfare reform', paper for Panel 10555-8FB: Redesigning Welfare Regimes: The Building Blocks of a New Architecture, Annual Meeting of the American Political Association (2002a).

R. Lister, 'The dilemmas of pendulum politics: balancing paid work, care and citizenship, *Economy and Society*, 31, 4 (2002b) 520–32.

T. Lloyd, *Working with Fathers* (London: Working with Men, 2001).

London Borough of Brent, *A Child in Trust: Report of the Panel of Inquiry Investigating the Circumstances Surrounding the Death of Jasmine Beckford* (London: London Borough of Brent, 1985).

J. Lovenduski and V. Randall, *Contemporary Feminist Politics* (Oxford: Oxford University Press, 1993).

C. Lupton and L. Barclay, *Constructing Fatherhood: Discourses and Experiences* (London: Sage, 1997).

M. MacLeod, ' "Don't just do it": children's access to help and protection', in Parton, N. and Wattam, C. (eds) *Child Sexual Abuse: Responding to the Experiences of Children* (Chichester: Wiley/NSPCC, 1999).

M. McKenzie, 'Engaging with empowerment: developing practice strategies in family social work', International Federation of Social Ware, International Assonates of Schools of Social Ware, Montreal, 29 July–2 August 2000.

E. McLaughlin and K. Murji, 'After the Stephen Lawrence Report', *Critical Social Policy*, 19, 3 (1999) 371–86.

A. McRobbie, 'Feminism and the Third Way', *Feminist Review*, 64 (2000) 97–112.

J. McTiernan, 'Future drivers of change', in Kendall, L. and Harker, L. (eds) *From Welfare to Wellbeing* (London: IPPR, 2002).

K. Mann and S. Roseneil, 'Poor choices? Gender, agency and the underclass debate', in Jagger, G. and Wright, C. (eds) *Changing Family Values* (London: Routledge, 1999).

P. Marsh and G. Crow, *Family Group Conferences in Child Welfare* (Oxford: Blackwell, 1998).

K. Millett, *Sexual Politics* (London: Virago, originally published in 1970, reprinted in 1985).

C. Milligan and A. Dowie, *What Do Children Need from Their Fathers?* Occasional Paper 42 (Edinburgh: University of Edinburgh, Centre for Theology and Public Issues, 1998).

J. Milner, 'Men's resistance to social workers', in Fawcett, B., Featherstone, B., Hearn, J. and Toft, C. (eds) *Violence and Gender Relations: Theories and Interventions* (London: Sage, 1996).

J. Mitchell, 'Reflections on twenty years of feminism', in Mitchell, J. and Oakley, A. (eds) *What is Feminism?* (Oxford: Blackwell, 1986).

S. Mitchell, 'Modernizing social services: the management challenge of the 1998 Social Services White Paper', in Hill, M. (ed.) *Local Authority Social Services: An Introduction* (Oxford: Blackwell, 2000).

D. Morgan, *Family Connections: An Introduction to Family Studies* (Cambridge: Polity, 1996).

P. Moss, J. Dillon and J. Statham, 'The 'child in need' and the 'rich child': discourses, constructions and practices', *Critical Social Policy*, 20, 2 (2000) 233–55.

A. Mullender, *Rethinking Domestic Violence* (London: Routledge, 1996).

A. Mullender and R. Morley (eds) *Putting the Abuse of Women on the Child Care Agenda* (London: Whiting & Birch, 1994).

J. Muncie, 'Institutionalized intolerance: youth justice and the 1998 Crime and Disorder Act', *Critical Social Policy*, 19, 2 (1999) 147–77.

C. Murray, *The Emerging British Underclass* (London, IEA Health and Welfare Unit, 1990).

National Family and Parenting Institute, *Family Policy Annual Digest 2001–2002* (London: National Family and Parenting Institute, 2002).

J. Newman, *Modernising Governance, New Labour, Policy and Society* (London: Sage, 2001).

L. Nicholson (ed.) *Feminism/Postmodernism* (London: Routledge, 1990).

A. Oakley and A. Rigby, 'Are men good for the welfare of women and children?', in Popay, J., Hearn, J. and Edwards, J. (eds) *Men, Gender Divisions and Welfare* (London: Routledge, 1998).

M. O'Brien and I. Shemilt, *Working Fathers: Earning and Caring* (London: Equal Opportunities Commission, 2003).

M. Pacey, 'Facing the childcare challenge', *Poverty*, 113 (2002) www.cpag.org.uk

R. Parker, *Torn in Two: The Experience of Maternal Ambivalence* (London: Virago, 1995).

R. Parker, 'The production of maternal ambivalence', in Hollway, W. and Featherstone, B. (eds) *Mothering and Ambivalence* (London: Routledge, 1997).

N. Parton, *The Politics of Child Abuse* (London: Macmillan – now Palgrave Macmillan, 1985).

N. Parton, 'Taking child abuse seriously', in Violence Against Children Study Group (eds) *Taking Child Abuse Seriously* (London: Unwin Hyman, 1990).

N. Parton, *Governing the Family: Child Care, Child Protection and the State* (London: Macmillan – now Palgrave Macmillan, 1991).

N. Parton, 'Child protection, family support and social work: a critical appraisal of the Department of Health research studies in child protection', *Child and Family Social Work*, 1 (1996) 3–11.

N. Parton, 'Child protection and family support: current debates and future prospects', in Parton, N. (ed.) *Child Protection and Family Support: Tensions, Contradictions and Possibilities* (London: Routledge, 1997).

E. Peled, 'Parenting by men who abuse women: issues and dilemmas', *British Journal of Social Work*, 30 (2000) 25–36.

H. Penn and D. Gough, 'The price of a loaf of bread: some conceptions of family support', *Children and Society*, 16 (2002) 17–32.

M. Peplar, *Family Matters: A History of Ideas about Family since 1945* (Harlow: Pearson Education, 2002).

S. Petrie, 'Working with families where there are child protection concerns', in Bell, M. and Stewart, K. (eds) *The Practitioner's Guide to Working with Families* (Basingstoke: Palgrave Macmillan, 2003).

J. Pinkerton, 'Emerging agendas for family support', in Canavan, J., Dolan, P. and Pinkerton, J. (eds) *Family Support: Direction from Diversity* (London: Jessica Kingsley, 2000).

L. Platt, *Parallel Lives? Poverty among Ethnic Minority Groups in Britain* (London: Child Poverty Action Group, 2003).

J. Popay, J. Hearn and J. Edwards (eds) *Men, Gender Divisions and Welfare* (London: Routledge, 1998).

M. Powell, *New Labour, New Welfare State?* (Bristol: Policy Press, 1999).

A. Prout, 'Researching children as social actors: introduction to the Children 5–16 Programme', *Children & Society*, 16, 2 (2001) 67–77.

G. Pugh, E. De'Ath and C. Smith, *Confident Parents: Confident Children* (London: National Children's Bureau, 1994).

T. Qureshi, D. Berridge and H. Wenman, *Family Support for South Asian Communities: A Case Study* (York: Joseph Rowntree Foundation, 2000).

K. Rake, 'Gender and New Labour's social policies', *Journal of Social Policy*, 30, 2 (2001) 209–32.

A. Rattansi (ed.) *Race, Culture and Difference* (London: Sage in association with the Open University, 1992).

T. Reynolds, 'Re-analysing the black family', in Carling, A., Duncan, S. and Edwards, R. (eds) *Analysing Families: Morality and Rationality in Policy and Practice* (London: Routledge, 2002).

A. Rich, *Of Woman Born: Motherhood as Experience and Institution* (New York: W.W. Norton, 1976).

B. Roche, *Today* programme, Radio 4, 6 December 2002.

J. Roche, 'The Children Act 1989 and children's rights: a critical reassessment', in Franklin, B. (ed.) *The New Handbook of Children's Rights: Comparative Policy and Practice* (London: Routledge, 2002).

B. Rogers and J. Pryor, *Divorce and Separation* (York: Joseph Rowntree Foundation, 1998).

S. Ruxton, *Men, Masculinities and Poverty in the UK* (Oxford: Oxfam, 2002).

M. Ryan, *Working with Fathers* (Abingdon: Radcliffe Medical Press, 2000).

J. Scourfield, *Gender and Child Protection* (Basingstoke: Palgrave Macmillan, 2003).

J. Scourfield and M. Drakeford, 'New Labour and the "problem of men"', *Critical Social Policy*, 22, 4 (2002) 619–41.

M. Seaton, 'Home work', *Guardian*, 25 January 2003.

F. Seebohm, *Report of the Committee on Local Authority and Allied Personal Social Services*, Cmnd. 3703 (London: HMSO, 1968).

L. Segal, *Is the Future Female? Troubled Thoughts on Contemporary Feminism* (London: Virago, 1987).

L. Segal, *Slow Motion: Changing Men, Changing Masculinities* (London: Virago, 1990).

L. Segal, 'Feminism and the family', in Burck, C. and Speed, B. (eds) *Gender, Power and Relationships* (London: Routledge, 1995).

L. Segal, *Why Feminism?* (Cambridge: Polity, 1999).

S. Seventuijsen, 'Caring in the third way', *Critical Social Policy*, 20, 1 (2000) 5–37.

S. Sharpe, *Just Like a Girl* (Harmondsworth: Penguin, 1994; first published 1976).

E.B. Silva and C. Smart, 'The 'new' practices and politics of family life', in Silva, E.B. and Smart, C. (eds) *The New Family?* (London: Sage, 1999).

G. Singh, 'Black children and the child protection system', in Violence Against Children Study Group (eds) *Children, Child Abuse and Child Protection* (Chichester: Wiley, 1999).

C. Skinner, 'The social political and welfare context for working with families', in Bell, M. and Stewart, K. (eds) *The Practitioner's Guide to Working with Families* (Basingstoke: Palgrave Macmillan, 2003).

C. Smart, 'The 'new' parenthood: fathers and mothers after divorce', in Silva, E.B. and Smart, C. (eds) *The New Family?* (London: Sage, 1999).

C. Smart and B. Neale, *Family Fragments?* (Cambridge: Polity, 1999).

C. Smart, B. Neale and A. Wade, *The Changing Experiences of Childhood: Families and Divorce* (Cambridge: Polity, 2001).

A. Snitow, 'Feminism and motherhood: an American reading', *Feminist Review*, 40, Spring (1992) 32–51.

J. Somerville, *Feminism and the Family: Politics and Society in the UK and USA* (Basingstoke: Palgrave Macmillan, 2000).

S. Speak, S. Cameron and R. Gilroy, *Young Single Fathers: Participation in Fatherhood – Bridges and Barriers* (London: Family Policy Studies Centre, 1997).

J. Stacey, 'Are feminists afraid to leave home? The challenge of conservative pro-family feminism', in Mitchell, J. and Oakley, A. (eds) *What is Feminism?* (Oxford: Blackwell, 1986).

J. Stacey, *Brave New Families* (New York: Basic Books, 1991).

J. Stacey, 'Dada-ism in the 1990s: getting past baby talk about fatherlessness', in Daniels, C.R. (ed.) *Lost Fathers: The Politics of Fatherlessness in America* (London: Macmillan – now Palgrave Macmillan, 1998).

K. Sternberg, 'Fathers, the missing parents in research on family violence' in M. Lamb (ed.) *The Role of the Father in Child Development*, 3rd edn (Chichester: Wiley, 1997).

O. Stevenson and P. Parsloe, *Community Care and Empowerment* (York: Joseph Rowntree Foundation, 1993).

J. Sudbury, 'Hidden struggles: black women's activism and black masculinity in the shadow of the windrush', *Soundings*, 10, Autumn (1998) 104–14.

D. Taylor, 'Social identity and social policy: engagements with postmodern theory', *Journal of Social Policy*, 27, 3 (1998) 329–50.

J. Thoburn, J. Wilding and J. Watcons, *Family Support in Cases of Emotional Maltreatment and Neglect* (London: The Stationery Office, 2000).

R. Tong, *Feminist Thought: A Comprehensive Introduction* (Boulder, Col.: Westview Press, 1989).

P. Toynbee and D. Walker, *Did Things Get Better?* (London: Penguin, 2001).

J. Tunstill, 'Implementing the family support clauses of the 1989 Children Act: Legislative, professional and organisational obstacles', in Parton, N. (ed.) *Child Protection and Family Support: Tensions, Contradictions and Possibilities* (London: Routledge, 1997).

J. Tunstill, 'Social services provision for children and young people: answer or problem?', in Tunstill, J. (ed.) *Children and the State: Whose Problem?* (London: Cassell, 1999).

J. Tunstill, 'Child care', in Hill, M. (ed.) *Local Authority Social Services: An Introduction* (Oxford: Blackwell, 2000).

S. Walby, *Theorising Patriarchy* (Oxford: Blackwell, 1990).

V. Walkerdine and H. Lucey, *Democracy in the Kitchen: Regulating Mothers and Socialising Daughters* (London: Virago, 1989).

V. Walkerdine, H. Lucey and J. Melody, *Growing Up Girl* (London: Virago, 2001).

N. Walter, *The New Feminism* (London: Virago, 1999).

J. Warin, Y. Solomon, C. Lewis and W. Langford, *Fathers, Work and Family Life* (London: Family Policy Studies Centre, 1999).

C. Wattam, 'Making inquiries under Section 47 of the Children Act 1989', in Wilson, K. and James, A. (eds) *The Child Protection Handbook*, 2nd edn (London: Baillière Tindall, 2002).

C. Wattam and C. Woodward, 'And do I abuse my children? ... No! – Learning about prevention from people who have experienced child abuse', *Childhood Matters: The Report of the National Commission of Inquiry into the Prevention of Child Abuse, Vol. 2: Background Papers* (London: HMSO, 1996).

J. Weeks, C. Donovan and B. Heaphy, *Families of Choice: Patterns of Non-heterosexual Relationships*, Social Science Research Papers (London: South Bank University, 1996).

A. Wilczynski 'Child killing by parents: a motivational model', *Child Abuse Review*, 4 (1995) 365–71.

F. Williams, *Social Policy: A Critical Introduction* (Cambridge: Polity, 1989).

F. Williams, 'Women with learning difficulties are women too', in Langan, M. and Day, L. (eds) *Women, Oppression and Social Work: Issues in Antidiscriminatory Practice* (London: Routledge, 1992).

F. Williams, 'Troubled masculinities in social policy discourses: fatherhood', in Popay, J., Hearn, J. and Edwards, J. (eds) *Men, Gender Divisions and Welfare* (London: Routledge, 1998).

F. Williams, 'Good enough principles for welfare', *Journal of Social Policy*, 28, 4 (1999) 667–89.

F. Williams, 'In and beyond New Labour: towards a new political ethics of care, *Critical Social Policy*, 21, 4, Issue 69 (2001) 467–94.

S. Wise, 'Feminist ethics in practice', in Hugman, R. and Smith, D. (eds) *Ethical Issues in Social Work* (London: Routledge, 1995).

Websites

http://www.nessbbk.ac.uk
http://www.nya.org.uk
http://www.statistics.gov.uk

Index

Aboriginal Head Start (Canada) 111
access visits 148, 149
accommodation systems 118
accounting mentality 140, 185
adoption 93, 131
adult literacy 113
adulthood: contrast with childhood 'eroded'
   171
adults 40, 173, 174, 176, 181
   lack of empathy for children 176, 181
   post-divorce parenting 83–4
   'trivialise children and young people's
      problems' 176, 180
   vulnerabilities 60
Advisory Group on Marriage and Relationship
   Support 93
age 53, 144, 147, 158
agency 38, 167
anger 148, 150, 168
anti-poverty strategies 124
anti-racism 174
anxiety 149, 150, 168, 177
assumptions 108, 160
   gendered 124, 130
   women and motherhood 165–6
Audit Commission (author) 2, 78
awkward family secrets 139

'Back to Basics' 92
Backett, K. 133
Bacon, H. 180
Bamford, T. 69
Bangladeshis 23, 138, 159
Barclay, L. 142
Barrett, M. 8, 45
Batchelor, J. 131, 133, 134
Bebbington, A. 72
Beck, U. 58, 159
Beck-Gernsheim, E. 58, 159
behaviour 103, 141
   abusive 152, 154, 182
   difficulties/problems 32, 34, 103
   policing 88
   violent 152, 182
behaviour control 114
benefit system 4, 65, 160
benefits 21, 163
Benn, M. 49, 50, 55
bereavement 103
Beresford, P. 166
Beveridge, Lord 117
Beveridge Report 66
Bhopal, K. 190
birth family 82
   modern defence 70, 71, 72, 74

birth fathers 145
birth mothers 130
birth parents 36
black workers 66
Blair, A.C.L. ('Tony') 5, 92, 96, 145
Blair, L. 145
blind people 68
Blunkett, D. 111, 117
Blyth, E. 35
Bowlby, J. 65, 73
boys 46, 181, 182, 184
   absence of father (deleterious consequences)
      38
   African 172
   African-Caribbean 172
   aged eleven-fourteen 171–4
   Asian 172
   constructed as 'problem' 180
   construction of parents 173
   disadvantages 8
   dissatisfaction with life 173
   eroticised gender difference 172,
      181
   friendships 175
   group discussions 174
   help-seeking 180
   policing role in relation to each other
      171–2
   problem-solving 175
   prospects 176–9
Brandwein, R. 103
Brannen, J. 187
Brannen, J. et al. 37, 190
   Bhopal, K. 190
   Heptinstall, E. 190
Brook, E. 166, 167
Brooker, C. 190
Bryson, V. 43, 44, 50, 51
bullying 175–6, 181
Burgess, A. 55
Burghes, L. et al. 143, 190
   Clarke, L. 190
   Cronin, N. 190
Busfield, J. 121, 122

Cameron, C. et al. 155, 190
   Moss, P. 190
   Owen, C. 190
Cameron, S. 200
Campbell, L. 123
Canada 97, 111
Canavan, J. et al. 2, 190
   Dolan, P. 190
   Pinkerton, J. 190
capitalism 45, 91

care   55, 80, 102, 183, 185–7
   gendered   186
   givers/recipients   46
   short-term provision   110
Care, Values and Future of Welfare (CAVA,
   University of Leeds)   50, 53
care-taking   7, 52
career: young women's attitudes   178
carer's income   50
carers   54, 164–5, 187
   primary   73
caring   24, 45, 62
   gendered settlements   52
caring responsibilities   26, 50, 101
   balance with paid work   143
casualisation   90
Cawson, P. et al.   175, 190
   Brooker, C.   190
   Kelly, G.   190
   Wattam, C.   190
census (April 2001)   21
charities   68, 72, 120
   NSPCC   120, 160
Cheal, D.   19
child abuse   2, 11, 67, 71–2, 79, 83, 84, 100,
   123–4, 133, 139, 151, 164, 180
   gendered dimensions   126
   parental   7
   step-parents   132
   women   140
child liberation   70, 71
child neglect   67
child poverty   87, 99, 100, 110, 111, 114, 120
child protection   7, 63–4, 67, 80, 84, 86, 110,
   115, 118–19, 119–20, 124, 125, 136, 163,
   185
   balance with family support   85
   state paternalism (1970s and 1980s)   70–4
Child Protection: Messages from Research
   (Department of Health, 1995)   78, 79, 83,
   119, 151
Child Protection Agency   119
child protection register   113, 114
child protection system: low levels of referrals
   by children themselves   179
child support/maintenance   76, 132, 147
Child Support Act (1991)   75–6, 89, 104
child welfare   73, 75, 80, 130, 137, 157, 167, 168,
   169
childbirth   148
childcare   4, 5, 46, 47, 49, 69, 81, 83, 96, 101–3,
   107, 154, 160, 185–6
   balance of responsibility   187
   constraints of provision   26
   cost   94
   flexible   112
   four perspectives   70
   gendered division   10, 162
   inadequate strategy   108
   liberal dilemma   67
   'men should be more involved'   178
   1990s   74–7
   public as well as private responsibility   94
   state provision   64
   unemployed men   28
   'childcare experts'   114
childhood   30, 170, 181
ChildLine   175, 179, 180
children   2, 4, 14, 19, 20, 23, 28, 40, 82, 87, 97,
   98, 130, 132, 136, 160–2, 166, 170–1,
   184–8
   adult responses   176, 180

African-Caribbean   138, 159
best interests   135
collective arrangements (Firestone)   44
constructions underpinning policy   181
difficult   105
difficult behaviour   165
effects of parental divorce   61
emotional well-being   35
equilibrium   32
evacuated   67
excluded at primary school   113
full-time care by men   148
healthy psychological development   31
heard   125
investment in   5, 88, 96, 99, 103, 110, 114
living apart from blood relatives   30
meanings attached to birth parents and step-
   parents   25
'might be endangered by desire to keep
   families together'   68
need to consult   179
needs   41, 159
performance at school   34
perspectives   167, 171
physical and emotional abuse (by women)   84
positioning re adults   13
post-divorce family life   52
pre-separation parental conflict   132
respect and liking for parents   37
rights to contact   137
strengths and capacities   181
struggle to be heard by adults   179–80
views on family change   36–8
vulnerabilities   60
well-being   62
Children Act (1948)   68
Children Act (1975)   71
Children Act (1989)   3–4, 6, 63, 74, 76, 83, 85,
   104, 110, 112, 118, 133, 135, 179, 181
   sections
      Part 1, Section 47   75, 78, 80, 119
      Part 3   78
      Part 3, Section 17   77, 78, 80, 119
      Schedule 2   77
   miscellaneous
      associated guidance   77
      binary approach   80
      family support   77–81
      implementation difficulties   7
      long-term difficulties   78
      priorities   78
      residence orders   131
'children in need'   6–7, 77, 85, 181
'rationing concept'   78
Children and Young Person's Act (1963)   68
children's centres   114
Children's Fund   95, 96, 115, 116, 120
Children's Officers   68
children's perspective   184
children's rights   70, 71, 82
Chodorow, N.   46, 54–5
'chronic hassles'   121
citizens/citizenship   24, 50, 101, 102
   'model citizen'   98
   'new subjects'   90
citizenship regime (Jenson and Saint-Martin)
   98
civic responsibilities   186
civil society   90
Clarke, J. et al.   64, 190
   Langan, M.   190
   Williams, F.   190

Clarke, L. 23, 190, 196
class 53, 59, 72, 73, 85, 163, 166, 176–7, 178
Cleveland events 74, 75
Cleveland Inquiry (1988) 74, 82–3, 84
Climbié, V. 80, 119
Clydeside 27
cohabitation 19, 21, 22, 32, 53, 93, 135
Colclough, L. v, 191
collectivisation 44, 45
Colwell, M. (d. 1973) 69–70
communitarianism 90–3
    many versions 91
    New Labour version 92–3
community care 2
community development 161
community involvement 160
'community leaders' 138
competitiveness 98
conferences 146, 162
conflict 60, 151
    absence of 146
    gendered 139–41
Connell, R. 55
Connexions 95, 96, 115, 116
Conservative Party 4, 6
    government of 1979–97 47, 66, 75, 90, 103, 104, 117, 185
    legacy to New Labour 88–9
    traditional authoritarianism 88
Contratto, S. 46
Corby, B. 74
counselling 89, 116, 163
'couples work' 139–41
court procedures/proceedings 60, 136
court-mandated programmes 152
Coward, R. 8–9, 26, 55, 168
crime 89, 98
Crime and Disorder Act (1998) 10, 95, 104, 108, 153, 162
Criminal Justice Act (1991) 75
criminalisation 170
criminality 5, 6, 30, 103, 110
Critical Studies of Men 142
Croft, S. 166
Cronin, N. 190
Crow, G. 9, 134–7, 141
culture 24, 107, 135, 141
Curtis Committee (1946) 67–8

'daddy quota' 102
Dads and Lads projects 174
Daniel, B. 152
Daniel, P. 67, 76, 99
Davis, A. 166, 167
Day, L. 166
day care 89
Day Care Trust (1980–) 47
Day Sclater, S. 60–1
Deater-Deckard, K. 36, 38
death 33
'debilitative power' (Smart and Neale) 53–4
debt problems 105
deficit model (of childhood) 7, 181
delinquency 68, 69
democratic families 13, 14, 41, 124–5, 140, 141, 143, 150
'democratic possibility' 29
democratisation
    family life 10–11, 39, 59, 129, 183, 184–5
    social work 166
Dennis, N. 106

Department for Education and Employment 120–1
Department of Health 118, 120–1
    statutory services 107
dependency 96
depression 122
deprivation 72, 94, 112, 130
developmental psychology 36
dialogue 181, 182, 185–7
Dillon, J. 198
Dinnerstein, D. 46
disability 27, 46, 53, 116
disabled parents 95, 96
disadvantage 113, 115, 131, 138
diversity 22, 38, 186
division of labour 29, 50
    domestic 44
    gendered 65, 107
divorce 19, 21–3, 30–4, 36, 47, 52, 56, 57, 101, 104, 121, 130, 137, 163, 171, 178
    contact arrangements (gendered approaches) 60
    emotional costs 60–1
    gendered causes and consequences 39
    psychoanalytic perspective 60
    psychological and emotional disturbance 32
    reasons 31, 58
Dolan, P. 190
domestic chores 28, 29, 45
domestic labour 122
domestic responsibilities 44
domestic violence 9, 11–12, 34, 35, 38, 58, 60, 80–5, 101, 109, 114, 121, 122, 150, 167, 171
    'destructive of self' 54
    one-off 54, 123
    potential trigger 59
Dominelli, L. 166
Donzelot, J. 3
Dowie, A. 145
Drakeford, M. 162
Drucker, C.B. 180
Driver, S. 91
Duncan, S. 53
Dunn, J. 36, 38
Dutt, R. 138, 139

early marriage 23
Early Years programme 115
economic
    crisis (mid-1970s) 69
    exploitation 44
    independence 56
    liberalism 88
    restructuring (impact upon men) 26
Economic and Social Research Council (ESRC)
    Children 5–16 Programme 171, 175
Edie 165
education 4, 64, 94–6, 98, 107, 112
    attainment 30, 158
Edwards, R. 53
Eekelaar, J. 76
Eisenstein, H. 42
elderly people 68
emotional
    difficulties 69
    literacy 150
    neglect 78
emotions (difficult) 168
employability 5, 6, 98, 99, 115, 116, 126, 165
    boys 108
    'integration of people into the market' 97
    parental 110

employers 5, 51, 89
employment 153, 170
  dead-end 98, 102
  full-time 122
  permanent 171
  prospects 178
  security 97
  women 25–6
  see also full employment
employment patterns 48, 107
  implications for family life 25–30
employment policies 143
employment practices 187
empowerment 2
'engaging fathers' 143, 150, 184
England 14n, 70, 95, 96, 109, 112, 131, 164, 178, 179
  family picture 21
  North 130
  North-East 27, 29, 106
equal opportunities legislation 136
equality 43, 49, 140
  of life chances 98
'essential family' 45
Erdos, G. 106
ethic of care 14, 50–1
ethnic minorities, see minority ethnic groups
ethnicity 22–3, 53, 58, 59, 138, 178
Etzioni, A. 103–4
eugenics 66
Europe 99
Exeter Family Society 58
expectations 145
  gendered 140

Fairclough, N. 87
families 69, 177, 186
  attempts to reinstate men's control over women and children 155
  broken-down 91
  reconstituted 79
  South Asian 23
'families'
  working with 129–41
'families of choice' 22
'families under stress' 100–1
family 45, 66, 64, 65, 91
  complexities of meanings and practices 188
  deconstruction of concept 80, 184
  'does not have singular meaning' 39
  flexible definition 135
  formation 38
  function 23–4, 25
  identification 135
  inclusive notions 137, 150
  as institution 183
  'meaning' 23–5
  natural 70
  new construction 79–80
  New Labour construction 88–9
  nuclear 24, 47, 73, 81
  postmodern 51
  reform or abolition 42–4
  socialising agent (decline as) 71
  two-parent 21, 22, 34, 37, 72, 92, 143, 144, 178
  young women's attitudes 178
'family' the 52, 91
  'imperfect model for political community' 92
family autonomy approach 74
'family breakdown' 101

family form 21, 37, 41, 51, 58, 61, 79, 85, 87, 133, 143, 183
  changes 8
  complexity and diversity 129–34
  diversity 129
  'inclusive notions' (Frost) 14
  links with poverty 129
  male breadwinner model 8–9, 20, 23, 25, 30, 39, 43, 44, 64–5, 66, 98, 144
  new normative guidelines 22
  non-stepfamilies 36
  non-traditional 31
  range 136
  'traditional' 22, 31
  undesirable 76
family group conferences 134–7
  independent coordinators 135, 136
family law 41, 60
Family Law Act (1996) 93
family leave policies 89
family life 13, 14, 19–40, 44, 48, 49, 60, 183, 186, 187
  bottom-up understandings 55
  changing world? 19–23
  deconstruction and multiplicity 45–7
  democratisation 10–11, 39
  'deterioration in quality' 19–20
  implications for family support 39–40
  multiple perspectives 55
  'no particular model to be promoted' 140
  paranoid exchanges 153
  post-divorce 133
  re-thinking 58
  reform or abandonment 45–7
family policy 41, 87
  Conservative 4
  family-friendly 50
  implicit 66
  landscape 13
family practices 10, 52, 183
  democratisation 184–5
family privacy 3
'family service' 69
family support 1–15, 39–40, 41, 130, 157, 183, 184, 187
  balance with child protection 85
  barriers and possibilities for social workers 150–3
  battle for hearts and minds 63
  battle for meaning 1–6
  book structure 13–15
  Children Act 1989 77–81
  complex and changing world 188
  context 79
  developments 180–1
  diverse picture 6–7
  diversity, contradictions, gaps 109–26
  'empty category' 2
  feminism 7–13, 56–61
  implications of young people's perspectives 179–82
  New Labour era (1997–) 87–108
  perspective 63–86
  policies and practices 185
  practices 59
  prevention and support (new services, new approach) 111–16
  refocusing project 80
  responsibilities and rights 67–70
  smaller initiatives 115–16
  statutory settings 117–20
  term emerged in 1980s 70

working with men 150–3
working with women 159–66
Family Support Grant 95, 115, 147
Family Support Programme 107, 116
family support projects 130, 165, 169
family values 88, 89
Farmer, E. 83, 164
fate of children removed 83
father figures 151
fatherhood 53, 133, 154
  cultural shifts in expectations 145
  'moved onto policy agenda' 142
  reclamation 55
fathering 10, 140, 152, 174, 180
  re-definition in situations of non-residence
    52
fathers 13, 36, 61, 93, 95, 130, 131, 160, 161, 165,
    174, 175, 187
  absent 38, 76, 151
  absent/distant 106–8
  absent/present 54–5
  behaviour 145
  boys' construction of 173
  children's perceptions 145
  contact with children 146
  critical of professional and judicial practices
    146
  demographic profile 143
  difficulties engaging with their children 180
  employed 144
  feared 145, 180
  full-time care of children 152
  'hard to reach' 116
  identity 144, 184
  'locating' 143–6
  men speaking out as 146–8
  non-biological 144, 145
  non-resident 141
  'often rely on mother to have relationship
    with children' 133
  'resources' for women and children' 152,
    153, 156
  risks 152, 156
  role 54
  terminology (exclusionary potential) 144
  themselves sexually-abused 180
  unmarried 147, 149
  violent men as 153
  vulnerable 152, 153, 156
  why and how to engage 155, 156
  work/home balance 145
  working 28
  young 147
Fathers Direct 95, 143, 174
Fathers Plus 29
fathers' rights 146
Fawcett, B. x, 192
Fawcett, B. et al. 83, 192
  Featherstone, B. 192
  Goddard, J. 192
Featherstone, B. ii, 12, 47, 84, 123, 129, 140,
    166, 192–3, 194
  interview with Edie 165
  interviews with men on parenting orders
    153
  interviews with mothers 160
  interviews with six young men 149–50
  involvement with MOSAIC 163
  physical violence towards children by their
    mothers (research project) 165
  research and voluntary work 13
  statutory social worker (early 1980s) 170

teaching and dialogue with practitioners 185
work as evaluator 126, 147, 148, 161
work as volunteer 126
Featherstone, B. et al. 165
'female biography' 159
Feminine Mystique (Friedan, 1963) 43
femininity 9, 164
feminism 1, 41–62, 94–5, 129, 139, 154–5, 166,
    178, 185
  assumed women could speak for children
    184
  backlash 44, 45
  'bourgeois triumphalism' 48
  critiques of New Labour 100–3, 108
  disciplinary project 185
  divisions/tensions 46–7, 48–9, 51
  family support 7–13, 56–61
  hostility 147
  internal divisions 42
  liberal 43, 44
  mapping complexity (1990s) 49–55
  marginalisation 74, 81
  marginalisation to revitalisation 81–5
  Marxist 45
  'midwife to needs of capitalist society' 56
  new confidence 49
  public face 48
  radical 42, 44, 45, 46, 48, 81
  reputation 41
  second-wave 8, 42
  socialist 42, 45, 48
  third wave 49
  usefulness 120–6
  winners and losers 47–9
feminist authoritarianism 185
feminist insight/analysis 14, 63, 64, 83, 84–5,
    166, 168, 169
  'four key issues' 9–13, 183–8
  'key argument' of book 120
  role 7
Ferguson, H. 11, 59, 84–5, 105, 124–5, 150, 152,
    163, 164
Ferri, E. 34
financial
  difficulties 132
  hardship 34
  support 54
Finch, J. 37, 53
Finer Report (1974) 71
Finlayson, G. 68
Firestone, S. 44
flexibility 97, 98
Forrest, S. 178
fostering 30, 37, 67, 69
  previously known as 'boarding out' 68
Fox Harding, L. 66, 70–1, 72, 73, 75, 81, 88, 104
Framework for Assessment of Children in Need and
    their Families (2000) 100, 122, 134, 138
Franks, S. 9, 25, 28, 29, 38, 49
Frazer, E. 92
Freely, M. 49, 55, 106, 131, 132, 145, 146, 185
Friedan, B. 43, 45
friends/friendship 22, 36, 37, 135, 175, 176, 186
Frosh, S. 153
Frosh, S. et al. 171–4, 175, 180, 181, 194
  Pattman, R. 194
  Phoenix, A. 194
Frost, N. x, 2, 3, 7, 12, 69, 84
Frost, N. et al. 2, 13, 194
  Jeffrey, L. 194
  Lloyd, A. 194
full employment 65, 98, 117

funding 93, 109, 112, 117, 120, 126, 134
further education 116

gaps 103, 109, 110, 150, 153
Gardner, R. 111, 118, 120, 160, 162, 165
Garrett, P. 116, 125
gender 5, 7, 10, 12, 13, 38, 41, 42, 53, 55, 59–62,
  65, 80, 83, 84, 100, 106, 122, 132, 136–8,
  156, 176, 180, 184
 government thinking 123
 language 188
 'opening up' 187
 smoking 162
gender boundaries 172
gender equality 5, 105, 99
 top–down understandings 181
gender equity 95, 153, 154–5, 157
gender identity 166, 167
gender issues 150
gender power 99–100
gender practices (older patterns) 176
gender relations 114, 176, 184
geographical areas 114
Ghate, H. 6, 95, 104–5
Giddens, A. 39, 56–60, 96–7
Gilligan, R. 2, 150, 159, 180
Gillis, J. 19–20
'girl power' 176–7
Gilroy, R. 200
girls 46, 172–3, 180, 181, 182, 184
 boys' attitudes 172
 eroticised gender difference 173, 181
 excluding behaviour 175
 friendships 175
 idealisation (by boys) 174, 175
 policing of each other 175
 problem-solving 175
 prospects 176–9
 social class 177
 views on gendered relations 172
Glass, N. 114
global capitalism 97
global market 98, 103
globalisation 90
Golombok, S. 31, 33–4, 35, 38
Golombok, S. et al. 35, 194
 Murray, C. 194
 Tasker, F. 194
Gordon, L. 12, 42, 81, 84
Gough, D. 2
government 111, 143, 162
government guidance 84, 125, 134, 137–8
government ministers 145
grandparents 36
Grier, J. 68
guardians ad litem 75

Hallett, C. et al. 175, 176, 181, 195
 Murray, C. 195
 Punch, S. 195
Hanks, H. 180
Hanmer, J. 166
hardness 172
Harker, L. 185
harm-ism phenomenon 36
harms (children suffer) 80, 110, 119, 120, 167
head of household: African-Caribbean women
  22–3, 138, 159
Head Start (USA) 111
healing 160, 163
health 64, 96, 98, 105, 112, 113, 151
Hearn, J. 142

help-seeking 179–80, 182, 184
Hendrick, H. 67, 68
Henricson, C. et al. 104, 109, 120, 139, 195
 Katz, I. 195
 Mesie, J. 195
 Sandison, M. 195
 Tunstill, J. 195
Henwood, K. 145
Heptinstall, E. 190
Hetherington, M. 34
Holland, J. 179
Holman, B. 72–3, 110, 120
home
 what happens 28–30
Home Office 95, 107, 116, 147
 author 120–1
Home Office Circular (1948) 68
home visiting 96
homosexuals
 couples 47, 93
 gays 22
 lesbians 22, 35, 47, 158
Hooper, C.-A. 84
households 131, 151
 jobless 113, 162
 lesbian 35
housing advice 163
human capital 97
human limitations 186
human nature 43
hypocrisy 92

identity 25, 26, 53, 58, 124, 162, 163, 165, 180,
  184
 boys 172
 fathers 146
 multiple 159–60
 traditional 152
ideology
 familial 45
 right-wing 88
illness
 mental 33
 physical 33
immigrants 178
imperialism 66
Income Support 72
independence (personal) 54, 96, 137
individual
 accountability 176
 autonomy 88; see also agency
 men 76
 self-sufficiency 186
individualisation 58
inequalities 44, 98, 158
 gendered 45
 social 73
 between women 48
 workplace 8
Institute for Public Policy Research 118
institutionalised racism 139
interdependence 186
interviews 130, 149, 153, 160, 171–3, 181
intimacy 24, 58
 restructuring 56–7
intimidation 136
'involved father' model 145
Ireland 15, 124, 164
Ivatts, J. 67, 76, 99

Jackson, R. 33
Jagger, G. 8, 42

Jeffrey, L. 114, 194
Jenson, J. 97–8, 99–100
Johnston, J. 123
Joshi, H. *et al.* 21, 196
  Clarke, L. 196
  Wiggins, D. 196
judicial practices 146
Just Like a Girl (Sharpe, 1976/1994) 177

Kaplan, E.-A. 159
Katz, I. 195
Kelly, G. 190
Kendall, L. 185
Kershaw, S. 35
Keynes, J.M. 117
kin/kinship 46, 51, 135, 186
knowledge economy 96, 116

labelling 170
Labour Governments (1945–51) 68
labour market 97, 176, 178
  changes 8–9
  gendered inequalities 34, 35, 102
  participation rates 98, 144
  pre-Second World War 65
laissez-faire 73, 88
Lamb, M.E. 31, 144
Laming, Lord 7, 80, 119, 125
Land, H. 4
Langan, M. 166, 190
language 9–10, 12, 13, 20, 24, 25, 45, 49, 53, 59,
    100, 105, 121, 125, 133, 144, 154, 167,
    183–4, 188
  gender-neutral 7, 33, 83–4, 161, 162, 184
law 25, 52
law and order 88, 103
Lawrence, S. 139
learning difficulties 116
LEAs (Local Education Authorities) 112
Lee, N. 170
Lees, S. 175, 177, 178–9
left-wing (politics) 74, 106
legislation 15
Lewis, J. 21, 22, 29, 53, 71
Libertarian Conservatism 88
Lister, R. x, 4, 50, 94, 99–102, 117
literature 125, 126
  family support 181
Lloyd, A. 194
Lloyd, T. 147–8, 174
local authorities 67–8, 77, 83, 118
  responsibility for personal social services
    (1948–) 68
local authority accommodation/care 69, 77
Local Authority Social Services Act (1970) 69
London 177
lone motherhood 19, 30, 34, 39–40, 158
lone mothers 45, 47, 53, 54, 76, 93, 102, 131,
    133, 148, 151, 163
  see also single mothers
lone parents 37, 43, 96, 105
  ten per cent of households 21
  ninety per cent women 21
lone-mother families/households 21, 37, 72,
    79, 144
'long hours' culture 28, 29
Lord Chancellor 93
love 57
low income 34
low warmth, high criticism 78
Lucey, H. 201
Lupton, C. 142

McIntosh, M. 8, 45
McKenzie, M. 136
McLeod, E. 166
MacLeod, M. 179
MacMurray, J. 92
Major, J. 88, 92
'managerial partnership state' 117
Mann, K. 38, 158
manufacturing industry 27
Maori people 134, 137
marginalisation 138
market forces 64, 88, 91
marriage 44, 47, 56, 57, 58, 60, 92–3, 159
  breakdown 23
  decline 106
  duration 21–2
  lifelong commitment 19, 39
  'partial disentangling with parenthood' 6,
    21, 83
  young women's views 177–8
married couples 53
Married Couples Tax Allowance (abolition) 93
Marsh, P. 9, 134–7, 141
Martell, L. 91
masculinity 9, 132, 142, 173
  hegemonic 172, 174
masculinity policy (New Labour) 106
material respect 187
maternity leave 94
media 48, 49
Melody, J. 201
men 44, 48, 54, 132, 142–56, 161, 181, 188
  abusive 64, 82
  changes/crises 148
  desire to father differently 150
  disadvantaged 8, 39
  economically inactive 26–7
  identity as fathers 147
  impact of economic restructuring 26
  involvement in violent behaviour 124
  issues 148–50
  marginalised 124
  needs and interests 41
  'not changed enough' 50
  older 152
  post-separation/divorce 137
  poverty 59
  'resources' in family life 55
  rights and needs as fathers 157–8
  role (feminist view) 55
  social workers' 'lack of confidence' dealing
    with 130
  speak out as fathers 146–8
  unemployed 9, 147
  unhappiest 29
  unmet needs 105, 153
  'unprepared for new role' 30
  victims 147
  violence 82, 123, 142
  vulnerabilities 60
  wishes and behaviour 55
'men pushing prams' 149
mental health/illness 2, 121, 122, 151
mentoring 116
Merseyside 27
Mesie, J. 195
Miles, J. 72
Millett, K. 44
Milligan, C. 145
minority ethnic groups 23, 27, 95, 116, 137–9
Mitchell, S. 118
'moral grammar' (Williams) 53

moral worth 186
Morley, R. 167
MOSAIC (project for mothers) v, 163–4
Moss, P. 7, 187, 190
Moss, P. *et al.* 181, 198
  Dillon, J. 198
  Statham, J. 198
'mother love' 65
motherhood 49, 53, 168
  difficult feelings 169
  models 167
  obstacles to equality at work 49–50
  sanitised notions 167, 169
  source of satisfaction 49
mothering 10, 11, 46, 84, 159, 164, 165, 166, 168
  contexts 158
  multiple meanings 169
mothers 3, 13, 26, 27, 61, 69, 83, 89, 100, 130,
    131, 133, 141, 158–60, 162, 163, 177, 180,
    186
  abusive behaviour towards children 47
  African-Caribbean 26
  ambivalence 168
  boys' construction of 173
  burden of responsibility 157
  death 33
  distancing techniques 169
  full-time work 148
  identity 184
  involvement with children 'not mediated
    through fathers' 149
  role as gatekeeper 149
  social workers engaging with 165
  unpaid work 65
  violence towards children 165
  women's interests 167
  working 29
Mullender, A. 167
Muncie, J. 104
Murray, C. 106, 194, 195

National Child Development Study 29
National Childcare Strategy 4, 94, 187
National Council of Voluntary Child Care
    Organisations 72–3
National Family and Parenting Institute 94, 95,
    109
national identity 66
National Organisation for Women 43
National Step Family Association 132
nationhood 88
Neale, B. 41, 52, 53, 58, 123, 136–7, 200
needs
  bottom-up approach 163
  definition 168–9
negotiation (intra-family) 29, 188
neo-liberalism 90, 91
New Labour Government (1997–) 4, 5–6, 12,
    15, 30, 49, 63, 84, 86, 109, 114, 118, 125,
    126, 150, 157, 185–6, 187
  attitude to the state 117
  building or overturning? 89–93
  child protection 110
  communitarianism 92–3
  Conservative legacy 88–9
  and 'the family' 88, 92
  family support 87–108, 160–1
  Green Paper on preventive services (planned)
    119, 120, 124
  manifesto (2001) 93
  'pessimistic policies' (on parenting) 162
  policy agenda 80

questions to be addressed 124
  see also Sure Start
New Right 3, 4, 88, 91, 117
New Zealand 134, 136, 137
Newman, J. 89–90, 92, 161
Norfolk 147
Northern Ireland 15
nursery 112, 187

O'Brien, M. 23
O'Neill, D. (*d.* 1945) 67
offending 170
Old Labour 89, 90
one-parent benefit 71
oppression 166, 167
Organisation of Women of African and Asian
    Descent (OWAAD) 139
outcomes for children 93, 146, 153, 161
  changing patterns of partnering 30–6
  placed in state care 83
  poor 104
Owen, C. 190
Owen, M. 83, 164

paedophiles 133
paid work 5, 12, 42–3, 47, 51, 52, 65, 90, 93, 94,
    96, 101, 102–3, 116, 158, 159, 160, 163–4,
    185, 187
  balance with caring responsibilities 8, 143
  mothers of young children 89
  parental involvement 114
  two-parent involvement 19
  women's involvement 56
Pakistanis 138
parent: 'gender-neutral'/'ungendered' term 7,
    10, 12, 122
parental leave 89, 94, 102
parental responsibility 4, 6, 60, 75, 77, 88, 93–6,
    103–6, 110
  Child Support Act (1991) 89
  economic 93
  gender neutrality 83
  gendered implications 76
  moral 92
  'ungendered term' 10
parenthood
  'dissociated from biology' 21
  gendered understandings 53
  'partial disentangling with marriage' 6, 21,
    83
parenting 2, 87, 104, 165, 180
  full-time 99
  'pessimistic policies' (New Labour) 162
  poor 186
  post-divorce 52, 54, 58, 83, 133, 144
  responsible 116
parenting group 165
parenting orders 110, 153, 162
parenting programmes 106
  gendered implications 105
  national evaluation 104–5
parenting services 109
parents 3, 4, 5, 87, 93–6, 119, 124, 135, 157,
    160–2, 173–6
  biological 73, 131
  'central to many strategies' 6
  conflict between 31, 132, 139; *see also* divorce
  professional class 28
  responsible 103–6
  safeguards in relation to legal interventions
    75
parents' needs 73

parents' rights 70, 71, 72, 74, 82
Parker, R. 168
Parton, N. x, 3, 69, 71, 74, 76–7, 84
paternal responsibility 103
paternity leave 94, 145
pathology 138
patriarchy 44, 46, 70, 76, 124
peer pressure 173
Peled, E. 153, 167
Penn, H. 2
Peplar, M. 19
'perfect mother' fantasy 46
personal advisers 116
pessimism 164–5
Phillips, M. 138, 139
Pinkerton, J. 2, 190
Platt, L. 23
play 96
'political ethics of care' 12, 51, 186
poor families 21, 23, 28, 39, 72, 73, 85
poor men 158–9
poor women 10, 162
post-natal depression 148
postmodernism 4, 48, 52
poverty 26, 33, 35, 38, 58–9, 72, 93, 105, 110,
    138, 144, 151, 158, 159, 162
  causes and consequences 114
  links with family form 129
  rediscovered (1960s) 69
power 11, 44, 53, 132, 136, 137, 142, 143, 153
  adult-children 181
  gendered 54
  imbalances in particular family arrangements
    183–4
'practices of care' 186
pragmatism 49, 92
pregnancy 112, 179
  smoking during 6, 113, 114, 161–2
  teenage 111
Prendergast, S. 178
prevention 3–4, 63, 64, 72, 78, 84, 85, 86,
    111–16, 119, 124
  of child leaving the family 68–9, 110
  of children going into care 77
  forerunner of 'family support' 70
  re-thinking 80
private sector 94
professional authority 74
protection, see child protection
Protection of Children Act (1999) 110
Prout, A. 171
Pryor, J. 36
psychoanalysis 46, 60, 69, 168, 173
psychological distress 122
psychology 73, 122, 123
psychosocial influence 135
public choice theory 117
Punch, S. 195
pure relationship (Giddens) 57, 58, 60
Putting Abuse of Women on Child Care Agenda
    (Mullender and Morley, 1994) 167

Quality Projects 117, 118

race 22–3, 46, 135, 136, 139, 144
Rake, K. 26
Ramalla, M. 6, 95, 104–5
Rape Crisis 82
Rattansi, A. 174
re-marriage 32
re-partnering 36
redistribution 98, 99

reflection 125–6
'reflexivity' 155
'refocusing' 118
relationship support 93
relationships
  ability to sustain 30
  abusive 160
  adult 29, 30, 177
  adult–child 180
  blood 24, 25
  break up/breakdown 58, 148
  equal 57–8
  familial 35
  intimate 32
  marital 24
  men and women 13, 20, 38, 39, 41, 140, 141
  men, women, children 129
  mother–child 36–7, 46
  between mothers 168
  negotiation 141, 149, 181, 188
  parent–child 133
  permanent 171
  post-divorce parenting 52, 133
  problems 105
  social 43
  stable adult family 170
  unsatisfying 101
  violent 157, 179
  between young people 176
religion 20, 58, 135
renegotiation 132, 133
residential care 30, 175
residential homes 83
resources 130, 153
respect 125, 136
Reynolds, T. 23
Rich, A. 46, 47, 54–5
Richardson, S. 180
right-wing (politics) 74, 106
Rogers, B. 36
role of state 7, 63, 64, 67, 68, 75, 76–7, 81, 88,
    89
  paternalism (1970s and 1980s) 70–4
roles 29, 140, 141, 160
Roseneil, S. 38, 158
Ruxton, S. 25, 26, 27, 29, 59
Ryan, M. 151

sacrifice of 'self' 165
safe-sex practices 179
safety 148, 153
Saint-Martin, D. 97–8, 99
Sandison, M. 195
schools 13, 160, 174, 177, 178
Scotland 15
Scourfield, J. 162
Seebohm Committee (1965) 69
Seen But Not Heard: Coordinating Community
    Child Health and Social Services for
    Children in Need (Audit Commission,
    1994) 78
Segal, L. 8, 9, 45, 48
self, notions of 159
self-esteem 30, 32, 54
self-fulfilment 159
self-interest 92
self-invention 176
self-reliance 90
separation
  marital 31, 33, 36, 52, 57, 58, 60, 103, 130,
    137, 163
  public and private spheres (break from) 94

service providers   28, 39, 130, 147, 148, 158, 164
    threat from violent or abusive men   152
    see also social services
service provision   165
service-users   130, 148, 159, 164, 168
    adult   161
    bottom-up challenges   166
    women   166, 167
Seventuijsen, S.   101
sexual
    behaviour   179
    contract   178
    intimacy   186
    offending   123
sexual abuse/violence   13, 44, 74, 78–80, 83–5,
        103, 111, 115, 121, 123, 124, 133, 153, 158,
        163, 175–6, 180
    causes   82
    space for children's voice to be heard   59
sexuality   53, 57, 82, 123, 144
Sharpe, S.   177
siblings   175, 176
sickness benefits   27
significant harm   75
significant others   135
Silva, E.B.   20–1, 23–5, 52
Singh, G.   138
single mothers   68
    African-Caribbean   22–3
    financially-secure   35
    poor   38
    see also lone mothers
single (never-married) people   21
single-father families   33
single-mother families   36
single-parent families   31–4
    separation, divorce, death   33
'situational power' (Smart and Neale)   54
skills   27, 130, 162
Skinner, C.   94
Smart, C.   20–1, 23–5, 41, 52, 53, 58, 123, 133,
        136–7
Smart, C. et al.   37, 52, 200
    Neale, B.   200
    Wade, A.   200
Snitow, A.   46
social
    capital   164
    care   119
    cohesion   5, 98, 99, 108, 110, 115, 126
    context   81
    control   12, 81
    democracy ('allegedly outdated')   91
    democratic thinking   117
    democrats   74
    divisions   73
    exclusion   96, 121
    identity   5
    justice   98
    order   71
    policy   25, 63
    process of care   186
    relations   166
    rights   98
    support   175
    unrest   106
'social investment state' (Giddens)   5, 88,
        96–100, 111, 117, 119, 187
    see also Sure Start
'social security'   96
social service departments   111, 118
    role   69

social services   151, 167
    challenges and possibilities   182
    for fathers   146
    reform   118
    for violent men who are fathers   150
    see also service providers
social services support   78
social work   179
    complexity and diversity   129–34
    feminist   166–9
    practice   70, 106, 125, 151
    premised upon notions of 'becoming' rather
        than 'being'   170
social workers   47, 79, 82, 118, 125, 129, 135–6,
        183–6
    attitudes and activities   80
    difficulties   131
    emotional equipment   141
    fathers critical of   146
    inclusive practice   141
    Maori   134
    project workers   130, 148–50
    skills   130
    staff shortages   126, 134
    Sure Start   115, 140
    working exclusively with women   157
    working with men   141, 142–56
    working with men in changing world
        142–56
    working with minority ethnic families
        137–9
    working with women   157–69
    see also women social workers
socialisation   123–4
    masculine   82, 85
socialism   90
society   92
    gendered debates and struggles   155
    'no such a thing'   91
socio-economic difficulties   31, 32, 33
sociology   37
solo mothers (Golombok)   33, 34–5
Somerville, J.   21, 42, 44, 49, 51
sources of legitimation   124
South Wales   27
South Yorkshire   27
Southall Black Sisters   139
space (personal)   54, 137, 162, 163, 184
    women-only   155, 157
Speak, S. et al.   147, 200
    Cameron, S.   200
    Gilroy, R.   200
special needs   96
speech and language problems   113
sperm-donors   35
Stacey, J.   51, 59
Stanley-Hagan, M.M.   34
state   3, 45, 51, 87, 158
    powers   82
    roll-back   117
state benefits   71, 102
state care   110, 136, 137, 138
state control   75, 82
state expenditure/resources   71, 75–6, 117,
        141
state intervention   100
state paternalism: childcare policy (1970s and
        1980s)   70–4
state power   44
Statham, D.   166
Statham, J.   198
status   27

statutory agencies 2
statutory interventions 138
statutory sector (social work) 3, 125, 126, 164, 169
Stein, M. 3, 69
step-children 131
step-families 23, 31, 32, 37, 40, 130, 131–4, 144, 151
  'stigma' 131
step-father families 36
step-fathers 131, 133
  feared 145, 180
step-mother/complex families 36
step-mothers 130
step-parenting 131, 132
  constraints 132
step-parents 32, 36, 133
  ex-step-parents 135
  'had to earn their significance' 38
stereotypical thinking 138
Sternberg, K. 132–3
stigma 131, 177
Stratton, P. 180
Straw, J. 103
stress 26, 120–2, 124
stress responses 121, 122
stressors 121, 122
substance misuse 105, 121
substitute care 71
Supporting Families: A Consultation Document (Home Office, 1998) 4, 87, 92–3, 95, 100, 107
Sure Start 6, 13, 95–6, 107–8, 111, 117–18, 125, 143, 153, 161–2, 169
  aim and objectives 112–15
  implementation 161
  importance of partnerships to New Labour 112
  monitoring and evaluation 114
  writer's personal involvement 161
  see also MOSAIC
Sure Start Plus 111–12
Sweden 4

targeting 4, 98, 114
targets 113, 114, 117, 125–6, 153, 161, 162
Tasker, F. 194
taxation and benefit systems 56, 93
Taylor, D. 166
Taylor, J. 152
teachers' attitudes 175
teenagers 111, 116
terminology 42
Thatcher, M. 48, 88, 117
  'no such thing as society' 91
  oblique reference 47
Thatcherism 89
Third Way 89, 91, 96–7
time 32, 102, 126, 130, 132, 134, 135, 149, 153, 163, 165
  in care 70
  future 97–8, 170, 171, 176–9
  present 97, 171–6
  spent by fathers with children 28–9
Tong, R. 42
tradition 58
traditional values 88
training 103, 116, 147, 153, 160, 162
Trinder, L. 123, 167
truancy 5, 103
trust 147, 186
Tunstill, J. 3, 77, 110, 118, 195

underclass 106
unemployment 26, 47, 59, 115, 121, 151
  jobless household 113, 162
  long-term 27, 152
  young fathers 108
  young men 141, 178
United Kingdom 3, 8, 23, 30, 38, 42, 47, 51–2, 71, 74, 92, 106, 111, 137, 142
  emergence of explicit family policy (1998) 87
United States of America 23, 31, 38, 42, 43, 51, 54, 66, 88, 92, 102
'universal caregiver' model 50, 102
unpaid labour 65, 81

value for money 117
Victorian values 22
violence 7, 48, 57, 103, 105, 122, 123, 137, 139, 151, 177, 181
  gendered 183, 185
  men 8, 124, 150
  to women 150, 167
  see also child abuse; domestic violence; sexual abuse/violence
visibility 65, 80
  'caring' work 12
voice 161, 184
voluntary sector 3, 68, 73, 80, 93, 101, 102, 109, 115, 160, 165, 169
vulnerability 137, 149–50, 152, 153

Wade, A. 200
wages 27, 90, 98
  gender gap 26
  housework 50
  male working-class 25
Walby, S. 44
Wales 15, 70, 95, 96, 109, 131, 179
  family picture 21
Walkerdine, V. *et al.* 176–7, 179, 201
  Lucey, H. 201
  Melody, J 201
Walter, N. 49, 55, 185
Wattam, C. 190
websites 112, 174, 202
welfare 142
  social democratic 69
welfare policies and practices 14
welfare reform 103
welfare state 4, 45, 73, 106
  assumptions 64–5
  'central to post-war reconstruction' 66
  'mixed economy of support' 65
  post-1945 (Beveridge model) 3, 14, 25, 63, 64–7, 91, 93, 97, 98, 108, 117
  post-1997 14, 88, 96–7
Wiggins, D. 196
Williams, F. 50, 53, 54, 55, 105, 143, 166, 186, 187, 190
women 61, 98, 105, 132, 161, 162, 177, 181, 188
  ability to make their voices heard 183
  African-Caribbean 22–3, 103, 138, 159
  antagonism to men 'being reproduced as victims' 123
  badly-paid jobs 26
  Bangladeshi 159
  black 43, 45–6, 139, 178
  'can be violent to men' 123
  changing aspirations 39
  child abuse 140
  complex differences 167–8
  'constructed solely as conduits for children's safety' 164

desires 45, 62, 137
disabled 46
disadvantaged 23
economic independence 47
entering paid labour force 185
'favoured in court setting' 146
financially secure 158
full-time employment 25–6
giving and receiving of care 187
happiest 29
hostility to social services for men 148
identity 184
inequalities 48
'judged' by social workers 164
location today 158–9
low-paid 66
needs 41, 159, 166, 167
non-married 177
organisational identity 168
outnumber men in paid employment 25
part-time employment 26, 28
private/public restrictions 44
reasons for having children 'on their own'
    31
right to stay at home to provide care 102
scarce resources taken away from 154
site of subordination 52
unpaid work 65
victimisation 8, 84
white, middle-class 43
worked with by women social workers
    130
working-class 43, 179
see also feminism
'women and social work' movement 81–2
women social workers 81–2, 130, 140, 148,
    166–8
anger/disappointment with men 154, 168
anxiety dealing with men 149
emotions 168
fear of violence 154
repressed feelings 168
working with fathers 147
Women's Aid 82, 114
women's studies 48
'women's work' 27, 50
Work and Parents: Competitiveness and Choice
    (Green Paper, 2001) 94–5
work-life balance 50, 51
working arrangements, flexible 94
working class 51, 65, 69
working with 'families' 129–41
working hours 102
antisocial 27–8, 39
matter to children 28
working practices 51
Working Together to Safeguard Children: A Guide to
    Interagency Working to Safeguard and
    Promote Welfare of Children (1999) 100,
    122
Wright, C. 8, 42

Yates, C. 60–1
young men 154
black 38
economic position 27
economic and social landscape 170
ideas and expectations 178
unemployed 141
young offenders 170
young people 171, 176, 180, 181
bullying 175
confidantes 175
need to consult 179
struggle to be heard by adults 179–80
young women 154, 176–7
Irish and African-Caribbean 178
middle- and working-class 177
youth justice system 95, 110, 113
Youth Offending Teams 95